Mastering Tableau

Smart Business Intelligence techniques to get maximum insights from your data

David Baldwin

BIRMINGHAM - MUMBAI

Mastering Tableau

First published: November 2016

Production reference: 1231116

Published by Packt Publishing Ltd.
Livery Place
35 Livery Street
Birmingham
B3 2PB, UK.
ISBN 978-1-78439-769-2

www.packtpub.com

Credits

Author

David Baldwin

Reviewer

Tamas Foldi

Commissioning Editor

Veena Pagare

Acquisition Editor

Vinay Argekar

Content Development Editor

Sumeet Sawant

Technical Editor

Akash Patel

Copy Editor

Vikrant Phadke

Project Coordinator

Shweta H Birwatkar

Proofreader

Safis Editing

Indexer

Aishwarya Gangawane

Graphics

Disha Haria

Production Coordinator

Nilesh Mohite

About the Author

David Baldwin has provided consulting in the business intelligence sector for 17 years. His experience includes Tableau training and consulting, developing BI solutions, project management, technical writing, and the web and graphic design. His vertical experience includes financial, healthcare, human resource, aerospace, energy, education, government, and entertainment industries. As a Tableau trainer and consultant, David enjoys serving a variety of clients throughout the USA. Tableau provides David a platform that collates his broad experience into a skill set that can service a diverse client base.

Many people provided invaluable support in the writing of this book. Although I cannot name everyone, there are those to whom I would like to draw special attention: My wife, Kara, was an unfailing encourager, supporter, and cheerleader throughout the writing journey. My children, Brent and Brooke, were very understanding of their dad's many long hours in front of a laptop at the dining room table. My mother, Bettye, was my first and best writing instructor and thus provided a foundation for clear communication. My father, Larry, taught me the importance of precise technical and mathematical thinking. My sister, Chelsea, modeled perseverance as she pursued and achieved advanced degrees. Also I'd like to thank my colleagues at Teknion for being ever willing to entertain questions, provide valuable feedback, and read rough drafts, particularly Bridget Cogley, Matthew Agee, Preston Howell, and especially Joshua Milligan.

www.Packtpub.com

For support files and downloads related to your book, please visit www.PacktPub.com.

Did you know that Packt offers eBook versions of every book published, with PDF and ePub files available? You can upgrade to the eBook version at www.PacktPub.com and as a print book customer, you are entitled to a discount on the eBook copy. Get in touch with us at service@packtpub.com for more details.

At www.PacktPub.com, you can also read a collection of free technical articles, sign up for a range of free newsletters and receive exclusive discounts and offers on Packt books and eBooks.

https://www.packtpub.com/mapt

Get the most in-demand software skills with Mapt. Mapt gives you full access to all Packt books and video courses, as well as industry-leading tools to help you plan your personal development and advance your career.

Why subscribe?

- Fully searchable across every book published by Packt
- Copy and paste, print, and bookmark content
- On demand and accessible via a web browser

Table of Contents

Preface

So what is this book about? The title certainly points in the right direction: *Mastering Tableau*. The word *Mastering* implies a journey to a level of competency beyond mere familiarity or superficial knowledge. The word *Tableau*, of course, limits the scope of a particular software package. Let's extend the title by one word in order to hone the focus: *Mastering Tableau Desktop*. The word *Desktop* further narrows consideration by communicating that this book is not focused on Tableau Server, although there is a chapter dedicated to interacting with Server. Nor does this book dive deep into topics beyond the realm of Tableau, though other technologies such as R and SQL are discussed as they pertain to Tableau. Furthermore, this book is not focused on data visualization or architectural theory per se, though these topics are explored and every attempt is made to adhere to sound methodology as technical problems are discussed. Instead, this book attempts to build on a foundation of an already basic understanding of Tableau Desktop so as to provide a theoretical and practical basis for solving real-world challenges in an efficient and elegant manner. Along the way, many tips and tricks for use in everyday work are discussed and exercises with careful step-by-step instructions and commentary are provided.

What this book covers

Chapter 1, *Getting Up to Speed - a Review of the Basics*, provides a quick on-ramp for those new to Tableau and a useful review for those with experience. For a more thorough consideration of fundamental topics, see *Learning Tableau*, written by Joshua Milligan and published by Packt Publishing.

Chapter 2, *All about Data - Getting Your Data Ready*, commences a series of three "All about Data" chapters. The chapter begins with a theoretical discussion of the Tableau data paradigm and data mining topics and then moves on to practical ways to use Tableau to survey and cleanse data.

Chapter 3, *All about Data - Joins, Blends, and Data Structures*, explores complex joins, data blending, and pivoting.

Chapter 4, *All about Data - Data Densification, Cubes, and Big Data*, ends the series of "All about Data" chapters by surveying a variety of data topics, including the undocumented world of data densification, working with cubes and big data considerations.

Chapter 5, *Table Calculations*, focuses on two questions: "What is the function?" and "How is the function applied?" These questions provide a framework for discussing directional and non-directional table calculations as well as partitioning and addressing.

Chapter 6, *Level of Detail Calculations*, begins with two playground environments created in Tableau designed to provide a foundation for understanding level-of-detail calculations and then moves on to practical application.

Chapter 7, *Beyond the Basic Chart Types*, looks at improving some popular visualization types and then considers the largely underexplored topic of using background images in Tableau. The workbook provided with this chapter also provides many additional visualization types.

Chapter 8, *Mapping*, begins by considering how to expand Tableau's native mapping capabilities without leaving the interface, and then explores extending Tableau mapping via other technologies, including connecting to WMS servers and MapBox. Lastly, the chapter demonstrates how to provide the end user options for choosing different maps and ends with a discussion on custom polygons.

Chapter 9, *Tableau for Presentations*, discusses techniques for integrating Tableau with PowerPoint as well as how to use Tableau as a standalone presentation tool via animation and story points.

Chapter 10, *Visualization Best Practices and Dashboard Design*, begins by considering design topics such as formatting, color, and visualization types and then addresses dashboard layout options. The chapter ends by exploring sheet swapping in some depth.

Chapter 11, *Improving Performance*, is the longest chapter of the book and attempts to systematically (though not exhaustively) cover options for optimizing Tableau performance.

Chapter 12, *Interacting with Tableau Server*, explores how to optimize Tableau Server architecture for best performance and easiest maintenance. The chapter also considers the web authoring environment, user filters, and accessing the Performance Recording dashboard via Tableau Server.

Chapter 13, *R Integration*, begins by considering how to install and integrate R with Tableau and then explores R and Tableau integration via a series of exercises. The chapter ends with a troubleshooting section.

What you need for this book

In order to make use of this book, an installation of Tableau 10 is required. The following technologies are mentioned and lightly utilized in this book but are not strictly required:

- Chapter 2, *All about Data - Getting Your Data Ready*, makes light use of Adobe Acrobat.
- Access to SQL Server is helpful in a few places, especially in Chapter 4, *All about Data - Data Densification, Cubes, and Big Data*.
- Chapter 7, *Beyond the Basic Chart* Types, assumes access to Inkscape to complete two exercises (Inkscape is an open source vector drawing application that is similar to Adobe Illustrator).
- Access to Tableau Server is helpful in a few places, especially Chapter 12, *Interacting with Tableau Server*, where permissions for publishing data sources and editing in the web authoring environment are assumed.
- Access to Rserve is assumed for Chapter 13, *R Integration*. RGui and RStudio are also helpful but not strictly required.

Who this book is for

Mastering Tableau targets persons with 5+ months of experience using Tableau. Although not strictly required, a thorough reading of the predecessor to this book, *Learning Tableau*, is helpful. Alternatively, the Desktop I and II training provided by Tableau provides a helpful foundation. A basic knowledge of SQL is helpful in a few sections. A basic knowledge of Excel is assumed.

Conventions

In this book, you will find a number of styles of text that distinguish between different kinds of information. Here are some examples of these styles, and an explanation of their meaning.

Code words in text, database table names, folder names, filenames, file extensions, pathnames, dummy URLs, user input and Twitter handles are shown as follows: "We can include other contexts through the use of the `include` directive. "

A block of code is set as follows:

```
IF [Actual/Forecast] = "Actual"
THEN SUM([World Indicators].[Country B Population])
ELSE PREVIOUS_VALUE(0) * [Select Country B Forecast] + PREVIOUS_VALUE(0)
END
```

When it is necessary to draw your attention to a particular part of a code block, the relevant lines or items are set in bold:

```
IF [Actual/Forecast] = "Actual"
THEN SUM([World Indicators].[Country B Population])
ELSE PREVIOUS_VALUE(0) * [Select Country B Forecast] + PREVIOUS_VALUE(0)
END
```

Any command-line input or output is written as follows:

```
# cd C:\Users\DavidBaldwin\Desktop\New_Directory
```

New terms and **important words** are shown in bold. Words that you see on the screen, in menus or dialog boxes, for example, appear in the text like this: "Clicking on the **Next** button moves you to the next screen".

Warnings or important notes appear in a box like this.

Tips and tricks appear like this.

Reader feedback

Feedback from our readers is always welcome. Let us know what you think about this book—what you liked or may have disliked. Reader feedback is important for us to develop titles that you really get the most out of.

To send us general feedback, simply send an e-mail to feedback@packtpub.com, and mention the book title via the subject of your message.

If there is a topic that you have expertise in and you are interested in either writing or contributing to a book, see our author guide on https://www.packtpub.com/books/info/packt/authors.

Customer support

Now that you are the proud owner of a Packt book, we have a number of things to help you to get the most from your purchase.

Downloading the example code

You can download the example code files for all Packt books you have purchased from your account at http://www.packtpub.com. If you purchased this book elsewhere, you can visit http://www.packtpub.com/support and register to have the files e-mailed directly to you.

You can download the code files by following these steps:

1. Log in or register to our website using your e-mail address and password.
2. Hover the mouse pointer on the **SUPPORT** tab at the top.
3. Click on **Code Downloads & Errata**.
4. Enter the name of the book in the **Search** box.
5. Select the book for which you're looking to download the code files.
6. Choose from the drop-down menu where you purchased this book from.
7. Click on **Code Download**.

Once the file is downloaded, please make sure that you unzip or extract the folder using the latest version of:

- WinRAR / 7-Zip for Windows
- Zipeg / iZip / UnRarX for Mac
- 7-Zip / PeaZip for Linux

The code bundle for the book is also hosted on GitHub at https://github.com/PacktPublishing/Mastering-Tableau. We also have other code bundles from our rich catalog of books and videos available at https://github.com/PacktPublishing/. Check them out!

Downloading the color images of this book

We also provide you a PDF file that has color images of the screenshots/diagrams used in this book. The color images will help you better understand the changes in the output. You can download this file from: `https://www.packtpub.com/sites/default/files/downloads/MasteringTableau_ColorImages.pdf`.

Errata

Although we have taken every care to ensure the accuracy of our content, mistakes do happen. If you find a mistake in one of our books—maybe a mistake in the text or the code—we would be grateful if you would report this to us. By doing so, you can save other readers from frustration and help us improve subsequent versions of this book. If you find any errata, please report them by visiting `http://www.packtpub.com/submit-errata`, selecting your book, clicking on the errata submission form link, and entering the details of your errata. Once your errata are verified, your submission will be accepted and the errata will be uploaded on our website, or added to any list of existing errata, under the Errata section of that title. Any existing errata can be viewed by selecting your title from `http://www.packtpub.com/support`.

Piracy

Piracy of copyright material on the Internet is an ongoing problem across all media. At Packt, we take the protection of our copyright and licenses very seriously. If you come across any illegal copies of our works, in any form, on the Internet, please provide us with the location address or website name immediately so that we can pursue a remedy.

Please contact us at `copyright@packtpub.com` with a link to the suspected pirated material.

We appreciate your help in protecting our authors, and our ability to bring you valuable content.

Questions

You can contact us at `questions@packtpub.com` if you are having a problem with any aspect of the book, and we will do our best to address it.

1
Getting Up to Speed – a Review of the Basics

The goal of this book is to empower you to become a Tableau master; in Tableau-speak, the term is Jedi. Yes, that is official Tableau terminology. Attend the yearly Tableau conference and you can sit in on Jedi classes. Of course, simply attending a class will not automatically bestow you with Jedi powers – nor will simply reading this book. Diligent work on real-world problems is absolutely essential. Couple this diligent work with industrious study and you will make it. You will become a Tableau Jedi. My hope is that this book will prove useful to you on your journey to mastery.

If you are a seasoned Tableau author, you may find this initial chapter elementary. (A person who creates Tableau workbooks is referred to as an author, not a developer.) For such persons, I recommend a quick, inspectional read. If after a few minutes you are satisfied you already possess a solid understanding of the concepts discussed, feel free to proceed to subsequent chapters. If, however, you find some of the content unfamiliar, it may be wise to read with greater attention.

Those who are fairly new to Tableau should find this chapter helpful in getting up to speed quickly; however, since this book targets advanced topics, relatively little time is spent considering the basics. For a more thorough consideration of fundamental topics, consider *Learning Tableau*, written by Joshua Milligan and published by Packt Publishing.

In this chapter, we will discuss the following:

- The Tableau universe
- Understanding the Tableau interface and basic terminology
- Worksheet and dashboard creation
- Connecting Tableau to your data

- Measure Names and Measure Values
- Three essential Tableau concepts

The Tableau universe

Tableau Software has a focused vision resulting in a small product line. The main product (and hence the center of the Tableau universe) is Tableau Desktop. Assuming you are a Tableau author, that's where almost all your time will be spent when working with Tableau. But of course you must be able to connect to data and output the results. Thus, as shown in the following figure, the Tableau universe encompasses data sources, Tableau Desktop, and output channels, which include the Tableau Server family and Tableau Reader:

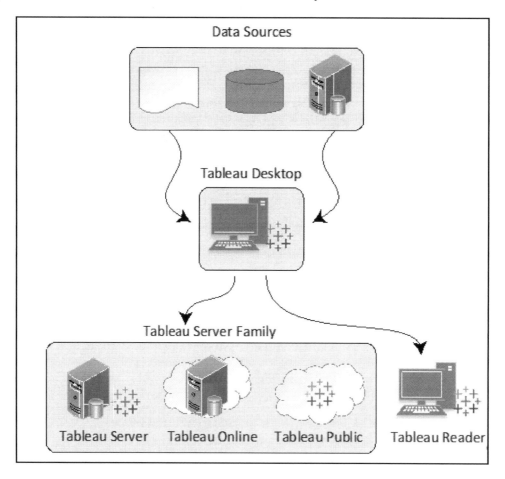

Data Sources	Tableau connects to many data sources. Those data sources will be discussed in more detail in the following section.
Tableau Desktop	Tableau Desktop is where visualizations are created. Although, as of Tableau 8.0, some authoring capabilities were introduced into the Tableau Server environment, that environment is limited. (See `Chapter 12`, *Interacting with Tableau Server* to learn more about authoring in the Tableau Server environment.) Thus, the heavy lifting is still done in Tableau Desktop.
Tableau Server Family	Once completed in Tableau Desktop, a workbook can be uploaded to Tableau Server for end-user access. Tableau Server provides a secure, web-based environment where end users can access visualizations created in Desktop either through a browser or via the Tableau Mobile app for Android and iPhone. Tableau Online is a cloud-based version of Tableau Server hosted by Tableau Software. It's an ideal solution for smaller organizations that need the security and flexibility of Server without the associated overheads. Tableau Public is, in reality, split into two products: the Tableau Public client, and a cloud-based, public-facing version of Tableau Server. The client has the capabilities of Desktop, with a few major exceptions: • The data sources you can connect to are very limited (for example, Excel, Access, text file formats and web data connectors) • You can only publish to Tableau Public • You are limited to 15 million rows of data per workbook
Tableau Reader	The relationship between Tableau Desktop and Tableau Reader is synonymous to that between Adobe Acrobat and Adobe Reader. Desktop is used for authoring; Reader is used for viewing. Desktop has an associated cost; Reader is free. A few brief notes regarding Reader: • Filters, dashboard actions, animation and parameters are all accessible on Reader, but no authoring is enabled • Reader is useful for presentations when Desktop is not available • Reader can only be used with packaged workbooks that do not contain live connections to other data sources

Understanding the Tableau interface and basic terminology

To begin our survey of the basics, let's consider the terminology and associated definitions of assets that make up the Tableau workspace. Lingering a little on these terms should prove helpful, since each is used throughout the book:

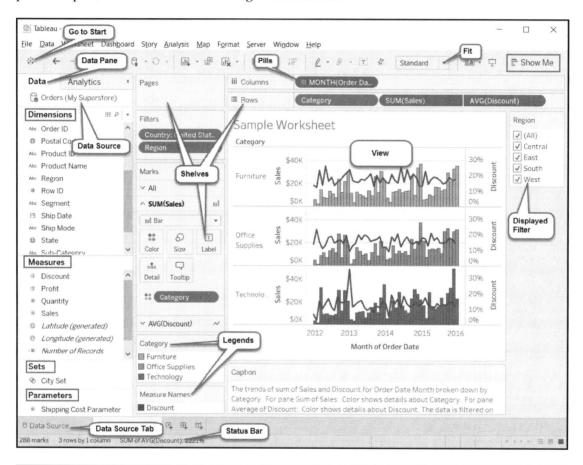

Go to Start	Click to toggle between the start page and the workspace.
Data Pane	Provides access to the data source, all fields, sets, and parameters, and displays the underlying data when the View Data icon is clicked.
Data Source	Lists all data sources and provides access to edit data sources, create data extracts, publish data sources, and more.

Dimensions	Lists all fields classified as **Dimensions**.
Measures	Lists all fields classified as **Measures**.
Sets	Lists all sets created by the Tableau author.
Parameters	Lists all parameters created by the Tableau author.
Data Source Tab	Provides access to the Data Source page.
Shelves	Areas where fields are placed to create views.
Legend	Serves the dual purpose of communicating **Color**, **Size**, and **Shape** information that exists in the view, as well as providing sorting, filtering, and highlighting capabilities.
Status Bar	Displays information about the current view.
Fit	Determines how a view is sized on the screen.
View	That which the end user sees via Tableau Server or Reader. Includes the visualization, legends, displayed filters, parameters, captions, and so on.
Pills	Fields, sets, or parameters that have been placed on one or more shelves. So named because the shape resembles a pill.
Show Me	Tool used to automatically create visualizations based on selected fields and any fields already placed on shelves.
Displayed Filter	A field exposed to the end user providing the ability to display/hide a numeric or date range of the field or display/hide members of the field. In earlier versions of Tableau this was referred to as a **Quick Filter**.

Worksheet and dashboard creation

At the heart of Tableau are worksheets and dashboards. Worksheets contain individual visualizations and dashboards contain one or more worksheets. Additionally, worksheets and dashboards may be combined into stories to communicate specific insights to the end user via a presentation environment. Lastly, all worksheets, dashboards, and stories are organized in workbooks that can be accessed via Tableau Desktop, Server, or Reader. In this section, we will look at worksheet and dashboard creation with the intent of not only communicating the basics, but also providing some insight that may prove helpful to even more seasoned Tableau authors.

Worksheet creation

At the most fundamental level, a visualization in Tableau is created by placing one or more fields on one or more shelves. To state this as a pseudo-equation:

Field(s) + shelf(s) = Viz

As an example, note that the visualization created in the following screenshot is generated by placing the **Sales** field on the **Text** shelf. Although the results are quite simple – a single number – this does qualify as a view. In other words, a **Field (Sales)** placed on a shelf (**Text**) has generated a Viz:

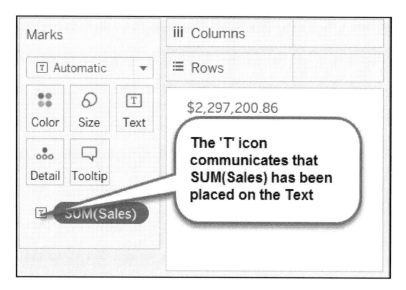

Exercise – fundamentals of visualizations

Let's explore the basics of creating a visualization via an exercise:

1. Navigate to `https://public.tableau.com/profile/david.baldwin#!/` to locate and download the workbook associated with this chapter.
2. In the workbook, find the tab labeled **Fundamentals of Visualizations**:

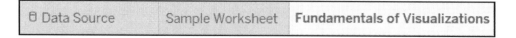

3. Locate **Region** within the **Dimensions** portion of the **Data** pane:

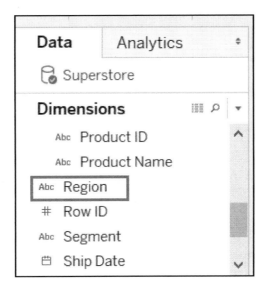

4. Drag **Region** to the **Color** shelf; that is, **Region** + **Color** shelf = what is shown in the following screenshot:

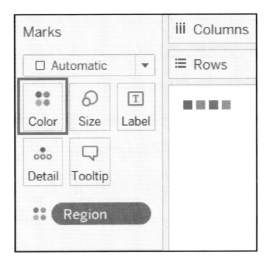

5. Click on the **Color** shelf and then on **Edit Colors...** to adjust colors as desired:

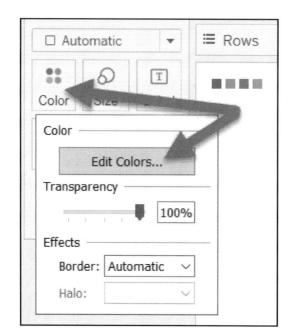

6. Next, move **Region** to the **Size**, **Label/Text**, **Detail**, **Columns**, and **Rows** shelves. After placing **Region** on each shelf, click on the shelf to access additional options.
7. Lastly, choose other fields to drop on various shelves to continue exploring Tableau's behavior.

As you continue exploring Tableau's behavior by dragging and dropping different fields onto different shelves, you will notice that Tableau responds with default behaviors. These defaults, however, can be overridden, which we will explore in the following section.

Beyond default behavior

Note that in the previous exercise, the **Marks** card perpetually reads **Automatic**. This means that Tableau is providing the default view. The default view can be easily overridden by choosing a different selection from the drop-down menu:

Another type of default behavior can be observed when dragging a field onto a shelf. For example, dragging and dropping a measure onto a shelf will typically result in the aggregation **Sum**. To override this default behavior, right click and drag a field from the **Data** pane and drop it onto a shelf. Tableau will respond by opening a dialog box with the possible options. An example of this is shown in the following screenshot, where the field **Region** has been placed on the **Rows** shelf via a right-click, drag and drop action:

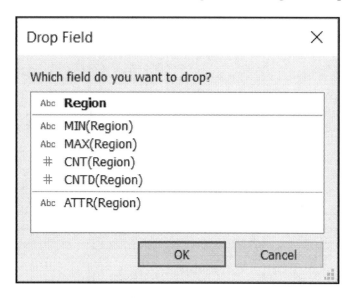

Exercise – overriding defaults

Let's walk through an exercise overriding the two default behaviors discussed previously:

1. In the workbook associated with this chapter, navigate to the Overriding Defaults worksheet, right-click and drag **Order Date** to the **Columns** shelf.

2. Within the resulting dialog box, choose the second instance of **MONTH(Order Date)**:

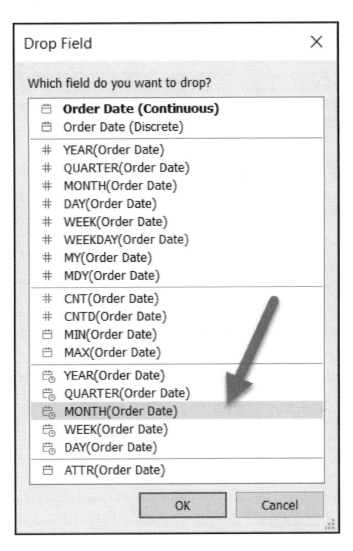

3. Place **Sales** on the **Rows** shelf and **Region** on the **Details** shelf.
4. Click on the dropdown in the **Marks** card and select **Area**:

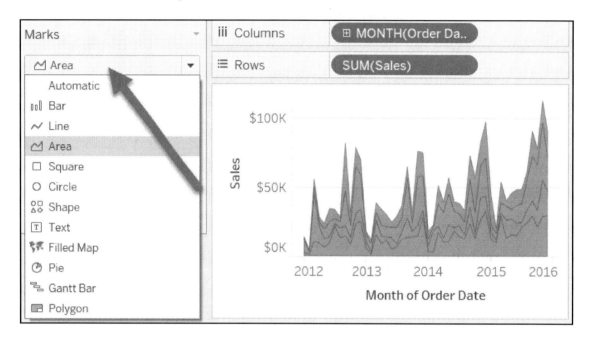

Show Me

Show Me allows the Tableau author to create visualizations at the click of a button. To understand how it works, consider the following screenshot:

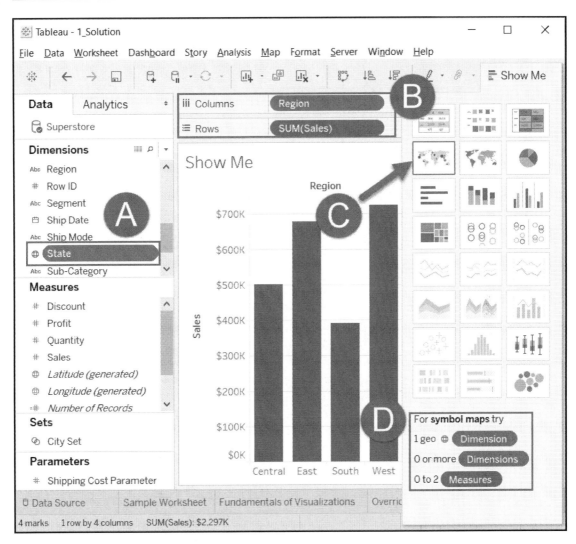

1. **A**: Selected field(s) in the **Data** pane.
2. **B**: Field(s) deployed in the view; that is, **Pills**.

3. **C**: The recommended view.

4. **D**: Help text communicating the requirements for creating the recommended view for any selection choice over which the cursor is placed.

5. Every icon in **Show Me** that is not grayed out represents a visualization that can be created simply by clicking on it. For example, in the preceding screenshot, the Tableau author may choose to click on the pie chart icon to create a pie chart based on the selected and deployed fields.

Show Me options are highlighted based on two criteria: the selected field(s) in the **Data** pane and the fields(s) deployed in the view.

6. **Show Me** may be effectively used for the following reasons:
   - **Efficiency**: The proficient Tableau author already knows how to create the basic visualization types. **Show Me** automates these basic types and thus may be used for quicker production.
   - **Inspiration**: Determining an effective way to visualize a dataset can be challenging. **Show Me** can help with this challenge by allowing the Tableau author to quickly consider various options.
   - **Education**: An inexperienced Tableau author may access **Show Me** to better understand how various visualizations are created. Much can be learned by reading the help text displayed at the bottom of **Show Me** and observing the results generated by clicking on various options.

7. These three reasons communicate the strong value that **Show Me** provides for worksheet creation; however, there is one reason for which it should not be used: as a crutch. The Tableau author who clicks on the various options without understanding how each visualization is created is not only shortchanging the educational process, but may generate results that are not well understood and could thus lead to detrimental business decisions.

Dashboard creation

Although, as stated previously, a dashboard contains one or more worksheets, dashboards are much more than static presentations. They are an essential part of Tableau's interactivity. In this section, we will populate a dashboard with worksheets and then deploy actions for interactivity.

Exercise – building a dashboard

1. In the workbook associated with this chapter, navigate to the tab entitled Building a Dashboard.

2. Within the **Dashboard** pane located on the left-hand portion of the screen, double-click on each of the following worksheets (in the order in which they are listed) to add them to the dashboard:
   - **US Sales**
   - **Customer Segment**
   - **Scatter Plot**
   - **Customers**

3. In the lower right-hand corner of the dashboard, click in the blank area below **Profit Ratio** to select the vertical container:
   - After clicking in the blank area, you should see a blue border around the filter and the legends. This indicates that the vertical container is selected.

4. As shown in the following screenshot, select the vertical container handle and drag it to the left-hand side of the **Customers** worksheet. Note the gray shading, which communicates where the container will be placed:

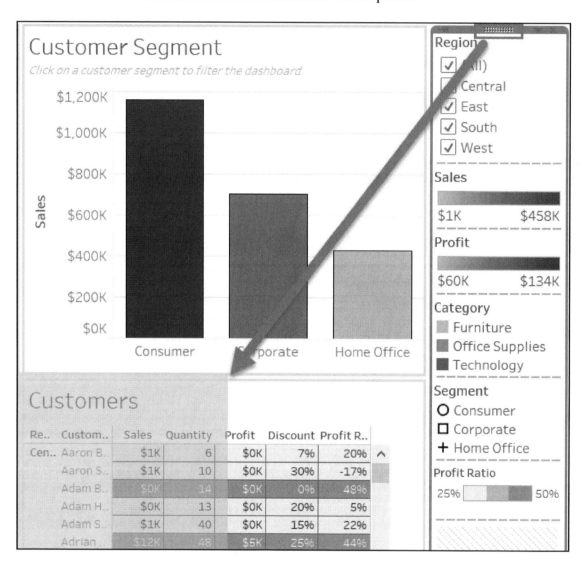

The gray shading (provided by Tableau when dragging elements such as worksheets and containers onto a dashboard) helpfully communicates where the element will be placed. Take your time and observe carefully when placing an element on a dashboard or the results may be unexpected.

5. Format the dashboard as desired. The following tips may prove helpful:
    1. Adjust the sizes of the elements on the screen by hovering over the edges between each element and then clicking and dragging as desired.
    2. Note that the **Sales** and **Profit** legends in the following screenshot are floating elements. Make an element float by right-clicking on the element handle and selecting **Floating**. (See the previous screenshot and note that the handle is located immediately above **Region**, in the upper-right-hand corner).
    3. Create **Horizontal** and **Vertical** containers by dragging those objects from the bottom portion of the **Dashboard** pane.
    4. Drag the edges of containers to adjust the size of each worksheet.

5. Display the dashboard title via **Dashboard | Show Title...**:

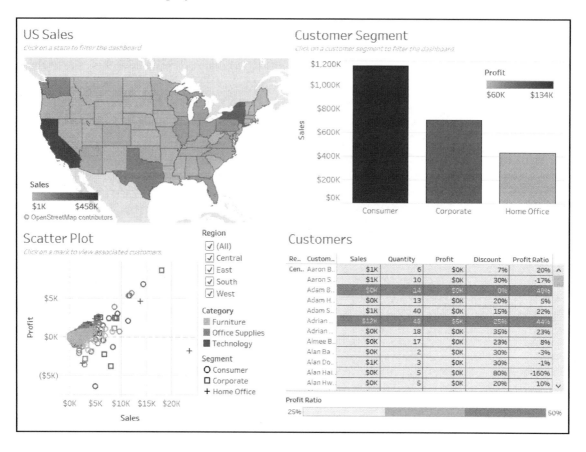

Exercise – adding interactivity to a dashboard

One of the primary benefits of Tableau is the interactivity it provides the end user. Dashboards are not simply for viewing; they are meant for interaction. In this exercise, we will add interactivity to the dashboard that was created in the previous exercise:

1. Starting where the previous exercise ended, click the drop-down menu associated with the **Region** filter and navigate to **Apply to Worksheets | All Using this Data Source**:

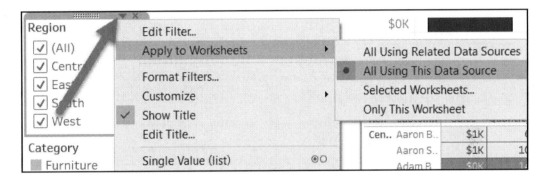

2. In order to use the map as a filter for the other worksheets on the dashboard, click the **Use as Filter** icon located in the top-right-hand corner of the **US Sales** worksheet:

3. Similarly, set **Customer Segment** to **Use as Filter**.
4. Navigate to the menu option **Dashboard | Actions**.

5. Within the dialog box, navigate to **Add Action** | **Filter** and create a filter like the one shown in the following screenshot:

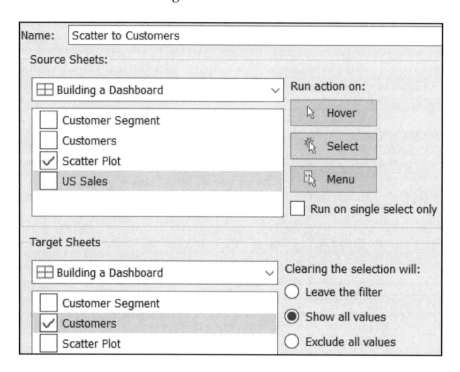

Having completed the preceding dashboard exercise, you should now be able to click on various objects on the dashboard and observe their interactivity. To learn advanced dashboarding techniques, be sure to check out `Chapter 10`, *Visualization Best Practices and Dashboard Design*.

Connecting Tableau to your data

At the time of writing, Tableau's Data Connection menu includes 50 different connection types, and that is somewhat of an understatement since some of those types contain multiple options. For example, the selection choice, **Other Files**, includes 21 options. Of course, we won't cover the details for every connection type, but we will cover the basics.

Upon opening a new instance of Tableau Desktop, you will note a link in the upper left-hand corner of the workspace. Clicking on that link will enable you to connect to data. Alternatively, you can simply click on the **New Data Source** icon on the toolbar:

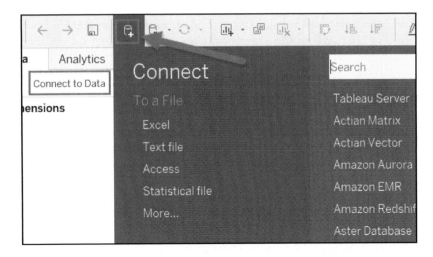

Although subsequent chapters will consider connecting to other data sources, here we will limit the discussion to considerations when connecting to Excel and text files.

Excel and text files

Upon choosing to connect to an Excel or text file, the Tableau author is presented with two choices. Note that those choices are somewhat hidden. As shown in the following screenshot, you will need to click on the arrow next to the **Open** button to access them:

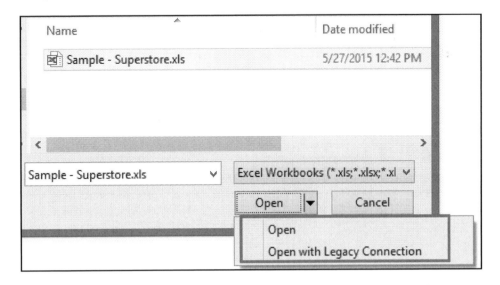

The **Open** option uses a native Tableau driver. The **Open with Legacy Connection** option accesses the Microsoft JET driver. Let's compare and contrast some of the differences between these two drivers.

Comparing and contrasting Native Tableau Driver and MS Jet Driver

Native Tableau Driver	MS Jet Driver
More set capabilities such as in/out and combined sets	Limited set capabilities
Count Distinct is allowed	Count Distinct is disallowed
Allows more than 255 columns	Columns are capped at 255
Special characters, such as brackets and quotation marks, are allowed in file and field names	Special characters are disallowed in file and field names
When connecting to Excel, the data type is determined by 95% of the first 10,000 rows	When connecting to Excel, the data type is determined by the first eight rows
Cannot connect to .xlsb files	Can connect to .xlsb files
File names can be any length	File names are limited to 64 characters
Custom SQL is not allowed	Custom SQL is allowed
Left and inner joins are allowed	Left, inner, and right joins are allowed
Pivot data from rows to columns	No pivoting feature
Improved header auto-detection	

Note that the preceding table is not complete. There are many other differences between the functionality of Native Tableau Driver and MS Jet Driver. Most of those, however, are less consequential.

So, when should you use Native Tableau Driver versus MS JET Driver? In short, use the native Tableau driver! In almost every case it will provide better performance and more functionality. One exception is when custom SQL is required. Tableau Software does not recommend using custom SQL in most cases because Tableau-generated SQL will run more efficiently; however, in some cases it may be necessary.

Connecting to a Tableau Server

Connecting to Tableau Server is perhaps the single most important server connection type to consider, since it is frequently used to provide better performance than may otherwise be possible. Additionally, connecting to Tableau Server enables the author to receive not only data, but information regarding how that data is to be interpreted, for example, whether a given field should be considered a measure or a dimension. Let's explore this further via two exercises.

Exercise – observing metadata differences

As a precursor to connecting to Tableau Server, let's compare and contrast the instance of the **Superstore** data source represented in the workbook associated with this chapter (that is, the Chapter 1 workbook) with a new connection to the same data.

Exercise steps

1. In a new instance of Tableau, navigate to **Data** | **New Data Source** | **Excel** to connect to the **Sample – Superstore** dataset that installs with Tableau desktop (it should be located on your hard drive under **My Tableau Repository** | **Datasources**).
2. Double-click on the **Orders** sheet.
3. Click on the **Sheet 1** tab.
4. Place **Discount** on the **Text** shelf.
5. Double-click on **Profit** and **Sales**.

6. Compare the results of the new worksheet to that of the worksheet entitled `Observing Metadata Differences` in the `Chapter 1` workbook:

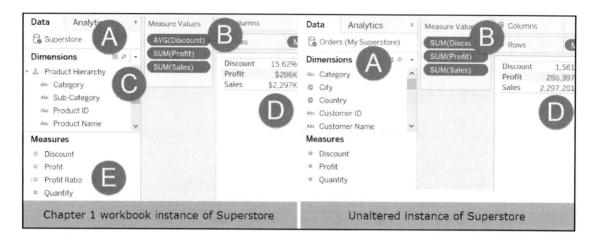

- **A**: The data source name has been altered in the `Chapter 1` workbook
- **B**: In the `Chapter 1` workbook, the default aggregation of **Discount** is **AVG**. In the unaltered instance the default is **SUM**
- **C**: **Product Hierarchy** exists only in the `Chapter 1` workbook
- **D**: The format of **Discount**, **Profit**, and **Sales** differs between the two instances
- **E**: **Profit Ratio** exists only in the `Chapter 1` workbook

Exercise – connecting to Tableau Server

In order to complete this exercise, access to an instance of Tableau Server is necessary. If you do not have access to Tableau Server, consider installing a trial version on your local computer:

1. In the workbook associated with this chapter, navigate to the `Connecting to Tableau Server` worksheet.
2. Right-click on the **Superstore** data source and select **Publish to Server**.
3. Log in to Tableau Server and follow the prompts to complete the publication of the data source.
4. After the data source has been published, open a new instance of Tableau Desktop and navigate to **Data** | **New Data Source** | **Tableau Server** to connect to the data source published in the previous step.

5. Click on **Sheet 1** in the new workbook and observe that the changes made in the Chapter 1 workbook have been preserved.

6. Within the **Data** pane, right-click on **Profit Ratio** and note that it is not directly editable.

Having completed the previous two exercises, let's discuss the most germane point; that is, metadata. Metadata is often defined as *data about the data*. In the preceding case, the data source name, default aggregation, default number formatting, and hierarchy are all examples of Tableau *remembering* changes made to the metadata. This is important because publishing a data connection allows for consistency across multiple Tableau authors. For example, if your company has a policy regarding the use of decimal points when displaying currency, that policy will be easily adhered to if all Tableau authors start building workbooks by pointing to data sources where all formatting has been predefined.

In the last exercise, the fact that the **Profit Ratio** calculated field was not directly editable when accessed via connecting to Tableau Server as a data source has important implications. Imagine the problems that would ensue if different Tableau authors defined **Profit Ratio** differently. End users would have no way of understanding what **Profit Ratio** truly means. However, by creating a workbook based on a published data source, the issue is alleviated. One version of **Profit Ratio** is defined and it can only be altered by changing the data source. This functionality can greatly improve consistency across the enterprise.

Connecting to saved data sources

Connecting to a saved data source on a local machine is much like connecting to a data source published on Tableau Server. Metadata definitions associated with the local data source are preserved, just like they are on Tableau Server. Of course, since the data source is local instead of remote, the publication process is different. Let's explore this via an exercise.

Exercise – creating a local data connection

1. In the workbook associated with this chapter, navigate to the tab entitled Local Data Connection.

2. In the **Data** pane, right-click on the **Superstore** data source and select **Add to Saved Data Sources**.

3. Using the resulting dialog box, save the data source as **Superstore** in **My Tableau Repository | Datasources**, located on your hard drive.

4. Click on the **Go to Start** icon located in the top-left corner of your screen and observe the new saved data source:

Note that you can save a local data source that points to a published data source on Tableau Server. First, connect to a published data source on Tableau Server. Next, right-click on the data source in your workspace and choose **Add to Saved Data Sources**. Now you can connect to Tableau Server directly from your **Start** page!

Measure Names and Measure Values

I've observed the following scenario frequently. A new Tableau author creates a worksheet and drags a measure to the **Text** shelf. They would like to create another row to display a second measure but do not know how. They drag the second measure to various places on the view and get results that seem entirely unpredictable. The experience is very frustrating for the author, since it's so easy to accomplish this in Excel! The good news is that it's also easy to accomplish in Tableau. It just requires a different approach. Let's explore the solution via an exercise.

Measure Names and Measure Values – the basics

Measure Names and Measure Values are generated fields in Tableau. They do not exist in the underlying data, but they are indispensable for creating many kinds of views. As may be guessed from its placement in the **Data** pane and its name, Measure Names is a dimension whose members are made up of the names of each measure in the underlying dataset. Measure Values contains the numbers or values of each measure in the dataset. Watch what happens below when measure names and measure values are used independently. Afterward observe how they work elegantly together to create a view.

Exercise – Measure Names and Measure Values

1. In the workbook associated with this chapter, navigate to the worksheet entitled `Measure Names/Values`.

2. Drag **Measure Values** to the **Text** shelf and observe the results:

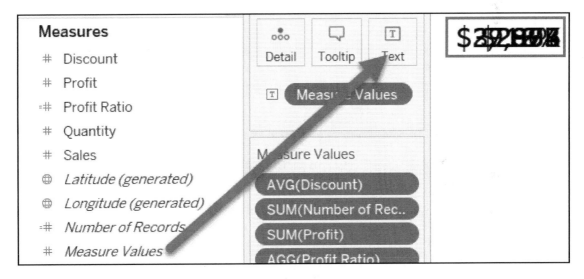

3. Clear the worksheet by clicking on the **Clear Sheet** icon on the toolbar:

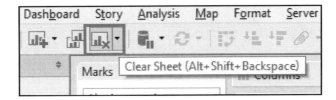

4. Drag **Measure Names** to the **Rows** shelf and observe that the view merely displays **No Measure Value**.
5. Drag **Measure Values** to the **Text** shelf. Note the list of measures and associated values.

Perhaps the interrelationship between **Measure Names** and **Measure Values** is best explained by an analogy. Consider several pairs of socks and a partitioned sock drawer. *Step 2* is the equivalent of throwing the socks into a pile. The results are, well, disorganized. *Step 4* is the equivalent of an empty sock drawer with partitions. The partitions are all in place but where are the socks? *Step 5* is a partitioned drawer full of nicely organized socks. Measure Names is like the partitioned sock drawer. Measure Values is like the socks. Independent of one another they are not of much use. Used together, they can be applied in many different ways.

Measure Names and Measure Values – shortcuts

Tableau provides various shortcuts to quickly create a desired visualization. If you are new to the software, this shortcut behavior may not seem intuitive, but with a little practice and a few pointers, you will quickly gain understanding. Let's use the following exercise to explore how you can use a shortcut to rapidly deploy Measure Names and Measure Values.

Exercise – Measure Names and Measure Values shortcuts

1. In the workbook associated with this chapter, navigate to the worksheet entitled `MeasureNames/Values ShrtCts`.
2. Drag **Sales** directly on top of the **Profit** number in the view:

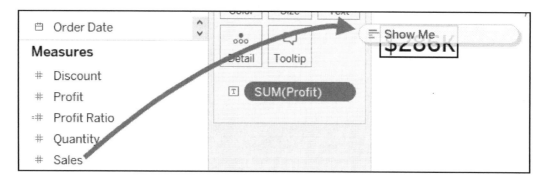

3. Observe the results, including the appearance of the **Measure Values** shelf, the deployment of **Measure Names** on the **Rows** and **Filters** shelves, and **Measure Values** on the **Text** shelf:

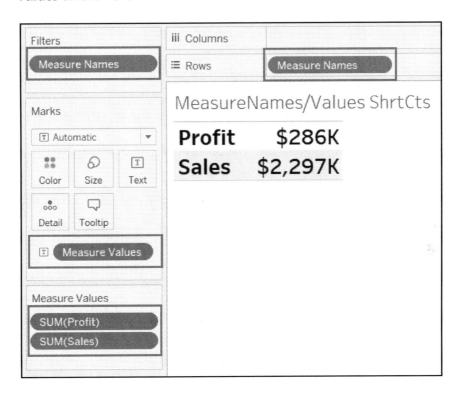

Exercise commentary

Several things happened in step 2. After placing **Sales** on top of the **Profit** number in the view, Tableau did the following:

1. Deployed **Measure Names** on the **Filters** shelf:
    *   Open the **Measure Names** filter and observe that only **Profit** and **Sales** are selected. This limits the view to display only those two measures.

2. Deployed **Measure Names** on the **Rows** shelf:
    *   **Measure Names** is acting like a partitioned container; that is, like the sock drawer in the preceding analogy. Because of the filter, the only rows that are displayed are for **Profit** and **Sales**.

3. Displayed the **Measure Values** shelf:
   - The **Measure Values** shelf is somewhat redundant. Although it clearly shows the measures that are displayed in the view, it essentially acts as an easy way to access the filter. You can simply drag measures on and off the **Measure Values** shelf to adjust the filter and thus display/hide additional **Measure Values**. You can also change the order within the **Measure Values** shelf to change the order of the measures in the view.

4. Deployed **Measure Values** on the **Text** shelf:
   - **Measure Values** simply defines the numbers that will be displayed for each row – in this case, the numbers associated with **Profit** and **Sales**.

If the visualization has an axis, the shortcut to deploy Measure Names and Measure Values requires the placement of a second measure on top of the axis of an initial measure, as shown in the following screenshot:

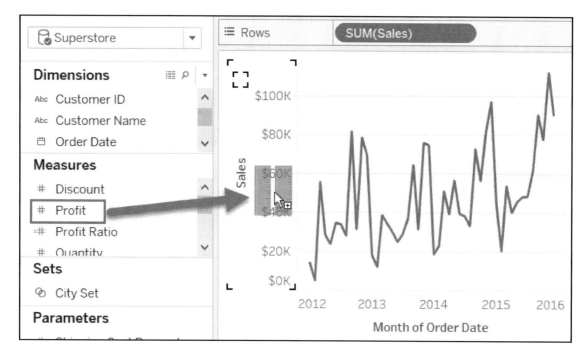

Three essential Tableau concepts

The road to the mastery of Tableau begins with three essential concepts. We will consider each of the following in turn:

- Dimensions and measures
- Row level, aggregate level, and table level
- Continuous and discrete

Essential concept 1 – dimensions and measures

Tableau categorizes every field from an underlying data source as either a dimension or a measure. A dimension is qualitative or, to use another word, categorical. A measure is quantitative or aggregable. A measure is usually a number but may be an aggregated, non-numeric field, such as **MAX(Order Date)**. A dimension is usually a text, Boolean, or date field, but may also be a number, such as **Order_ID**. Dimensions provide meaning to numbers by slicing those numbers into separate parts/categories. Measures without dimensions are mostly meaningless.

Let's consider an example to better understand this concept.

Exercise – dimensions and measures

1. In the workbook associated with this chapter, navigate to the worksheet entitled `Dimensions and Measures`.
2. Drag **Sales** to the **Rows** shelf.

3. Place **Order Date** and **Category** on the **Columns** shelf:

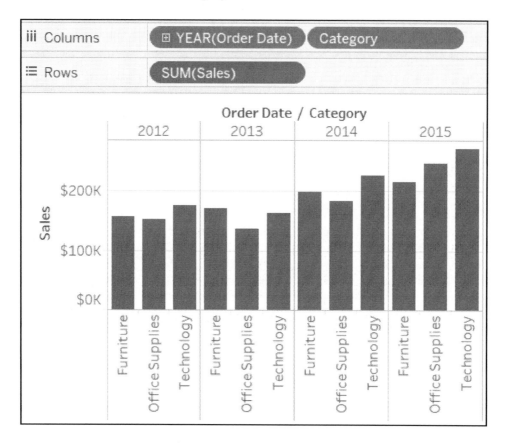

The result of step 2 is mostly meaningless. The measure **Sales** is about $2.3 million, but without the context supplied by slicing the measure with one or more dimensions, there is no way to understand what it means. Step 2 brings meaning. Placing **Order Date** and **Category** on the **Columns** shelf provides context, which imparts meaning to the visualization.

Essential concept 2 – Row Level, Aggregate Level, and Table Level

There are three levels of calculations in Tableau: Row, Aggregate, and Table. To understand how these three levels function, it is important to be familiar with the Tableau process flow:

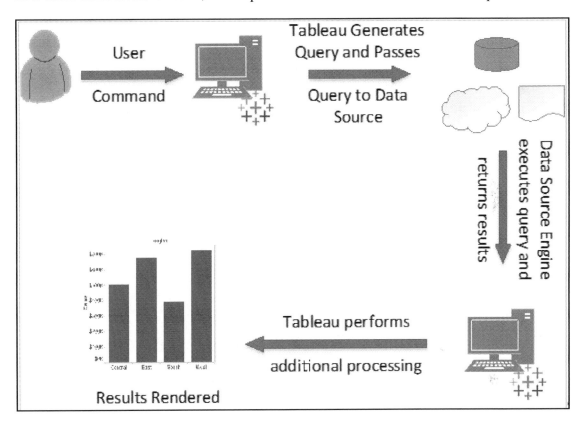

Let's follow the flow of the preceding figure to understand where the three levels of calculations take place. We will do so via an example considering the fields **Profit** and **Sales**. Assuming SQL, consider the following calculation types, calculated fields, and queries. Note that the SQL is simplified for the sake of the example:

Calculation type	Calculated field in Tableau	Query passed to Data Source
Row level	`Profit/Sales`	`SELECT SUM(Profit / Sales)` `FROM Orders$`

Aggregate level	`Sum(Profit)/Sum(Sales)`	`SELECT SUM(Profit),`
		`SUM(Sales)`
		`FROM Orders$`

Table level	`WINDOW_AVG(Sum([Number of Records])/Sum(Quantity))`	`SELECT SUM(Profit),`
		`SUM(Sales)`
		`FROM Orders$`

For the row-level calculation, the computation is actually completed by the data-source engine. Tableau merely displays the results. For the aggregate level calculation, Tableau does a little bit more than display the results; it also divides the two numbers that are returned by the data-source engine. For the table-level calculation, Tableau may perform additional computations on the returned results. Let's explore further via an exercise using the similar calculated fields.

Exercise – Row Level, Aggregate Level, and Table Level

1. In the workbook associated with this chapter, navigate to the worksheet entitled `Row_Agg_Tbl`.
2. Navigate to **Analysis** | **Create Calculated Field** to create the following calculated fields. Note that each must be created separately; it is not possible in this context to create a single calculated field containing all three calculations:

Name	Calculation
Lev – Row	`[Number of Records]/[Quantity]`
Lev – Agg	`SUM([Number of Records])/SUM(Quantity)`
Lev – Tab	`WINDOW_AVG([Lev - Agg])`

3. In the **Data** pane, right-click on the three calculated fields you just created and navigate to **Default Properties** | **Number format**.
4. In the resulting dialog box, select **Percentage** and click **OK**.
5. Place **Order Date** on the **Columns** shelf.
6. Place **Measure Names** on the **Rows** shelf and **Measure Values** on the **Text** shelf.
7. Exclude all values except for **Lev – Row**, **Lev – Agg**, and **Lev – Tab**:

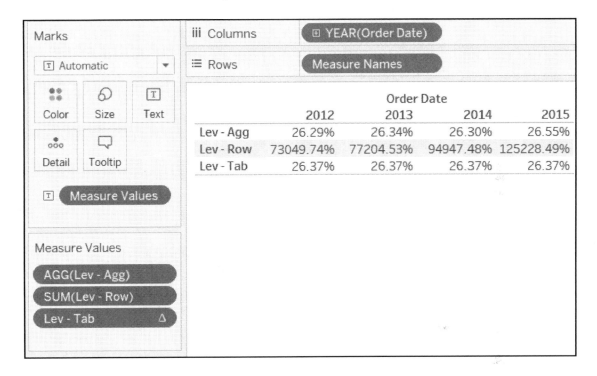

Exercise commentary

Lev – Agg is an aggregate-level calculation. The aggregated results of [Number of Records] and [Quantity] are returned by the data-source engine. Tableau divides those results and displays values for each year.

Lev – Row is a row-level calculation. The computation is completed by the data-source engine. [Number of Records] is divided by [Quantity] for each row of the underlying data. The results are then summed across all rows. Of course, in this case, the row-level calculation does not provide useful results; however, since a new Tableau author may mistakenly create a row-level calculation when an aggregate-level calculation is what is really needed, the example is included here.

Lev – Tab is a table-level calculation. Some of the computation is completed by the data-source engine; that is, the aggregation. Tableau completes additional computation on the results returned from the data-source engine. Specifically, the results of **Lev – Agg** are summed and then divided by the number of members in the dimension. For the preceding example, this is (26.29% + 26.34% + 26.30% + 26.55%)/4. Once again, the results in this case are not particularly helpful, but they do demonstrate knowledge the budding Tableau author should possess.

Essential concept 3 – continuous and discrete

Continuous and discrete are not concepts that are unique to Tableau. Indeed, both can be observed in many arenas. Consider the following example:

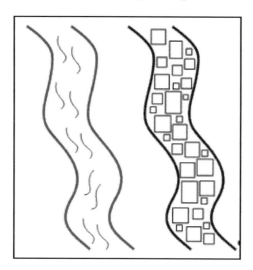

This is an image of two rivers – River-Left and River-Right. Water is flowing in River-Left. River-Right is composed of ice cubes. Could you theoretically sort the ice cubes in River-Right? Yes! Is there any way to sort the water in River-Left? In other words, could you take buckets of water from the bottom of the river, cart those buckets upstream and pour the water back into River-Left and thereby say, I have sorted the water in the river? No. The H_2O in River-Left is in continuous form; that is, water. The H_2O in River-Right is in discrete form; that is, ice.

Having considered an example of continuous and discrete in natural phenomena, let's turn our attention back to Tableau. Continuous and discrete in Tableau can be more clearly understood via the following seven considerations:

1. Continuous is green. Discrete is blue. Select any field in the **Data** pane or place any field on a shelf and you will note that it is either green or blue. Also, the icons associated with fields are either green or blue.
2. Continuous is always numeric. Discrete may be a string.
3. Continuous and discrete are not synonymous with dimension and measure. It is common for new Tableau authors to confuse continuous with measure and discrete with dimension. They are not synonymous. A measure may be either discrete or continuous. Also, a dimension, if it is a number, may be discrete or continuous. To prove the point, right-click on any numeric or date field in Tableau and note that you can convert it:

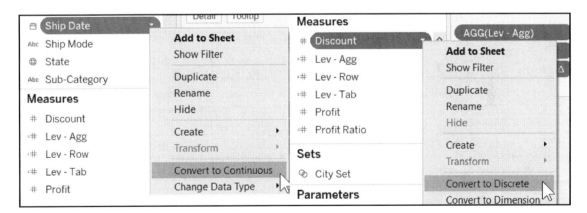

4. Discrete is sortable. Continuous is not sortable. Sortable/not sortable behavior is most easily observed with dates, as shown in the following screenshot:

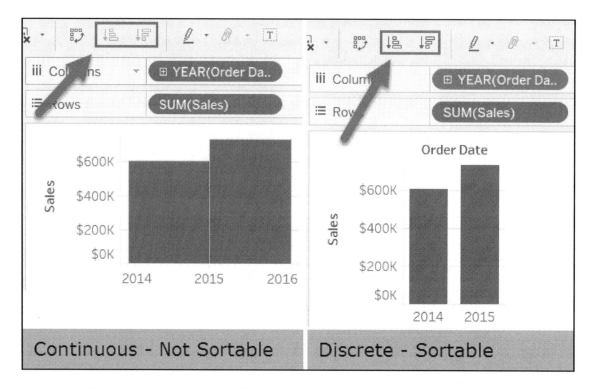

5. Continuous colors are gradients. Discrete colors are distinct. The following example shows **Profit** as continuous and then as discrete. Note the difference in how colors are rendered. The left portion of the following screenshot demonstrates that continuous results in gradients and the right portion demonstrates that discrete results in distinct colors:

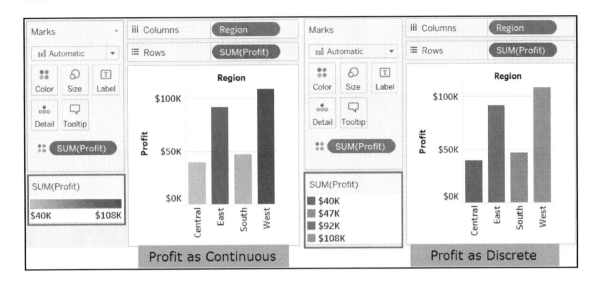

6. Continuous pills can be placed to the right of discrete pills, but not to the left. In the following screenshot, note that the Tableau author *can place* **Region** to the right of **Year** when **Year** is discrete. Further note that the Tableau author *is unable to place* **Region** to the right of **Year** when **Year** is continuous:

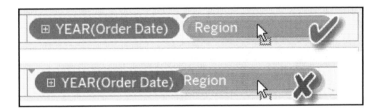

7. Continuous creates axes. Discrete creates headers. Note that in the left portion of the following screenshot, **Year(Order Date)** is continuous and the **Year of Order Date** axis is selected. Since **Year of Order Date** is an axis, the entire *x*-plane is selected. In the right portion of the screenshot, **Year(Order Date)** is discrete and **2014** is selected. Since **2014** is a header, only it is selected and not the entire *x*-plane:

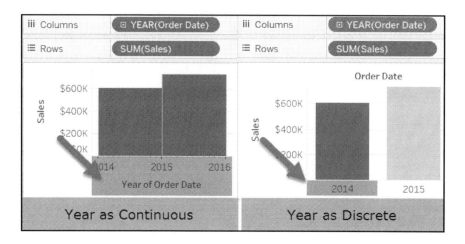

Summary

In this chapter, we looked at the basics of Tableau. We began our survey by considering the Tableau universe, as well as the Tableau interface and some basic terminology. This is important, since definitions given here will be used throughout the book and are prevalent in any discussion concerning Tableau.

Next we considered the basics of creating worksheets and dashboards. We focused on default behavior and how to override that behavior, and we also considered best practices, particularly with regard to the prudent use of **Show Me**.

Next we reviewed **Measure Names** and **Measure Values**. Note that this is often an area where new Tableau authors stumble. If you struggle with proper utilization of Measure Names and Values, consider repeating the exercises and constructing some of your own to ensure clear comprehension.

Finally, we considered three essential Tableau concepts: dimensions and measures; row, aggregate, and table levels; and continuous and discrete. Of particular importance is the understanding that row- and aggregate-level calculations are computed by the data-source engine, while table-level calculations are handled by Tableau. Also, a clear understanding of the seven considerations regarding continuous and discrete should prove helpful.

We will continue our exploration of Tableau with a series of chapters that are *all about the data*. In these chapters, we will consider how to prepare your data for Tableau; joins, blends, and data structures; and data densification, cubes, and big data.

2
All about Data – Getting Your Data Ready

Perhaps the most pertinent and frequent question I'm asked when teaching Tableau is, *How do I get my data ready for Tableau?* I find this difficult to answer for two reasons. Firstly, it's hard to know exactly what the student means by the question, and secondly, it's outside the scope of the class. Let's consider both these reasons.

There is a range of possible meanings for *How do I get my data ready for Tableau?* At the simplest end of the spectrum, some who ask this question just want to know what an Excel spreadsheet prepared for use with Tableau should look like. It suffices to show such students the *Sample Superstore* dataset that installs with Tableau and explain that the addition of human-readable content, such as comments and text boxes, may make the file difficult or impossible to connect to and that the inclusion of totals in the body of the spreadsheet would skew results. Other students wish to understand the basic data structure required by Tableau to work well with relational data. For those people, demonstrating the Tableau Excel plugin and the Data Interpreter can be very helpful. Still others need to address more complex challenges, such as working with cubes or reproducing star schemas. Conversations surrounding these more difficult topics can become quite extended and exploratory.

Questions about getting data ready for Tableau are beyond the scope of most Tableau training.

Training provided by Tableau Software includes well-structured, clean data. This is reasonable, since it's important to spend class time focused on the tool and not on cleaning and restructuring data. Students attending Tableau classes may or may not have extensive data knowledge, but they almost always lack the knowledge to efficiently and effectively navigate the tool. This is why they attend class! Spending significant class time on topics not specific to Tableau does not serve students well.

Because I do not have the liberty to lead focused discussions on data readiness in most training settings, it is with pleasure that I include the topic in this book. The truism **garbage in garbage out** (GIGO) is applicable here. Beautiful, engaging visualizations showing wrong results are just a quicker way to make bad decisions.

A few notes before we press on to the content. This chapter and the following two chapters are *all about data*. As a whole, they represent a significant percentage of this book. This focus on the data is intended to give the reader a firm understanding of basic data approaches, methodology, and challenges, and how to overcome those challenges, especially with regard to working with Tableau. Such a foundation will empower the Tableau author to create workbooks that better support business processes, enhance the overall data environment, and perform more efficiently.

The first part of this chapter is theoretically oriented and does not include exercises. A careful reading of this information is encouraged, since it provides a foundation for greater insight. The later portion of the chapter provides various exercises specifically focused on data preparation.

Now let's dive into this fascinating topic with the goal of enriching our understanding and becoming ever-better data stewards.

In this chapter, we will discuss the following:

- Understanding Tableau's data-handling engine
- Data mining and knowledge-discovery process models
- CRISP-DM
- Focusing on data preparation

Understanding Tableau's data-handling engine

Tableau's data-handling engine is usually not well comprehended by even advanced authors because it's not an overt part of day-to-day activities; however, for the author who wants to truly grasp how to ready data for Tableau, this understanding is indispensable. In this section, we will explore Tableau's data-handling engine and how it enables structured yet organic data mining processes in the enterprise.

To begin, let's clarify a term. The phrase **Data-Handling Engine (DHE)** in this context references how Tableau interfaces with and processes data. This interfacing and processing is comprised of three major parts: Connection, Metadata, and VizQL. Each part is described in detail in the following section. In other publications, Tableau's DHE may be referred to as a **metadata model** or the **Tableau infrastructure**. I've elected not to use either term because each is frequently defined differently in different contexts, which can be quite confusing.

Tableau's DHE (that is, the engine for interfacing with and processing data) differs from other broadly considered solutions in the marketplace. **Legacy business intelligence solutions** often start with structuring the data for an entire enterprise. Data sources are identified, connections are established, metadata is defined, a model is created, and more. The upfront challenges this approach presents are obvious: highly skilled professionals, time-intensive rollout, and associated high startup costs. The payoff is a scalable, structured solution with detailed documentation and process control.

Many *next generation business intelligence platforms* claim to minimize or completely do away with the need for structuring data. The upfront challenges are minimized: specialized skillsets are not required and the rollout time and associated startup costs are low. However, the initial honeymoon is short-lived, since the total cost of ownership advances significantly when difficulties are encountered trying to maintain and scale the solution.

Tableau's infrastructure represents a hybrid approach, which attempts to combine the advantages of legacy business intelligence solutions with those of next-generation platforms, while minimizing the shortcomings of both. The philosophical underpinnings of Tableau's hybrid approach include the following:

- Infrastructure present in current systems should be utilized when advantageous
- Data models should be accessible by Tableau but not required
- DHE components as represented in Tableau should be easy to modify
- DHE components should be adjustable by business users

The Tableau Data-Handling Engine

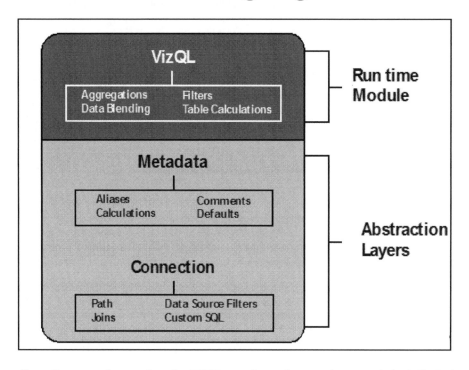

The preceding diagram shows that the DHE consists of a run time module (**VizQL**) and two layers of abstraction (**Metadata** and **Connection**). Let's begin at the bottom of the graphic by considering the first layer of abstraction, Connection.

The most fundamental aspect of the Connection is a path to the data source. The path should include attributes for the database, tables, and views as applicable. The Connection may also include joins, custom SQL, data-source filters, and more. In keeping with Tableau's philosophy of *easy to modify and adjustable by business users* (see the previous section), each of these aspects of the Connection is easily modifiable. For example, an author may choose to add an additional table to a join or modify a data-source filter. Note that the Connection does not contain any of the actual data. Although an author may choose to create a data extract based on data accessed by the Connection, that extract is separate from the connection.

The next layer of abstraction is the metadata. The most fundamental aspect of the Metadata layer is the determination of each field as a measure or dimension. When connecting to relational data, Tableau makes the measure/dimension determination based on heuristics that consider the data itself as well as the data source's data types. Other aspects of the metadata include aliases, data types, defaults, roles, and more. Additionally, the Metadata layer encompasses author-generated fields such as calculations, sets, groups, hierarchies, bins, and so on. Because the Metadata layer is completely separate from the Connection layer, it can be used with other Connection layers; that is, the same metadata definitions can be used with different data sources.

VizQL is generated when a user places a field on a shelf. The VizQL is then translated into **Structured Query Language (SQL)**, **Multidimensional Expressions(MDX)**, or **Tableau Query Language (TQL)** and passed to the backend data source via a driver. The following two aspects of the VizQL module are of primary importance:

- VizQL allows the author to change field attributions on the fly
- VizQL enables table calculations

Let's consider each of these aspects of VizQL via examples:

Changing field attribution example

An analyst is considering infant mortality rates around the world. Using data from `http://data.worldbank.org/`, they create the following worksheet by placing **AVG(Infant Mortality Rate)** and **Country** on the **Columns** and **Rows** shelves, respectively. **AVG(Infant Mortality Rate)** is, of course, treated as a measure in this case:

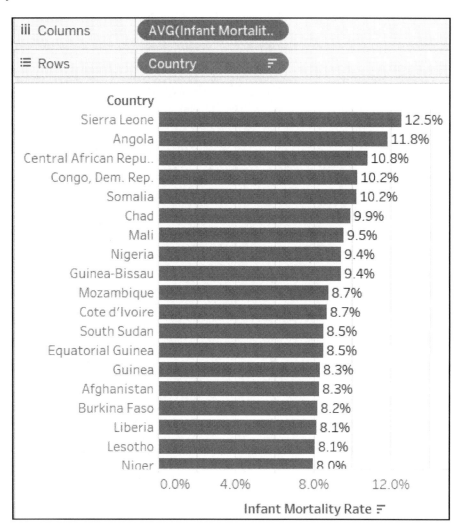

Next they create a second worksheet to analyze the relationship between **Infant Mortality Rate** and **Health Exp/Capita** (that is, health expenditure per capita). In order to accomplish this, they define **Infant Mortality Rate** as a dimension, as shown in the following screenshot:

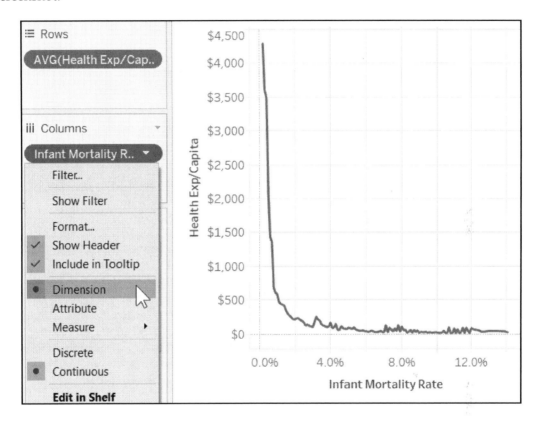

Studying the SQL generated by VizQL to create the preceding visualization is particularly insightful:

```
SELECT ['World Indicators$'].[Infant Mortality Rate] AS [Infant Mortality
Rate],
AVG(['World Indicators$'].[Health Exp/Capita]) AS [avg:Health
Exp/Capita:ok]
FROM [dbo].['World Indicators$'] ['World Indicators$']
GROUP BY ['World Indicators$'].[Infant Mortality Rate]
```

The Group By clause clearly communicates that **Infant Mortality Rate** is treated as a dimension. The takeaway is to note that VizQL enabled the analyst to change the field usage from measure to dimension without adjusting the source metadata. This *on-the-fly* ability enables creative exploration of the data not possible with other tools and avoids lengthy exercises attempting to define all possible uses for each field.

You can view the code generated by Tableau that is passed to the data source via the Performance Recorder, which is accessible via **Help | Settings and Performance | Start Performance Recording**. See Chapter 11, *Improving Performance*, for additional details.

Table calculation example

In the following example, note that **Sales** on the right axis is set to **Quick Table Calculation | Moving Average**. Calculating a moving average, running total, or other such comparison calculations, can be quite challenging to accomplish in a data source. Not only must a data architect consider what comparison calculations to include in the data source, but they must also determine dimensions for which these calculations are relevant. VizQL greatly simplifies such challenges via table calculations:

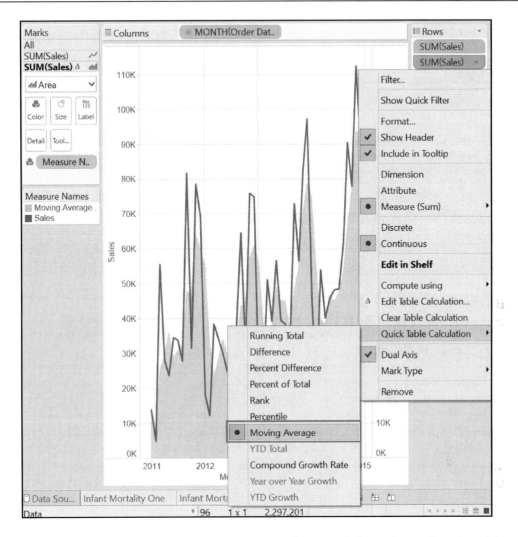

The relevant portion of SQL generated by the preceding worksheet shows that the table calculation is not performed by the data source. Instead, it is performed in Tableau by the VizQL module:

```
SELECT SUM([Orders$].[Sales]) AS [sum:Sales:ok],
  DATEADD(month, DATEDIFF(month, 0, [Orders$].[Order Date]), 0) AS
[tmn:Order Date:ok]
FROM [dbo].[Orders$] [Orders$]
GROUP BY DATEADD(month, DATEDIFF(month, 0, [Orders$].[Order Date]), 0)
```

To reiterate, nothing in the preceding call to the data source generates the moving average. Only an aggregated total is returned and Tableau calculates the moving average via VizQL.

DHE takeaways

This overview of the Tableau **Data-Handling Engine** (**DHE**) demonstrates a flexible approach to interfacing with data. Knowledge of the DHE is helpful for understanding the parameters for Tableau data readiness. Two major takeaways from this section are as follows:

- It is not necessary to explicitly define data types and roles for optimal Tableau usage
- Comparison calculations such as moving averages and running totals can be addressed by table calculations in Tableau and thus do not need to be calculated in advance

Knowledge of these two takeaways can reduce data preparation and data modeling efforts, and thus help streamline the overall data mining lifecycle.

Data-mining and knowledge-discovery process models

Data modeling, data preparation, database design, data architecture; how do these and other, similar terms fit together? This is no easy question to answer! Terms may be used interchangeably in some contexts and be quite distinct in others. Also, understanding the interconnectivity of any technical jargon can be challenging. In the data world, data mining and knowledge-discovery process models attempt to consistently define terms and contextually position and define the various data sub-disciplines. Since the early 1990s, various models have been proposed. The following list is adapted from *A Survey of Knowledge Discovery and Data Mining Process Models* by Lukasz A. Kurgan and Petr Musilek, published in *The Knowledge Engineering Review Volume 21 Issue 1, March 2006*.

Survey of the process models

	Fayyad et al.	KDD	CRISP-DM	Cios et al	SEMMA
	Developing and Understanding of the Application Domain	Selection	Business Understanding	Understanding the Data	Sample
	Creating a Target Data Set Data Cleaning and Pre-processing	Pre-processing	Data Understanding	Understanding the Data	Explore
Steps	Data Reduction and Projection	Transformation	Data Preparation	Preparation of the Data	Modify
	Choosing the DM Task Choosing the DM Algorithm	Data Mining	Data Preparation	Preparation of the Data	Modify
	DM	DM	Modeling	DM	Model
	Interpreting mined Patterns Consolidating Discovered Knowledge	Interpretation/Evaluation	Evaluation Deployment	Evaluation of the Discovered Knowledge Using the Discovered Knowledge	Assess

Only three of these models are currently in use: KDD, CRISP-DM, and SEMMA. Since CRISP-DM is used by four to five times the number of people as the closest competing model (SEMMA), it is the model we will consider in this chapter. For more information, see `http://www.kdnuggets.com/2014/10/crisp-dm-top-methodology-analytics-data-mining-data-science-projects.html`.

The important takeaway is that each of these models grapples with the same problems, particularly, understanding, preparing, modeling, and interpreting data.

CRISP-DM

The **Cross Industry Standard Process for Data Mining (CRISP-DM)** model was created between 1996 and 2000 as a result of a consortium including SPSS, Teradata, Daimler AG, NCR Corporation, and OHRA. It divides the process of data mining into six major phases, as shown in the following CRISP-DM reference model. This model provides a bird's-eye view of a data-mining project lifecycle. Although the sequence of the phases shown in the diagram is typical, it is not rigid; that is, jumping back and forth from phase to phase is allowed and expected. Note that the outer circle communicates the ongoing data-mining lifecycle. Data mining does not cease upon the completion of a particular project. Instead, it exists as long as the business exists and should be constantly revisited to answer new questions as they arise:

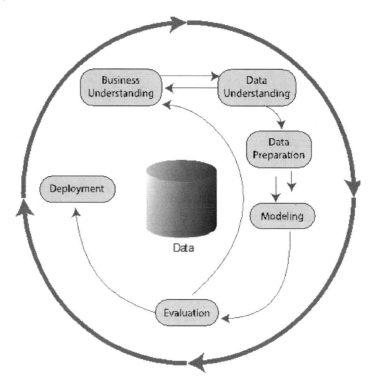

We will consider each of the six phases that comprise CRISP-DM and explore how Tableau can be used effectively throughout the lifecycle. We will particularly focus on the **Data Preparation** phase as that is the phase encompassing data cleansing. As Tableau has evolved over the years, more and more data cleansing capabilities have been introduced.

CRISP-DM phases

The following list briefly defines each of the six CRISP-DM phases and includes high-level information on how Tableau might be used:

- **Phase 1**: Business Understanding
  - This phase determines the business objectives and corresponding data-mining goals. It also assesses risks, costs, and contingencies, and culminates in a project plan.
  - Tableau is a natural fit for presenting information to enhance business understanding.

- **Phase 2**: Data Understanding
  - This phase begins with an initial data-collection exercise. The data is then explored to discover first insights and identify data quality issues.
  - Once the data is collected into one or more relational data sources, Tableau can be used to effectively explore the data and enhance data understanding.

- **Phase 3**: Data Preparation
  - This phase includes data selection, cleansing, construction, merging and formatting.
  - Tableau can be effectively used to identify the preparation tasks that need to occur; that is, Tableau can be used to quickly identify the data selection, cleansing, merging, and so on that should be addressed. Additionally, Tableau can sometimes be used to do actual data preparation. We will walk through some examples here.

As Tableau has evolved, functionality has been introduced that enables it to be used to not just identify data preparation tasks, but also to do more and more of the actual data preparation work.

- **Phase 4**: Modeling
  - In this phase, data-modeling methods and techniques are considered and implemented in one or more data sources. It is important to choose an approach that works well with Tableau. For example, as discussed in `Chapter 4`, *All about Data – Data Densification, Cubes, and Big Data*, Tableau works better with relational data sources than with cubes.

- Tableau has some limited data-modeling capabilities such as pivoting datasets via the Data Source page. Note, however, that this functionality is only available for use with Excel, text files, and Google Sheets. The following chapter addresses pivoting. Also, see *Learning Tableau* by Joshua Milligan for more information.

- **Phase 5**: Evaluation
  - The Evaluation phase considers the results and processes, and determines next steps.
  - Tableau is an excellent fit for considering the results during this phase.

- **Phase 6**: Deployment
  - This phase should begin with a carefully considered plan to ensure a smooth rollout. That plan should include ongoing monitoring and maintenance to ensure continued streamlined access to quality data. Although the phase officially ends with a final report and accompanying review, the data-mining process, as stated in the previous section, continues for the life of the business. Therefore, this phase will always lead to the previous five phases.
  - Tableau should certainly be considered a part of the Deployment phase. Not only is it an excellent vehicle for delivering end-user reporting, it can also be used to report on the data-mining process itself. For instance, Tableau can be used to report on the performance of the overall data-delivery system and thus be an asset for ongoing monitoring and maintenance.

Focusing on data preparation

As discussed previously, Tableau can be effectively used throughout the CRISP-DM phases. Unfortunately, a single chapter is not sufficient to thoroughly explore how Tableau can be used in each phase. Indeed, such a thorough exploration may be worthy of an entire book! Our focus, therefore, will be directed to data preparation, since that phase has historically accounted for up to 60% of the data-mining effort. Our goal will be to learn how Tableau can be used to streamline that effort.

Surveying data

Tableau can be a very effective tool for simply surveying data. Sometimes in the survey process, you may discover ways to clean the data or populate incomplete data based on existing fields. Sometimes, regretfully, there are simply not enough pieces of the puzzle to put together an entire dataset. In such cases, Tableau can be useful to communicate exactly what the gaps are and this, in turn, may create initiative for the organization to more fully populate the underlying data.

In this exercise, we will explore how to use Tableau to quickly discover the percentage of null values for each field in a dataset. Next, we'll explore how data might be extrapolated from existing fields to fill in the gaps.

Exercise – surveying data

1. Navigate to `https://public.tableau.com/profile/david.baldwin#!/` to locate and download the workbook associated with this chapter.
2. Navigate to the worksheet entitled `Surveying and Extrapolating Data`.
3. In the **Data** pane, select the **Data with Nulls** data source.
4. Drag **Manager** and **Territory** to the **Rows** shelf. Observe that in some cases the **Manager** field has null values for given territories:

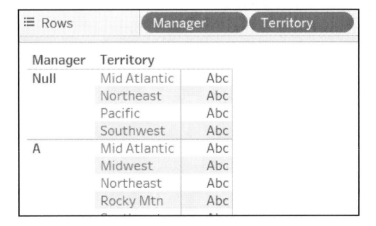

5. Create and show a parameter entitled `Select Field` with **Data type** set to `Integer` and a list that contains an entry for each field name in the dataset:

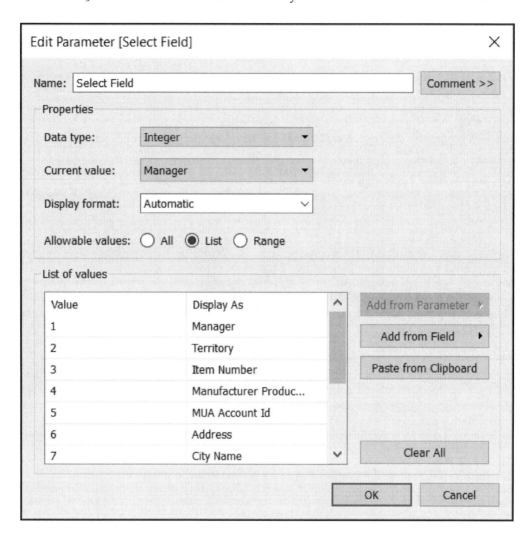

6. In the **Data** pane, right-click on the parameter just created and select **Show Parameter Control**.

7. Create a calculated field entitled **% Populated** and write the following code:

```
SUM([Number of Records]) / TOTAL(SUM([Number of Records]))
```

8. In the **Data** pane, right-click on **% Populated** and select **Default Properties** | **Number Format**.

9. In the resulting dialog box, choose **Percentage**.

10. Create a calculated field entitled **Null & Populated** and write the following code. Note that the complete case statement is fairly lengthy, but it is also repetitive. The following lines represent only a percentage of the total but should be sufficient to enable you to produce the whole.

 In cases requiring a lengthy but repetitive calculation, consider using Excel to write the code more quickly and accurately. By using Excel's Concatenate function, you may be able to save time and avoid typos.

```
CASE [Select Field]
WHEN 1 THEN IF ISNULL ([Manager]) THEN 'Null Values'
ELSE 'Populated Values'
END
WHEN 2 THEN IF ISNULL ([Territory]) THEN 'Null Values'
ELSE ' Populated Values'
END WHEN 3 THEN IF ISNULL ([Item Number]) THEN 'Null Values'
ELSE 'Populated Values'
END
//complete the case statement with the remaining fields
in the data set
END
```

11. Remove **Manager** and **Territory** from the **Rows** shelf.

12. Place **Null &Populated** on the **Rows** and **Color** shelves and **% Populated** on the **Columns** and **Label** shelves.

13. Select various choices in the **Select Field** parameter and note that some fields have a high percentage of null values. For example, in the following screenshot, **24.5%** of records do not have a value for **Manager**:

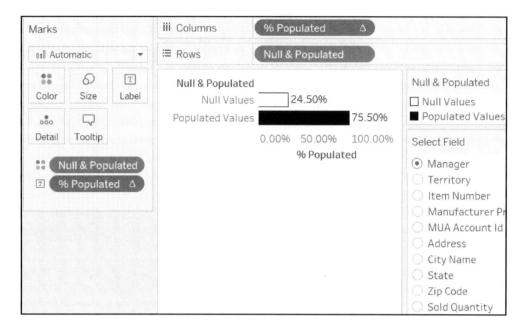

Commentary will be provided for the exercise just completed. Before doing so, however, we'll explore how we might cleanse and extrapolate data from existing data using the same dataset.

Exercise – extrapolating data

This exercise will expand on the previous exercise by cleansing existing data and populating some of the missing data from known information. We will assume that we know which manager is responsible for a given territory; for example, Manager A is responsible for the Midwest, Pacific, and Rocky Mountain territories. We'll use that knowledge to fix errors in the **Manager** field and fill in the gaps (that is, replace the null values) using Tableau:

1. Starting where the previous exercise ended, create a calculated field entitled **Manager Extrapolated** with the following code:

```
CASE [Territory]
WHEN 'Midwest' THEN 'A'
```

```
WHEN 'Pacific' THEN 'A'
WHEN 'Rocky Mtn' THEN 'A'
WHEN 'Mideast' THEN 'B'
WHEN 'Northeast' THEN 'B'
WHEN 'Southwest' THEN 'C'
WHEN 'Mid Atlantic' THEN 'C'
WHEN 'Southeast' THEN 'C'
END
```

2. Add a **Manager Extrapolated** option to the **Select Field** parameter:

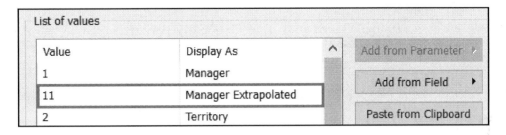

3. Add the following code to the **Null & Populated** calculated field:

```
WHEN 11 THEN IF ISNULL ([Manager Extrapolated])
THEN 'Null Values' ELSE 'Populated Values' END
```

4. Note that the **Manager Extrapolated** field is now fully populated:

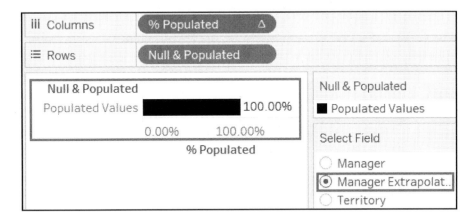

Exercise commentary

Now let's consider some of the specifics from the previous two exercises. Take a look at the following code:

```
CASE [% Populated]
WHEN 1 THEN IF ISNULL ([Manager]) THEN 'Null Values'
ELSE 'Populated Values'
END
```

- Note that the complete case statement is several lines long. The preceding is a representative portion.
- This case statement is a row-level calculation that considers each field in the dataset and determines which rows are populated and which are not. For example, in the preceding representative lines of code, every row of the field **Manager** is evaluated for nulls:

```
SUM([Number of Records]) / TOTAL(SUM([Number of Records]))
```

- This code is the equivalent of the quick-table calculation **Percent of Total**. In conjunction with the **Null & Populated** calculated field, it allows us to see what percentage of our fields are actually populated with values:

It's a good idea to get in the habit of writing table calculations from scratch even if an equivalent quick-table calculation is available. This will help you more clearly understand table calculations.

```
CASE [Territory]
WHEN 'Midwest' THEN 'A'
...
END
```

- This case statement is an example of how you might use one or more fields to extrapolate what another field should be. For example, the **Manager** field in the dataset has a large percentage of null values, and even the existing data has errors. Based on our knowledge of the business (that is, which managers are in charge of each territory) we were able to use the **Territory** field to achieve 100% population with accurate information.

Nulls are a part of almost every extensive *real* dataset. Understanding how many nulls are present in each field can be vital to ensuring that you provide accurate business intelligence. It may be acceptable to tolerate some null values when the final results will not be substantially impacted. Too many nulls invalidate results. Also, as demonstrated in the previous exercise, in some cases one or more fields can be used to extrapolate the values that should be in an underpopulated or erroneously populated field.

 The ability to use Tableau to effectively communicate to your data team what values are missing, which are erroneous, and possible workarounds can be invaluable to the overall data-mining effort.

Cleaning the data

The United States government provides helpful documentation for various bureaucratic processes. For example, the **Department of Health and Human Services (HHS)** provides lists of ICD-9 codes, otherwise known as *International Statistical Classification of Diseases and Related Health Problems* codes. Unfortunately, these codes are not always in easily accessible formats. Often, only PDF documents are provided. How can you connect Tableau to a PDF document? You can't! However, you can export data from a PDF document to a text file with software such as Adobe Acrobat. It may then be possible to extract the desired data. As an example, let's consider an actual HHS document known as R756OTN.

Exercise – cleaning the data

Note that the first three steps below require locating the data, preparing the data, and then connecting Tableau to the data. To complete this exercise, you can skip these steps and simply reference the data in the workbook provided with this chapter.

Exercise steps

1. Locate and download `R756OTN.pdf` via a search engine.
2. Open `R756OTN.pdf` within a PDF editor and export to text. Using Adobe Acrobat Pro DC, the menu path is **File | Export To... | Text (Plain)**.
3. Within the resulting text file, remove all data previous to the section entitled `Diagnosis Code Description`. Note that some additional cleanup may be required before connecting Tableau to the text file.

4. Within the workbook associated with this chapter, navigate to the worksheet entitled `Cleaning the Data`.

5. Navigate to the worksheet entitled `Cleaning the Data`.

6. Within the **Data** pane, select the data source **R756OTN Raw**.

7. Drag **Diagnosis** to the **Rows** shelf and observe the text in the view. Note the junk data that occurs in some rows:

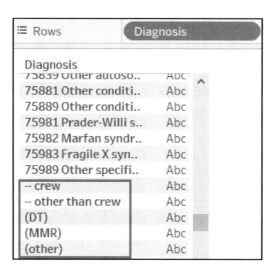

8. Create a calculated field named `DX` with the following code:

```
SPLIT( [Diagnosis], " ", 1 )
```

9. Create a calculated field named `Null Hunting` with the following code:

```
INT(MID([DX],2,1))
```

10. In the **Data** pane, drag `Null Hunting` from **Measures** to **Dimensions**.

11. Drag `DX` and `Null Hunting` to the **Rows** shelf after **Diagnosis**. Observe that **Null** is returned when the second character in the **Diagnosis** field is not numeric:

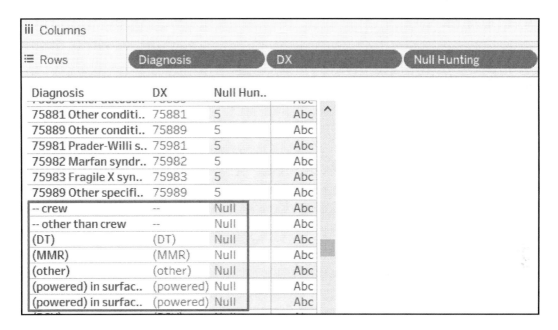

12. Create a calculated field named `Exclude from ICD Codes` with the following code:

```
ISNULL([Null Hunting])
```

13. Clear the sheet of all fields and set the **Marks** card to **Shape**.

14. Place `Exclude from ICD Codes` on the **Rows, Color**, and **Shape** shelves, and then place `DX` on the **Rows** shelf. Observe the rows labeled as **True**:

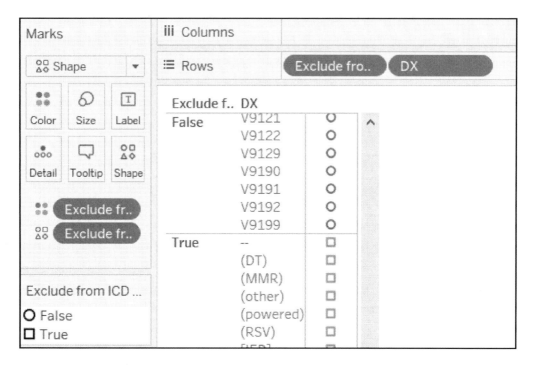

15. To exclude the junk data (that is, those rows where `Exclude from ICD Codes` equates to `TRUE`), place `Exclude from ICD Codes` on the **Filter** shelf and deselect `TRUE`.

16. Create a calculated field named `Diagnosis Text` with the following code:

```
REPLACE([Diagnosis],[DX] + " ","")
```

17. Place `Diagnosis Text` on the **Rows** shelf after `DX`. Also, remove `Exclude from ICD Codes` from the **Rows** shelf:

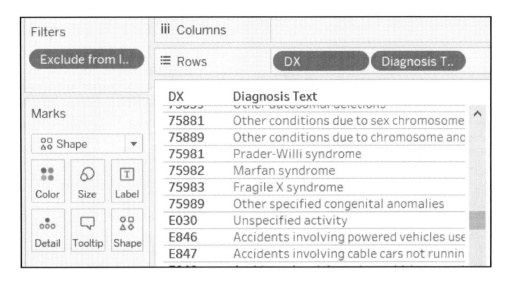

Exercise commentary

Now that we've completed the exercise, let's take a moment to consider the code:

- The `SPLIT` function was introduced in Tableau 9.0:

```
SPLIT( [Diagnosis], " ", 1 )
```

As described in the help documentation, this function:

Returns a substring from a string, as determined by the delimiter extracting the characters from the beginning or end of the string.

- To add a point of clarification to the preceding description, to extract characters from the end of the string, the token number (that is, the number at the end of the function) must be negative:

```
INT(MID([DX],2,1))
```

- The use of `MID` is quite straightforward and is much the same as the corresponding function in Excel. The use of `INT` in this case, however, may be confusing. Casting an alpha character with an `INT` function will result in Tableau returning `Null`. This satisfactorily fulfills our purpose, since we simply need to discover those rows not starting with an integer by locating the nulls:

```
ISNULL([Null Hunting])
```

- ISNULL is a Boolean function that simply returns TRUE in the case of Null.

  ```
  REPLACE([Diagnosis],[DX] + " ","")
  ```

- This calculated field uses the ICD-9 codes isolated in DX to remove those same codes from the **Diagnosis** field and thus provide a fairly clean description. Note the phrase *fairly clean*. The rows that were removed were initially associated with longer descriptions that included a carriage return. The resulting additional rows are what we removed in this exercise. Therefore, the longer descriptions are truncated in this solution.

The final output for this exercise could be to export the data from Tableau as additional source data. This data could then be used by Tableau and other tools for future reporting needs. For example, the DX field could be useful in data blending. If nothing else, a technique for translating the many government-issued PDFs into more data-friendly formats is quite useful.

Does Tableau offer a better approach that might solve the issue of truncated data associated with the previous solution? Yes! Let's turn our attention to the next exercise, where we will consider Regular Expression functions.

Exercise – extracting data

Although, as shown in the previous section, the SPLIT function can be useful for cleaning data, Regular Expression functions are far more powerful and represent a broadening of the scope from Tableau's traditional focus on visualization and analytics to also include data-cleansing capabilities. Let's look at an example that requires us to deal with some pretty messy data in Tableau. Our objective will be to extract phone numbers.

Exercise steps

1. If you have not already done so, search for `Mastering Tableau` on Tableau Public to locate and download the workbook associated with this chapter.
2. Select the **Extracting the Data** tab.
3. In the **Data** pane, select the data source **String of Data** and drag the **String of Data** field to the **Rows** shelf. Observe the challenges associated with extracting the phone number:

4. Access the underlying data and copy several rows:

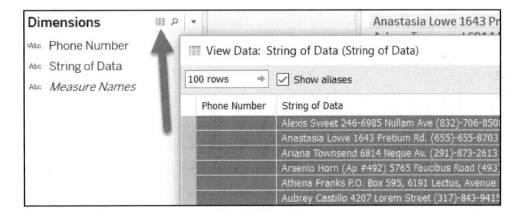

5. Navigate to `http://regexpal.com/` and paste the data into the pane labeled `Test String`; that is, the second pane:

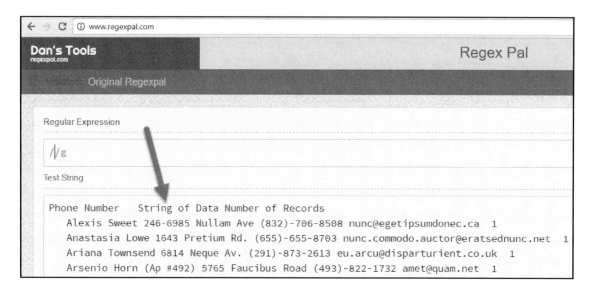

6. In the first pane (that is, the one labeled **Regular Expression**), type the following:

```
\([0-9]{3}\)-[0-9]{3}-[0-9]{4}
```

7. Return to Tableau and create a calculated field called **Phone Number** with the following code:

```
REGEXP_EXTRACT([String of Data],'(\([0-9]{3}\)-[0-9]
{3}-[0-9]{4})')
```

8. Note the regular expression nested in the calculated field.

9. Place **Phone Number** on the **Text** shelf:

Exercise commentary

Now let's consider some of the specifics in more detail from the preceding exercise:

```
REGEXP_EXTRACT([String of Data],'()')
```

- The expression pattern is purposely excluded here as it will be covered in detail in the following section. The `'()'` code acts as a placeholder for the expression pattern.
- The `REGEXP_EXTRACT` function used in this example is described in the help documentation as follows:

Returns a substring of the given string that matches the capturing group within the regular expression pattern.

- Note that at the time of writing, the Tableau documentation does not communicate details on how to ensure that the pattern input section of the function is properly delimited. For this example, be sure to include `'()'` around the pattern input section to avoid a `Null` output.

```
http://regexpal.com/.
```

- There are numerous Regular Expression websites that allow you to enter your own code and *help you out*, so to speak, by providing immediate feedback based on sample data that you provide. One such site is `http://regexpal.com/`, but you can search as desired to find one that meets your needs:

```
\([0-9]{3}\)-[0-9]{3}-[0-9]{4}
```

- In this context, the `\` indicates that the next character should not be treated as special but as literal. For our example, we are literally looking for an open parenthesis.

- [0-9] simply declares that we are looking for one or more digital characters. Alternatively, consider \d to achieve the same results.
- The {3} immediately after [0-9] designates that we are looking for three consecutive digits.
- As with the opening parenthesis at the beginning of the pattern, the \ character designates the closing parenthesis as a literal.
- The – is a literal that specifically looks for a hyphen.
- The rest of the expression pattern should be decipherable based on the preceding information.

After reviewing the preceding exercise and accompanying commentary, you may be curious about how to return just the e-mail address. According to http://www.regular-ex pressions.info/email.html, the regular expression for e-mail addresses adhering to the RFC 5322 standard is as shown here:

 E-mails do not always adhere to RFC 5322 standards, so additional work may be required to truly clean e-mail address data.

```
(?:[a-z0-9!#$%&'*+/=?^_`{|}~-]+(?:\.[a-z0-9!#$%&'*+/=?^_`{|}~-
]+)*|"(?:[\x01-\x08\x0b\x0c\x0e-\x1f\x21\x23-\x5b\x5d-\x7f]|\\[\x01-
\x09\x0b\x0c\x0e-\x7f])*")@(?:(?:[a-z0-9](?:[a-z0-9-]*[a-z0-9])?\.)+[a-
z0-9](?:[a-z0-9-]*[a-
z0-9])?|\[(?:(?:25[0-5]|2[0-4][0-9]|[01]?[0-9][0-9]?)\.){3}(?:25[0-5]|2[0-4
][0-9]|[01]?[0-9][0-9]?|[a-z0-9-]*[a-z0-9]:(?:[\x01-\x08\x0b\x0c\x0e-
\x1f\x21\x5a\x53-\x7f]|\\[\x01-\x09\x0b\x0c\x0e-\x7f])+)\])
```

Although I won't attempt a detailed explanation of this code, you can read all about it at ht tp://www.regular-expressions.info/email.html, which is a great resource for learning more about regular expressions. If you make frequent use of this website for your regular expression code, be sure to leave a donation. I did! Also, YouTube has several helpful regular expression tutorials.

The final output for this exercise should probably be used to enhance existing source data. Data dumps such as this example represents do not belong in data warehouses; however, important and even necessary data can be hidden in such dumps and Tableau can be effectively used to extract it.

Summary

We began this chapter with a discussion of the Tableau **Data-Handling Engine (DHE)**. This illustrated the flexibility Tableau provides in working with data. It is important to understand the DHE in order to ensure that data-mining efforts are intelligently focused. Otherwise, effort may be wasted on activities not relevant to Tableau.

Next we discussed data-mining and knowledge-discovery process models with an emphasis on CRISP-DM. The purpose of this discussion was to get an appropriate bird's-eye view of the scope of the entire data-mining effort. Tableau authors (and certainly end users) can become so focused on the reporting produced in deployment that they forget or short-change the other phases, particularly Data Preparation.

Our last focus in this chapter was on the phase that can be the most time consuming and labor intensive, namely, Data Preparation. We considered using Tableau for surveying and cleansing data. The data-cleansing capabilities represented by the regular expression functions are particularly intriguing.

Having completed our first data-centric discussion, we'll continue with another chapter that also includes *all about the data* in the title. Since we have now laid a foundation, we are well equipped to explore challenges associated with joins, blends, and data structures.

3

All about Data – Joins, Blends, and Data Structures

Connecting Tableau to data often means more than connecting to a single table in a single data source. You may need to use Tableau to join multiple tables from a single data source. As of Tableau 10, you can also join tables from disparate data sources. Sometimes, you may need to merge data that does not share a common row-level key. In such cases, you will need to blend the data. Also, you may find instances where it is necessary to create multiple connections to a single data source in order to pivot the data in different ways. This may be required in order to discover answers to questions that are difficult or simply not possible to address with a single data structure.

In this chapter, we will discuss the following:

- Complex joins
- Data blending
- Data structures

About joins

This book assumes basic knowledge of joins, specifically inner, left-outer, right-outer, and full-outer joins. If you are not familiar with join basics, consider taking the SQL tutorial at h ttp://www.w3schools.com/. The basics are not difficult, so it won't take you long to get up to speed.

Complex joins

The terms **simple join** and **complex join** mean different things in different contexts. For our purposes, we will consider a simple join to be a single join between two tables. Every other instance of joining will be considered complex.

Let's look at a star schema as an example of a complex join:

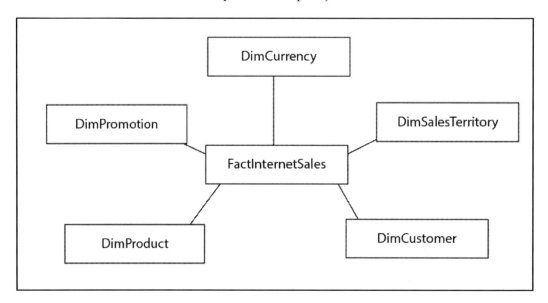

A star schema consists of a fact table referencing one or more dimension tables. The fact table typically contains measures, whereas dimension tables, as the name suggests, contain dimensions. Star schemas are an important part of data warehousing, since their structure is optimal for reporting.

The star schema pictured is based on the Adventure Works data warehouse for MS SQL Server 2014. The workbook associated with this chapter does not include the SQL Server database. Also, to keep the file size of the workbook small, the extract has been filtered to only include data for the United Kingdom. Access to the database may prove helpful when working through some of the exercises in this chapter.

You can download variations of Adventure Works for SQL Server and Access at http://www.codeplex.com/.

Exercise – observing join culling

Note that in order to view the SQL generated by Tableau in the following examples, you will need to point to a SQL data source. Queries to an extract (that is, a .tde file) will cause Tableau to generate TQL.

The following screenshot is a representation of the preceding star schema graphic on the Tableau Data Source page. Of course, viewing the joins as shown in the preceding star schema presupposes that you have connected to a database as opposed to using the extracted data sources provided with the workbook:

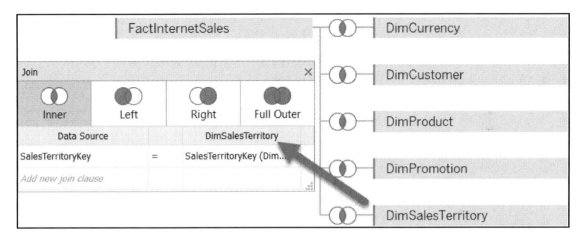

The preceding screenshot communicates an inner join between the fact table (**FactInternetSales**) and various dimension tables. **FactInternetSales** and **DimSalesTerritory** are connected via an inner join on the common key, **SalesTerritoryKey**. In this exercise, we will look at the SQL generated by Tableau when building a simple view using these two tables.

Exercise steps

1. Navigate to `https://public.tableau.com/profile/david.baldwin#!/` to locate and download the workbook associated with this chapter.
2. Select the `Joins w/o Snowflaking` worksheet and click on the `AdventureWorks_wo_Snowflaking` data source.
3. Drag **Sales Territory Country** to the Rows shelf and place **SalesAmount** on the **Text** shelf.

4. From the menu, navigate to **Help** | **Settings and Performance** | **Start Performance Recording**.
5. Press the F5 key to refresh the view.
6. Stop the recording via **Help** | **Settings and Performance** | **Stop Performance Recording**.
7. In the resulting **Performance Summary** dashboard that is displayed, drag the time slider to **0.00** and select **Query** to see the SQL generated by Tableau:

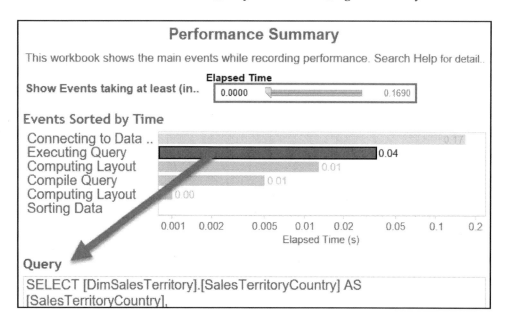

Exercise commentary

Let's look at the SQL query in detail:

```
SELECT [DimSalesTerritory].[SalesTerritoryCountry] AS
[SalesTerritoryCountry],
SUM([FactInternetSales].[SalesAmount]) AS [sum:SalesAmount:ok]
FROM [dbo].[FactInternetSales] [FactInternetSales]
INNER JOIN [dbo].[DimSalesTerritory] [DimSalesTerritory] ON
([FactInternetSales].[SalesTerritoryKey] =
[DimSalesTerritory].[SalesTerritoryKey])
GROUP BY [DimSalesTerritory].[SalesTerritoryCountry]
```

Note that a single inner join was generated; that is, between **FactInternetSales** and **DimSalesTerritory**. Despite the presence of a complex join, Tableau only generated the SQL necessary to create the view. This is **join culling** in action.

 In Tableau, join culling assumes tables in the database have referential integrity; that is, a join between the fact table and a dimension table does not require joins to other dimension tables. Join culling ensures that if a query requires only data from one table, other joined tables will not be referenced. The end result is better performance.

As shown in the following screenshot, let's make one small change to the star schema and add the dimension **DimProductSubcategory**. In the workbook provided with this chapter, the worksheet is entitled `Joins w/o Snowflaking`. As in the preceding case, viewing the joins presupposes that you have connected to a database, as opposed to using the extracted data sources provided with the workbook:

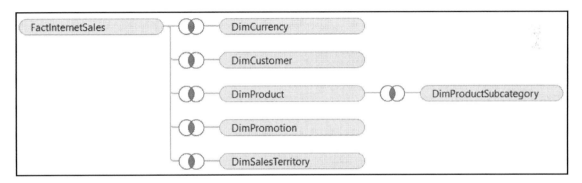

Note that there is no common key between **FactInternetSales** and **DimProductSubcategory**. The only way to join this additional table is to connect it to **DimProduct**. Let's repeat the steps listed above for observing the underlying SQL and consider the results:

```
SELECT [DimSalesTerritory].[SalesTerritoryCountry] AS
[SalesTerritoryCountry],
SUM([FactInternetSales].[SalesAmount]) AS [sum:SalesAmount:ok]
FROM [dbo].[FactInternetSales] [FactInternetSales]
INNER JOIN [dbo].[DimProduct] [DimProduct] ON
([FactInternetSales].[ProductKey] = [DimProduct].[ProductKey])
INNER JOIN [dbo].[DimSalesTerritory] [DimSalesTerritory] ON
([FactInternetSales].[SalesTerritoryKey] =
[DimSalesTerritory].[SalesTerritoryKey])
WHERE (NOT ([DimProduct].[ProductSubcategoryKey] IS NULL))
GROUP BY [DimSalesTerritory].[SalesTerritoryCountry]
```

Although our view does not require the `DimProduct` table, an additional join was generated for the `DimProduct` table. Additionally, a `Where` clause was included. What's going on? The additional inner join was created because of snowflaking.

 Snowflaking normalizes a dimension table by moving attributes into one or more additional tables that are joined on a foreign key.

As a result of the snowflaking, Tableau is limited in its ability to exercise join culling. The resulting query is less efficient. The same is true for any secondary join.

Now let's consider the query that is generated for the same visualization if we connect to an extract as opposed to MS SQL:

 The following query is **Tableau Query Language** (TQL).

```
(restrict
(aggregate
(project
(table [Extract].[Extract])
(([SalesTerritoryCountry] [SalesTerritoryCountry])))
(([SalesTerritoryCountry] [SalesTerritoryCountry]))
(([sum:SalesAmount:ok] (sum [SalesAmount]))))
([SalesTerritoryCountry] [sum:SalesAmount:ok]))
```

Note that this query does not include any reference to **DimProduct** or **DimProductSubcategory**. This tells us that the extract has materialized and flattened the view.

 A materialized view is the result of a query that is physically stored in a database. It differs from a view in that a view requires the associated query to be run every time it needs to be accessed.
In Tableau, an extract is always de-normalized or flattened; that is, no joins are included.

The germane points to remember from this section are as follows:

- Using secondary joins limits Tableau's ability to employ join culling. This results in less efficient queries to the underlying data source.
- Creating an extract materializes all joins. Thus, even if secondary joins are used when connecting to the data source, any extract from that data source will be denormalized or flattened. This means that any query to an extract will not include joins and may thus perform better.

Data blending

In a nutshell, data blending allows you to merge multiple, disparate data sources in a single view. Understanding the four following points will give you a basic grasp of data blending:

- Data blending is typically used to merge data from multiple data sources:
    - Although as of Tableau 10, joining is possible between multiple data sources, there are still cases where data blending is the only possible option to merge data from two or more sources. The following **Pants & Shirts** example demonstrates such a case.
- Data blending requires a shared dimension:
    - A **date** dimension is often a good candidate for blending multiple data sources.
- Data blending aggregates and then matches. Joining matches and then aggregates:
    - This point will be covered in detail in the following section
- Data blending does not enable dimensions from a secondary data source:
    - Attempting to use dimensions from a secondary data source will result in a * or null in the view. There is an exception to this rule, which we will discuss further on in the chapter.

Order of operations for aggregating and matching

Isn't a data blend the same thing as a left join? This is a question new Tableau authors often ask. The answer, of course, is no, but let's explore the differences. The following example is simple, even light-hearted, but does demonstrate serious consequences that can result from incorrect aggregation resulting from an erroneous join.

Exercise – a data blend versus a left join

One day soon you may move to fulfill a lifelong desire to open a brick and mortar store:

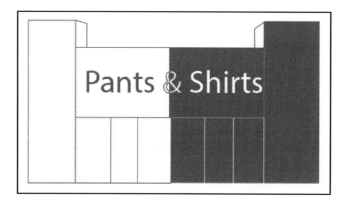

Let's assume that you will open a clothing store specializing in pants and shirts. Because of the fastidious tendencies you developed as a result of years of working with data, you are planning to keep everything quite separate. In a word, you plan to **normalize** your business. As evidenced by the preceding image, the pants and shirts you sell in your store will be quite separated. Also, as shown here, you intend to keep your data stored in separate tables, although these tables will exist in the same data source:

Pants Table		Shirts Table	
Sales Person	**Pants Amount**	**Sales Associate**	**Shirt Amount**
Tanya	100	Tanya	50
Zhang	100	Zhang	50
Tanya	100	Tanya	50
Zhang	100	Zhang	50

Note the following: in these tables, two people are listed – **Tanya** and **Zhang**. In one table, these people are members of the **Sales Person** dimension and in the other they are members of the **Sales Associate** dimension. Furthermore, Tanya sold $200 in pants and $100 in shirts. **Ditto** for **Zhang**. Let's explore different ways Tableau could connect to this data to better understand joining and data blending. When looking at the spreadsheets associated with this exercise, you will notice additional columns not referenced in the preceding tables. These columns will be used in a later exercise.

Exercise steps

1. In the workbook associated with this chapter, right-click on the **Pants** data source and select **Edit Data Source**. Make sure that the data interpreter is on. This is necessary because the Excel file contains extraneous information (the rows that read **Pants Table** and **Rows Table**). This will return odd results if the data interpreter is not on:

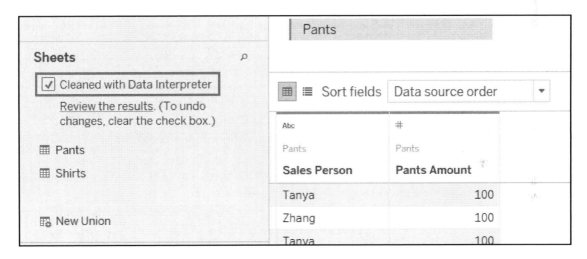

2. Do the same for the **Shirts** data source.

3. Open the **Join** data source and observe the join between the **Pants** and **Shirts** tables using **Sales Person/Sales Associate** as the common key:

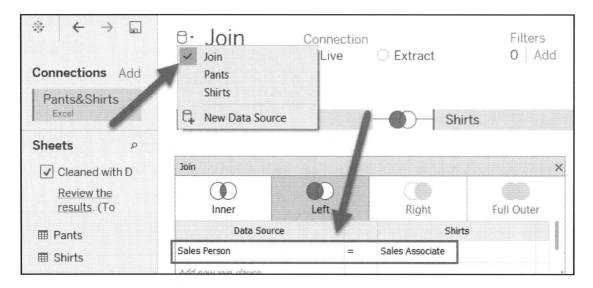

4. On the worksheet entitled **Pants**, select the **Pants** data source and place **Sales Person** on the **Rows** shelf and **Pants Amount** on the **Text** shelf.

5. On the worksheet entitled **Shirts**, select the **Shirts** data source and place **Sales Associate** on the **Rows** shelf and **Shirt Amount** on the **Text** shelf.

6. On the worksheet entitled **Join**, select the **Join** data source and place **Sales Person** on the **Rows** shelf. Next, double-click **Pants Amount** and **Shirt Amount** to place both on the view.

7. On the worksheet entitled `Blend - Pants Primary`, select the **Pants** data source and place **Sales Person** on the **Rows** shelf and **Pants Amount** on the **Text** shelf. Next, select the **Shirts** data source and double-click on **Shirt Amount**.

8. Note that Tableau responds with a warning. Close the warning dialog box.

9. Select **Data | Edit Relationships**.

10. In the resulting dialog box, click on the **Custom** radio button.
11. Click **Add**.
12. In the left-hand column, select **Sales Person**, and in the right-hand column, select **Sales Associate**.
13. Click **OK** and then remove the link between each instance of **Material Type**.
14. The results in the dialog box should match what is displayed in the following screenshot:

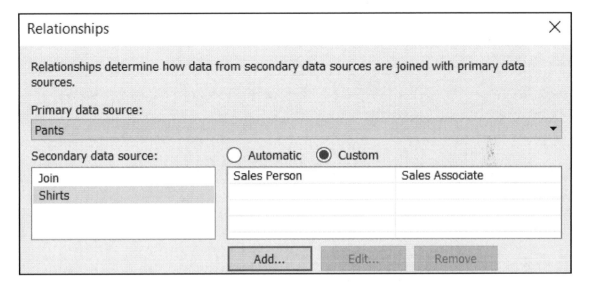

15. On the worksheet entitled `Blend - Shirts Primary`, select the **Shirts** data source and place **Sales Associate** on the **Rows** shelf and **Shirt Amount** on the **Text** shelf. Next, select the **Pants** data source and double-click **Pants Amount**.
16. Place all five worksheets on a dashboard. Format and arrange as desired.

17. Now let's compare the results between the five worksheets:

Pants / Shirts

Sales Person		Sales Associate	
Tanya	$200	Tanya	$100
Zhang	$200	Zhang	$100

Join

Sales Person	Pants Amount	Shirt Amount
Tanya	$400	$200
Zhang	$400	$200

Blend - Pants Primary / Blend - Shirts Primary

Sales Person	Pants Amount	Shirt Amount	Sales Associate	Pants Amount	Shirt Amount
Tanya	$200	$100	Tanya	$200	$100
Zhang	$200	$100	Zhang	$200	$100

Understanding the join

Note that in the preceding screenshot, the worksheet named **Join** has double the expected results. Why? Because a join first matches on the common key (in this case, **Sales Person/Sales Associate**) and then aggregates the results. The more matches found on a common key, the worse the problem will become. If multiple matches are found on a common key, the results will grow exponentially. Two matches will result in squared results, three matches will result in cubed results, and so on. This exponential effect is represented graphically as follows:

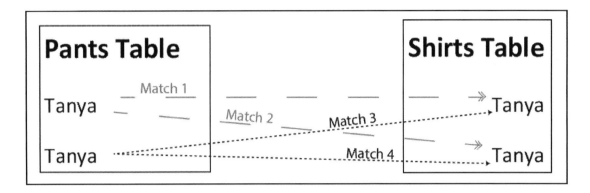

Understanding the data blend

Before the blend could function properly, we had to edit the data relationship so that Tableau could connect the two data sources using the fields **Sales Person** and **Sales Associate**. If the two fields had been identically named (for example, **Sales Person**), Tableau would have automatically provided an option to blend between the data sources using those fields.

The results for the worksheets `Blend - Pants Primary` and `Blend - Shirts Primary` are correct. There is no exponential effect. Why? Because data blending first aggregates the results from both data sources and then matches the results on a common dimension (in this case, **Sales Person/Sales Associate**), as demonstrated in the following figure:

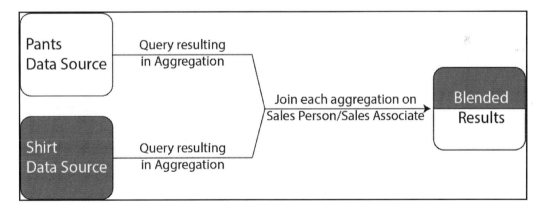

No dimensions from a secondary source

Data blending, although very useful for connecting disparate data sources, has limitations. The most important limitation to be aware of is that data blending does not enable dimensions from a secondary data source. There is an exception to this limitation; that is, there is one way you can add a dimension from a secondary data source. Let's explore further.

Exercise – adding secondary dimensions

As mentioned previously, there are other fields besides **Sales Person/Sales Associate** and **Shirt Amount/Pants Amount** in the data sources. We will reference those fields in this exercise:

1. In the workbook associated with this chapter, select the worksheet entitled **Adding Secondary Dimensions**.
2. Select the **Shirts** data source.
3. Add a relationship between the **Shirts** and **Pants** data sources for **Material Type**. The required steps are as follows:
    1. Select **Data | Edit Relationships**.
    2. Ensure that **Shirts** is the primary data source and **Pants** is the secondary data source.
    3. Select the **Custom** radio button.
    4. Click **Add**.
    5. Select **Material Type** in both the left- and right-hand columns.
    6. Click **OK** to return to the view.
4. Place **Material Type** on the **Rows** shelf.
5. Select the **Pants** data source. Make sure that the chain-link icon next to **Material Type** in the **Data** pane is activated and that the chain-link icon next to **Sales Person** is deactivated. If the icon is a gray, broken chain-link, it is not activated. If it is an orange, connected chain-link, it is activated.

6. Place **Material Cat** before **Material Type** on the **Rows** shelf.
7. Place **Fastener** after **Material Type** on the **Rows** shelf:

≣ Rows	Material Cat ⬢	Material Type	Fastener ⬢

Adding Secondary Dimensions

Material Cat	Material Type	Fastener	
Tech	Acrylic	Button	Abc
	Polyester	Velcro	Abc
Traditional	Wool	*	Abc

Material Cat is a dimension from a secondary data source. The limitation stated previously is that data blending does not enable dimensions from a secondary data source. Why does it work in this case? There are a few reasons, as follows:

- There is a one-to-many relationship between **Material Cat** and **Material Type**; that is, each member of the **Material Type** dimension is matched with one, and only one, member of the **Material Cat** dimension.
- The view is blended on **Material Type**, not **Material Cat**.
    - This is important, because **Material Type** is at a lower level of granularity than **Material Cat**. Attempting to blend the view on **Material Cat** will not enable **Material Type** as a secondary dimension.
- Every member of the **Material Type** dimension within the primary data source also exists in the secondary data source.

Fastener is also a dimension from the secondary data source. In the preceding screenshot, it displays an asterisk in one of the cells, thus demonstrating that **Fastener** is not working as a dimension should; that is, it is not *slicing* the data as discussed in Chapter 1, *Getting Up to Speed – a Review of the Basics*. The reason an asterisk is displayed is because there are multiple fastener types associated with the **Wool**. **Button**, and **Velcro** display because **Acrylic** and **Polyester** each have only one fastener type in the underlying data.

Scaffolding

Scaffolding is a technique that introduces a second data source via blending for the purpose of reshaping and/or extending the initial data source. Scaffolding enables capabilities that extend Tableau to meet visualization and analytical needs, which may otherwise be very difficult or altogether impossible. Joe Mako, the gentleman who pioneered scaffolding in Tableau, tells a story in which he used the technique to recreate a dashboard using four worksheets. The original dashboard, which did not use scaffolding, required 80 worksheets, painstakingly aligned, pixel by pixel.

Exercise – enhanced forecasting via scaffolding

Among the many possibilities scaffolding enables is extending Tableau's forecasting functionality. Tableau's native forecasting capabilities are sometimes criticized for lacking sophistication. Scaffolding can be used to mitigate this criticism:

1. In the workbook associated with this chapter, select the `Scaffolding` worksheet and connect to the **World Indicators** data source.
2. Using Excel or a text editor, create a **Records** dataset. The following two-row table represents the **Records** dataset in its entirety:

Records
1
2

3. Connect Tableau to the **Records** dataset.
4. To be expedient, consider copying the dataset using *Ctrl + C* and pasting it directly in Tableau using *Ctrl + V*.
5. In Tableau, create a **Start Date** parameter with the following settings. In particular, notice the highlighted sections in the following screenshot, by which you can set the desired display format:

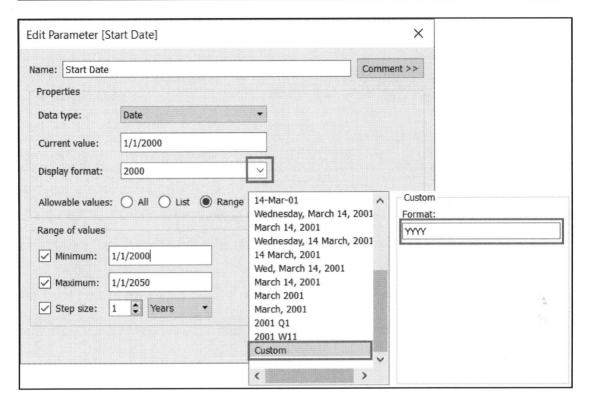

6. Create another parameter named **End Date** with identical settings.
7. In the **Data** pane, right-click on the **Start Date** and **End Date** parameters you just created, and select **Show Parameter Control**.
8. Set the start and end dates as desired; for example, 2000 – 2005.
9. Select the **Records** data source and create the following calculated field:

Calculated field name	Calculated field code
Date	IIF([Records]=1,[Start Date],[End Date])

10. Place the **Date** field on the **Rows** shelf.
11. Right-click on the **Date** field on the **Rows** shelf and select **Show Missing Values**.

12. Note that all the dates between the start and end date settings are now displayed:

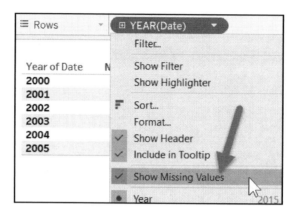

13. Create a parameter named **Select Country A** with the settings shown in the following screenshot. In particular, note that the list of countries was added using the **Add from Field** button:

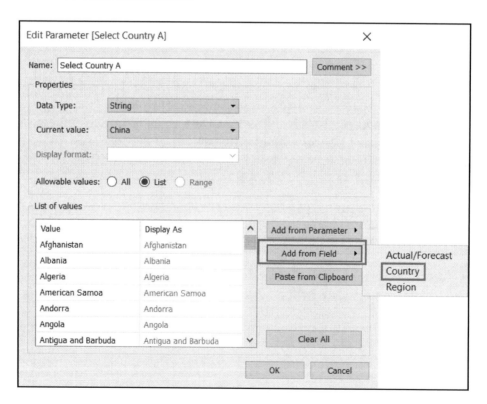

14. Create another parameter named `Select Country B` with identical settings.

15. Create a parameter named **Select Country A Forecast** with the following settings. In particular, notice the highlighted sections, by which you can set the desired display format:

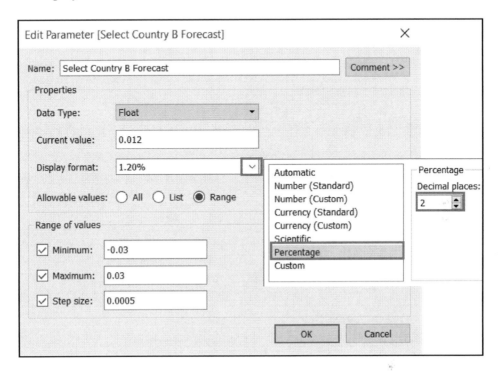

16. Create another parameter named `Select Country B Forecast` with identical settings.

17. In the **Data** pane, right-click on the four parameters you just created (**Select Country A**, **Select Country B**, **Select Country A Forecast**, and **Select Country B Forecast**) and select **Show Parameter Control**.

18. Make sure that the **Date** field in the **World Indicators** data source has the orange chain icon deployed. This indicates it's used as a linking field:

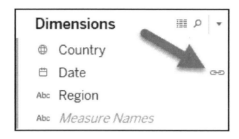

19. Within the **World Indicators** dataset, create the following calculated fields:

Calculated field name	Calculated field code
Country A Population	IIF([Country] = [Select Country A],[Population Total],NULL)
Country B Population	IIF([Country] = [Select Country B],[Population Total],NULL)

20. Within the **Records** dataset, create the following calculated fields:

Calculated field name	Calculated field code
Actual/Forecast	IIF(ISNULL(AVG([World Indicators].[Population Total])),"Forecast","Actual")
Country A Population	IF [Actual/Forecast] = "Actual" THEN SUM([World Indicators].[Country A Population]) ELSE PREVIOUS_VALUE(0) *[Select Country A Forecast] + PREVIOUS_VALUE(0) END
Country A YOY Change	([Country A Population] – LOOKUP([Country A Population], -1)) / ABS(LOOKUP([Country A Population], -1))
Country B Population	IF [Actual/Forecast] = "Actual" THEN SUM([World Indicators].[Country B Population]) ELSE PREVIOUS_VALUE(0) *[Select Country B Forecast] + PREVIOUS_VALUE(0) END

Country B YOY Change	([Country B Population] - LOOKUP([Country B Population], -1)) / ABS(LOOKUP([Country B Population], -1))
Country A-B Diff	[Country A Population] - [Country B Population]
Country A-B % Diff	[Country A-B Diff]/[Country A Population]

21. Within the **Data** pane, right-click on **Country A YOY Change**, **Country B YOY Change**, and **Country A-B % Diff**, and select **Default Properties | Number Format** to change the default number format to percentage, as shown in the following screenshot:

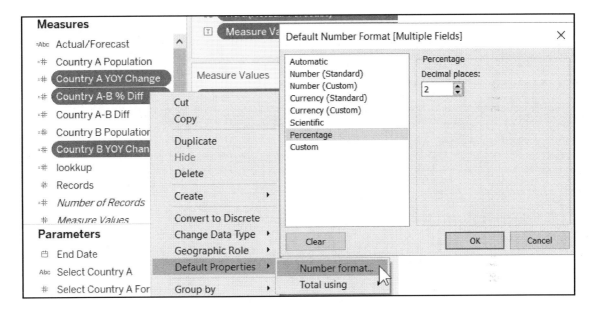

22. With the **Records** data source selected, place the following fields on their respective shelves:

Field	Shelf
Actual/Forecast	Color
Measure Values	Label/Text
Measure Names	Columns

23. Adjust the **Measure Values** shelf so that the fields displayed are identical to the following screenshot. Also, ensure that **Compute Using** for each of these fields is set to **Table (down)**:

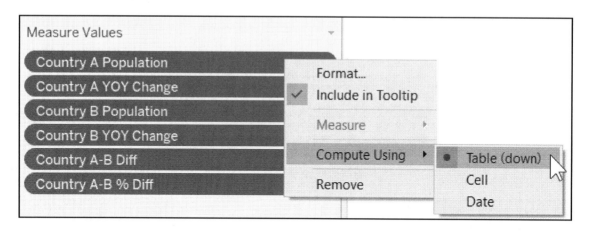

24. Let's ask the question, *When will the population of India overtake that of China?* Set the parameters as desired and observe the results. My results are the year 2024. What are yours?:

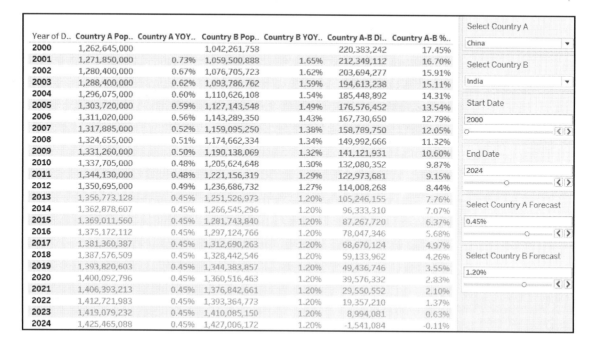

One key to this exercise is data densification. Data densification produces data that doesn't exist in the data source. The **World Indicators** dataset only includes dates from **2000 – 2012** and obviously, the **Record** dataset does not contain any dates. By using the **Start Date** and **End Date** parameters coupled with the calculated field **Date**, we were able to produce any set of dates desired. The actual data densification occurred upon selecting **Show Missing Values** from the **Date** field dropdown after it was placed on the **Rows** shelf. This allowed every year between **Start Date** and **End Date** to display, even when there were no matching years in the underlying data. The following chapter will consider data densification in more detail.

Let's look at a few of the calculated fields in more depth to better understand how the forecasting works in this exercise.

Calculated field – Actual/Forecast

```
IIF(ISNULL(AVG([World Indicators].[Population Total])),"Forecast","Actual")
```

This code determines whether or not data exists in the **World Indicators** dataset. If the date is after 2012, no data exists and thus `Forecast` is returned.

Calculated field – Country A Population

```
IF [Actual/Forecast] = "Actual" THEN
SUM([World Indicators].[Country A Population])
ELSE PREVIOUS_VALUE(0)
 *[Select Country A Forecast] + PREVIOUS_VALUE(0)
END
```

If forecasting is necessary for determining the value (that is, if the date is after 2012), the `ELSE` portion of this code is exercised. The `PREVIOUS_VALUE` function returns the value of the previous row, multiplies the results by the forecast, and then adds the previous row.

See the following table for an example of this:

Previous Row Value (PRV)	1000
Forecast (F)	0.01
PRV * F	10
Current Row Value	1010

One important thing to note in the **Country A Population** calculated field is that the forecast is quite simple; that is, multiply the previous population by a given forecast number and tally the results. Without changing the overall structure of the logic, this section of code could be modified with more sophisticated forecasting.

Data structures

The right data structure is not easily definable. True, there are ground rules. For instance, tall data is generally better than wide data. A wide dataset with lots of columns can be difficult to work with, whereas the same data structured in a tall format with fewer columns but more rows is usually easier to work with. But this isn't always the case! Some business questions are more easily answered with wide data structures, and that's the crux of the matter. Business questions determine the right data structure. If one structure answers all questions, great! However, your questions may require multiple data structures. The pivot feature in Tableau helps you adjust data structure on the fly, in order to answer different business questions.

Before beginning the exercise, understanding the points in the following information box will be important.

Pivoting in Tableau is limited to Excel, text files, and Google Sheets. Pivot in Tableau is referred to as unpivot in database terminology.

Exercise – adjusting data structure for different questions

As a business analyst for a hospital, you are connecting Tableau to a daily snapshot of patient data. You have two questions:

- How many events occur on any given date? For example, how many patients check in on a given day?
- How much time passes between events? For example, what is the average stay for those patients who are in the hospital multiple days?

Exercise steps – part 1

1. Within the starter workbook associated with this chapter, select the `Time Frames` worksheet and within the **Data** pane, select the **Patient_Snapshot** data source.
2. Click on the dropdown in the **Marks View** card and select **Bar**.

3. Right-click in the **Data** pane to create a parameter named `Select Time Frame` with the settings displayed in the following screenshot:

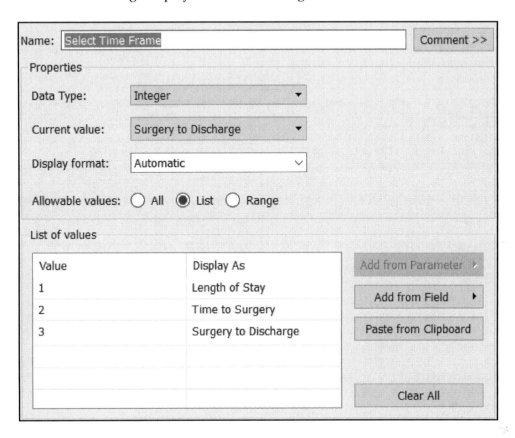

4. Right-click on the parameter just created and select **Show Parameter Control**.
5. Right-click in the **Data** pane to create the following calculated field:

Calculated field name	Calculated field code

Selected Time Frame	```CASE [Select Time Frame]```
	```WHEN 1 THEN DATEDIFF('day',[Check-in Date],[Discharge Date])```
	```WHEN 2 THEN DATEDIFF('day',[Surgery Date],[Discharge Date])```
	```WHEN 3 THEN DATEDIFF('day',[Check-in Date],[Surgery Date])```
	```END```

6. Drag the following fields to the associated shelves and define as directed:

Field name	Shelf directions
Patient Type	Drag to the **Filter** shelf and check **Inpatient**.
Check-in Date	Drag to the **Filter** shelf and select **Range of dates**. Also, right-click on the resulting filter and select **Show Filter**.
Check-in Date	Right-click and drag to the **Columns** shelf and select **MDY**.
Selected Time Frame	Right-click and drag to the **Rows** shelf and select **AVG**.
Selected Time Frame	Right-click and drag to the **Color** shelf and select **AVG**. Set colors as desired.

7. Right-click on the **Avg Selected Time Frame** axis and select **Edit Axis…**. Next, delete the title:

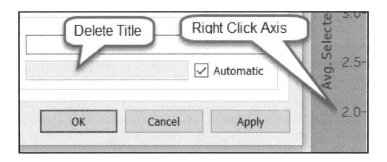

8. Select **Worksheet** | **Show Title**. Edit the title by inserting the parameter, as shown in the following screenshot:

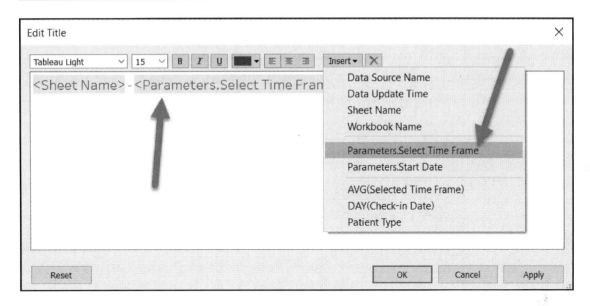

The data structure was ideal for the first part of this exercise. You were likely able to create the visualization quickly. The only section of moderate interest was setting up the **Selected Time Frame** calculated field with the associated parameter. This allows the end user to choose which timeframe they would like to view.

But what happens if you need to find out how much time passes between events? This question is rather difficult to answer using the current data structure. (Try it and you will understand!) In the second part of the exercise, we'll try a different approach by pivoting the data.

Exercise steps – part 2

1. Within the starter workbook associated with this chapter, select the Events Per Date worksheet.
2. Within the **Data** pane, right-click the **Patient_Snapshot** data source and choose **Duplicate**.
3. Rename the duplicate **Events**.

4. Right-click on the **Events** data source and choose **Edit Data Source...**:

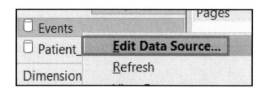

5. Review the highlighted areas of the following screenshot and take the following steps:

      1. Click on the **Manage metadata** icon.

      2. Select all five of the date fields using *Shift* or *Ctrl* + click.

      3. Select the drop-down option for any of the selected fields and choose **Pivot**:

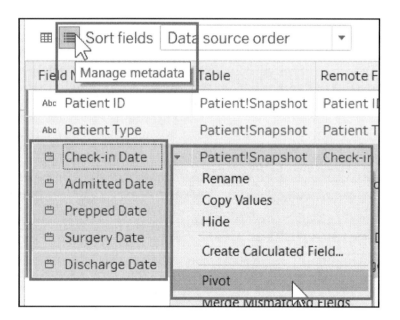

6. Rename the pivoted fields to Event Type and Event Date.

7. Select the `Events Per Date` worksheet, place the following fields on the associated shelves, and define as directed:

Field name	Shelf directions
Event Date	Right-click and drag to the **Rows** shelf and select **MDY**.
Event Type	Place after **Event Date** on the **Rows** shelf.
Patient Type	Right-click and select **Show Filter**.
Number of Records	Drag to the **Columns** shelf.

The original data structure was not well-suited for this exercise; however, after duplicating the data source and pivoting, the task was quite simple. That's the main takeaway. If you find yourself struggling to create a visualization to answer a seemingly simple business question, consider pivoting.

Summary

We began this chapter with a discussion on complex joins and discovered that when possible, Tableau uses join culling to generate efficient queries of the data source. A secondary join, however, limits Tableau's ability to employ join culling. An extract results in a materialized, flattened view, which eliminates the need for joins to be included in any queries.

Next we reviewed data blending to clearly understand how data blending differs from joining. We discovered that the primary limitation in data blending is that no dimensions are allowed from a secondary source; however, we also discovered that there are exceptions to this rule. We also discussed scaffolding, which can make data blending surprisingly fruitful.

Finally, we discussed data structures and learned how pivoting can make difficult or seemingly impossible visualizations easy.

Having completed our second data-centric discussion, we will continue with another chapter that also includes *All about Data* in the title. Specifically, we will explore data densification, cubes, and big data.

4

All about Data – Data Densification, Cubes, and Big Data

Often, when teaching Tableau classes, I'm asked questions that don't fall under the purview of data topics discussed in the previous two chapters. In other words, these are questions that don't fall neatly into the categories of data preparation, joins, blends, or data structure. Here are a few example questions:

- I just created a table calculation and observe that the view displays numbers that doesn't exist in the underlying data. Why?
- We use SAP BW in my organization. What should I know about how Tableau works with cubes?
- I work for a Fortune 100 company. Can you tell me how Tableau works with big data?

This chapter will continue the data discussion from the previous two chapters by addressing the topics these three questions target. Those topics are as follows:

- About data densification
- Working with cubes
- Tableau and big data

There are a few people I'd especially like to thank who have worked diligently to provide resources that I found very helpful while writing this chapter. Joe Mako has championed data densification understanding more than anyone else in the Tableau community. Be sure to check out his video on Vimeo for a deep dive into this challenging topic. The **Tableau Knowledge Base Team** has an invaluable series of articles and accompanying workbooks for understanding the ins and outs of working with OLAP Cubes. Lastly, Ben Sullins has provided an excellent resource on Tableau and big data at Pluralsight.

About data densification

Data densification is a largely undocumented aspect of Tableau that can be useful in many circumstances but can also be confusing when encountered unexpectedly. This section will provide information about data densification with the intent of dispelling confusion and providing the Tableau author with sufficient knowledge to use this feature advantageously.

To begin to understand data densification, four terms should be defined. **Data densification**, **sparse data**, **domain completion**, and **domain padding**. The first two terms will be defined immediately, and the last two within the context of the rest of this section of the chapter. In addition to the definitions, each term will be discussed in detail via examples to help improve understanding.

Data densification: A behavior wherein Tableau displays marks in the view for which there is no corresponding underlying data.
Sparse data: An intersection of one or more dimensions and one measure for which there is no value.

Domain completion

There are two types of data densification, domain completion, and domain padding. Domain completion is the more complex of the two and can be deployed cleverly to solve sparse data issues, but may also appear unexpectedly and prove a challenge to address. Consider the following definition.

Domain completion: The addition of marks on a sparsely populated view causing all possible dimension/measure combinations to display results.

Grasping domain completion requires a good understanding of dimensions and measures, discrete and continuous, and partitioning and addressing within table calculations. The first two sets of terms, dimensions/measures and discrete/continuous, are discussed in the first chapter of this book, Chapter 1, *Getting Up to Speed – a Review of the Basics*. The last set of terms, partitioning and addressing, is discussed in detail in Chapter 5, *Table Calculations*.

Now let's consider how domain completion can be deployed, when it's helpful, and when it's a problem.

How domain completion can be deployed

Domain completion can be activated in numerous and sometimes perhaps surprising and confusing ways. Adjusting the arrangement of pills on the shelves, toggling dimensions between discrete and continuous, switching view types on the **Marks View** card, adjusting partitioning and addressing and other changes can impact domain completion activation. Although examples for every activation possibility will not be covered in this book, a review of typical domain completion scenarios should prove helpful.

Exercise – activating domain completion in a crosstab part I

This exercise demonstrates how the deployment of a table calculation in a crosstab view can activate domain completion. Immediately following this exercise is an explanation that should aid understanding:

1. Navigate to https://public.tableau.com/profile/david.baldwin#!/ to locate and download the workbook associated with this chapter.
2. Navigate to the worksheet entitled DC - Crosstab.
3. Insure that **Analysis | Table Layout | Show Empty Rows** and **Show Empty Columns** are both deselected.
4. In the **Superstore** data source, create a calculated field named **Index** with the code INDEX().
5. Place **Customer Name** on the **Rows** shelf and add a filter to view only the first five customers when sorted alphabetically.

6. Place **Order Date** on the **Columns** shelf. Note, as shown in the following screenshot, the view is sparsely populated:

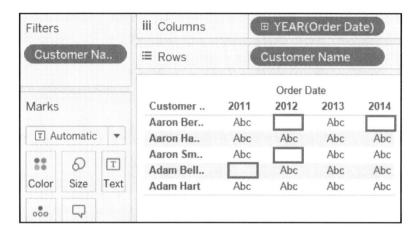

7. Place **Index** on the **Detail** shelf. Note in the following screenshot that the view now reflects domain completion; that is, the view is fully populated:

8. Right click on **YEAR(Order Date)** and select **Continuous**. Note that data densification is deactivated:

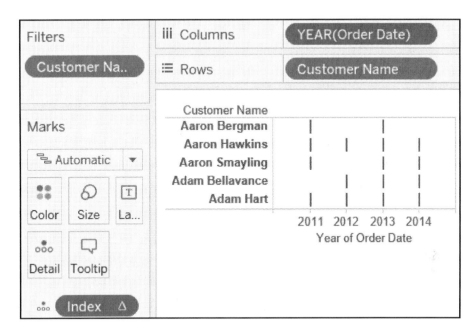

9. Reset **YEAR(Order Date)** to **Discrete** and then right-click on **Index** and select **Edit Table Calculation**.

10. In the resulting dialog box, select **Specific Dimensions** and then observe the results for each of the following selections:

Select specific dimension	Data densification activated/deactivated
Customer Name	Activated
Year of Order Date	Activated
Customer Name and **Year of Order Date**	Deactivated
No selection	Deactivated

The preceding exercise illustrates the following rule for deploying domain completion.

 Given a crosstab with discrete dimensions on the **Rows** and **Columns** shelves, utilizing a table calculation in which at least one dimension is addressed (but not all dimensions) activates domain completion.

One word in the previous rule may have been confusing – *addressed*. Partitioning and addressing were briefly mentioned previously and will be defined here to insure understanding. This is what the Tableau documentation says:

> *"The dimensions that define how to group the calculation, that is, define the scope of data it is performed on, are called partitioning fields. The table calculation is performed separately within each partition. The remaining dimensions, upon which the table calculation is performed, are called addressing fields, and determine the direction of the calculation."*

When editing a table calculation, you can choose to select/deselect **Specific Dimensions**. When a dimension is selected, that dimension is used to address the table calculation. When a dimension is not selected, the dimension is used to partition the table calculation. The following screenshot shows an example of the dialog box that is used to edit a table calculation. It demonstrates partitioning on **Year of Order Date** and addressing **Customer Name**:

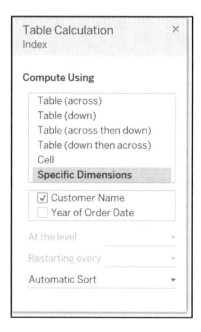

Exercise – activating domain completion in a crosstab part II

1. Duplicate the worksheet from the previous exercise, DC - Crosstab I. Name the new worksheet DC - Crosstab II.
2. Right click on **Index** and select **Compute Using** | **Cell**. Note that the view is sparsely populated.
3. Select **Analysis** | **Table Layout** | **Show Empty Columns**. The view is now fully populated.

The preceding exercise illustrates the following rules for deploying domain completion:

Given a crosstab with discrete dimensions on the **Rows** and **Columns** shelves, selecting **Compute Using** | **Cell** deactivates domain completion. Given a crosstab with discrete dimensions on the **Rows** and **Columns** shelves, selecting **Analysis** | **Table Layout** | **Show Empty Rows/Columns** activates domain completion.

The step in the preceding exercise in which **Compute Using** is set to **Cell** may give rise to a question. What about the other **Compute Using** options such as **Table (Across)**, **Table(Down)**, and so on? These options are actually all variations on partitioning and addressing.

Exercise – activating domain completion via View Types

This exercise demonstrates that deploying various view types can activate or deactivate domain completion:

1. Duplicate the worksheet from the previous exercise, DC - Crosstab II. Name the new worksheet DC - View Types.
2. Remove **Index** from the **Marks View** card and deselect **Analysis** | **Table Layout** | **Show Empty Columns**. The view is now sparsely populated with only 16 marks.

3. Change the **Marks View** card from **Automatic** to **Line**. The view is now fully populated with **20 marks**:

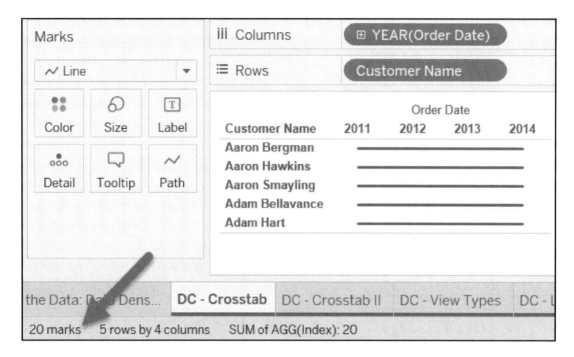

 Choose each view type option on the **Marks View** card and observe which View Types activate domain completion and which do not.

The preceding exercise illustrates the following rule for deploying data completion:

- Given a view with discrete dimensions on the **Rows** and **Columns** shelves, selecting the **Line**, **Area**, and **Polygon** View Types from the **Marks View** card activates domain completion

How domain completion is useful

Domain completion can be useful in many circumstances. In fact, you may have gleaned some uses from the previous exercises even though they were designed merely for illustration purposes. The following exercise demonstrates one of the many ways that domain completion can be useful.

Exercise – labelling nulls

This exercise demonstrates how to use domain completion to display **No Data** for cells without a value in a sparsely populated view:

1. Duplicate the worksheet from the previous exercise, DC - View Types. Name the new worksheet DC - Labelling Nulls.

2. Adjust the duplicated worksheet so that the View Types is set to **Text**. Also insure that only **Customer Name** and **YEAR(Order Date)** are deployed on the view. Be sure to leave **Customer Name** on the **Filters** shelf so that only the first five customers are displayed:

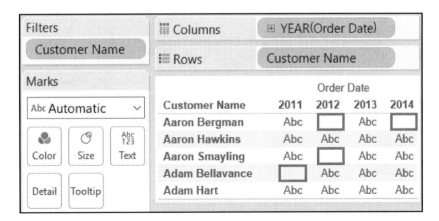

3. Create a calculated field named **No Data** with the following code:

```
IF ISNULL(SUM([Sales])) THEN 'No Data' END
```

4. Place **Sales** and **No Data** on the **Text** shelf. Note that the text **No Data** *is not* displayed.

5. Place **Index** on the **Detail** shelf. Note that the text **No Data** *is* displayed. The domain completion portion of the exercise is now complete but consider making the visualization more appealing by utilizing a shape such as is shown in the following screenshot:

When domain completion is a problem

After being made aware of domain completion, a user will no longer be confused when unwanted marks display in the view. But how to get those unwanted marks to not display can be a challenge. The following exercise shows an occasion of undesired domain completion and how to address the problem.

Exercise – unwanted domain completion

The goal of this exercise is to display each year a given country reported tourism revenue with an accompanying filter to adjust the countries that display based on the number of years data is available:

1. In the workbook associated with this chapter, navigate to the worksheet entitled DC - Year Count.

2. Select the **World Indicators** dataset in the **Data** pane.

3. Place **Country** and **Year** on the **Columns** shelf and **Tourism Inbound** on the **Text** shelf. Format as desired. Note the missing values for **Afghanistan** as shown in the following screenshot. This is not an instance of data densification since the dataset actually has these null values:

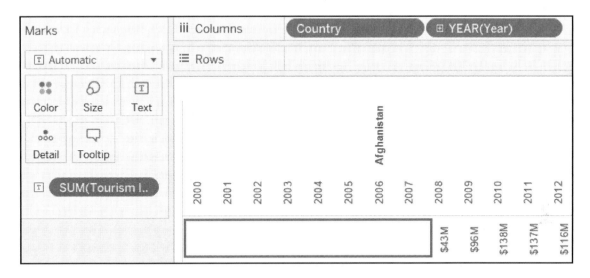

4. In order to remove the null values, click on the drop-down list associated with **SUM(Tourism Inbound)** and select **Filter**. In the resulting dialog box, select **Special** and **Non-null values**:

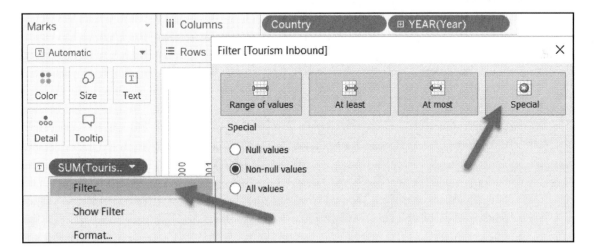

5. Create a table calculation named **Year Count** with the following code:

```
SIZE()
```

6. Place a discrete instance of **Year Count** on the **Columns** shelf to the right of **Country** and **Year**. Note that the resulting number represents every column in the view.

7. Right-click on **Year Count** and select **Compute Using | Year**. It appears as if the problem discussed in the second step has returned. However, although the issue looks the same in the view, the underlying problem differs. **Year Count** is a table calculation and has caused domain completion.

8. Right-click on **Year Count** and select **Edit Table Calculation**.

9. In the resulting dialog box select **Specific Dimensions**. Make sure that **Country** and **Year of Year** are both checked and in the order shown in the following dialog box. Leave **At the level** to **Deepest** and set **Restarting every** to **Country**:

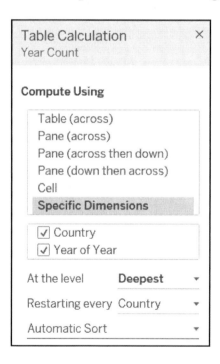

10. Complete the exercise by moving **Year Count** from the **Columns** shelf to the **Filters** shelf. Change **Year Count** to continuous and display the filter. Format as desired:

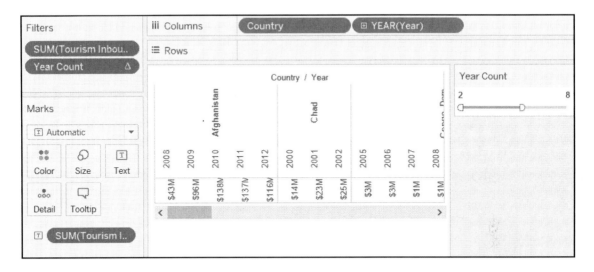

This exercise illustrates the first rule of domain completion. As a reminder, that rule is as follows:

 Given a crosstab with discrete dimensions on the **Rows** and **Columns** shelves, utilizing a table calculation in which at least one dimension is addressed (but not all dimensions) activates domain completion.

The relevant section in the preceding rule for this exercise is *a table calculation in which at least one dimension is addressed (but not all dimensions) activates domain completion*. The domain completion occurred when first deploying **Year Count**, which is a table calculation. Upon changing the addressing and partitioning of **Year Count** so that all dimensions were addressed (that is, no dimensions were partitioned), the issue was resolved.

Domain padding

The second type of data densification, domain padding, is fairly straightforward and, unlike domain completion, is discussed in Tableau documentation. We will proceed with a definition and then consider how domain padding is deployed and when it's useful.

 Domain padding: The addition of marks to the view via the **Show Missing Values** option on range aware dimensions (that is, date and bin) and **Analysis | Table Layout | Show Empty Rows/Columns**, even when there is no underlying data associated with those marks.

Deploying domain padding via Show Empty Rows/Columns

You may recall that one of the ways to deploy domain completion was **Analysis | Table Layout | Show Empty Rows/Columns**. The same is true of domain padding, as is illustrated in the following exercise.

Exercise – activating domain padding via Show Empty Rows/Columns

This exercise demonstrates how to toggle domain padding on and off:

1. In the workbook associated with this chapter, select **Data | New Data Source** and connect to the Superstore Excel workbook that ships with Tableau. It is located in **My Tableau Repository | Datasources**.
2. In the resulting instance of the **Data Source** page, double-click on **Orders and Returns**. This will cause an inner join to be created on the field **Order ID**.
3. Name the data source Superstore - Returns.
4. Navigate to the worksheet entitled DP - Show Missing Values and select the Superstore - Returns data source that was just created.
5. Place **Ship Mode** and **Region** on the **Rows** shelf. Next, place **Sales** on the **Text** shelf. Note that the **South** region does not display for **Same Day**.

6. Navigate to **Analysis** | **Table Layout** | **Show Missing Rows**:

Initially, it was necessary to point to a live data source, such as the instance of Superstore that ships with Tableau, because using an extract would not, in this case, activate domain padding even if **Analysis** | **Table Layout** | **Show Missing Rows** was selected. The end result of the exercise, as displayed in the screenshot, is that the **South** region is now displayed, even though there is no associated value.

How domain padding is useful

Domain padding is often useful when working with dates with gaps. Such gaps occur when some dates have associated values and some dates do not. As shown in the following example, returns do not occur every day in the Superstore dataset. Since a visualization displaying dates with gaps could be confusing, it might be helpful to fill in those gaps.

Exercise – domain padding – filling date gaps

This exercise demonstrates how to use domain padding to force every date to appear within a given range, even if dates are sparsely populated within the underlying data source:

1. In the workbook associated with this chapter, navigate to the worksheet entitled `DP - Filling Date Gaps`.
2. Select the `Superstore - Returns` data source that was created in the previous exercise.

3. Place a discrete instance of **MDY(Order Date)** on the **Columns** shelf and place **Sales** on the **Rows** shelf. Note that every mark in the view is equally spaced regardless of the length of time between dates:

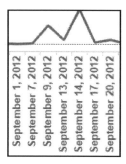

4. Right-click on **MDY(Order Date)** and select **Show Missing Values**.
5. Right-click on **SUM(Sales)** in the **Rows** shelf and select **Format**. In the resulting format window, choose the **Pane** tab and set **Marks** as **Show at Default Value**. Note that the distance between marks is now based on the length of time between dates. All dates with no value display at the zero line:

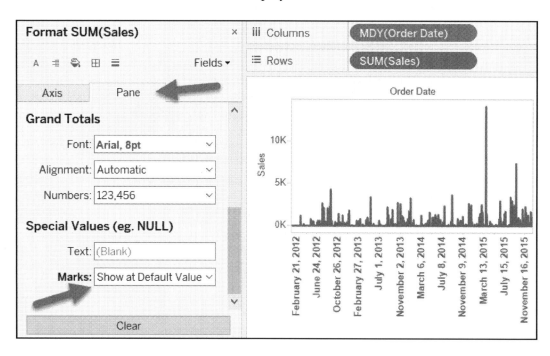

When domain padding is a problem

Since domain padding can be toggled on or off via specific commands in Tableau (that is, **Show Missing Values** and **Show Empty Rows/Columns**), it's typically not a problem. There are a few scenarios, however, when domain padding may cause confusion.

Exercise – from a domain padded visualization to a crosstab

This brief exercise demonstrates an instance when domain confusion is confusing and should thus be toggled off:

1. In the workbook associated with this chapter, navigate to the worksheet entitled `DP - From Viz to Crosstab`.
2. Select the `Superstore` dataset.
3. Right-click on **Discount** and select **Create | Bins**. In the resulting dialog box choose a bin size of `0.05`.
4. Place the newly created **Discount (bin)** dimension on the **Columns** shelf.
5. Right-click on **Discount (bin)** and ensure that **Show Missing Values** is selected.
6. Right-click and drag the **Discount** measure from the **Data** pane to the **Rows** shelf. Select **CNT** in the resulting dialog box. Note that some of the bins have no values. For example, as shown in the following screenshot, the 35% bin has no associated value:

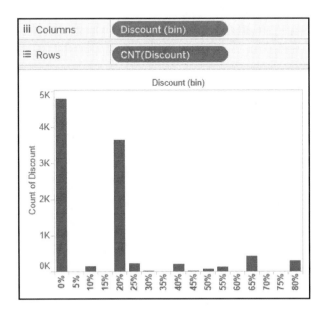

7. Duplicate the sheet as a crosstab by right-clicking on the worksheet tab and selecting **Duplicate as Crosstab**. Note that **Show Missing Values** is still activated:

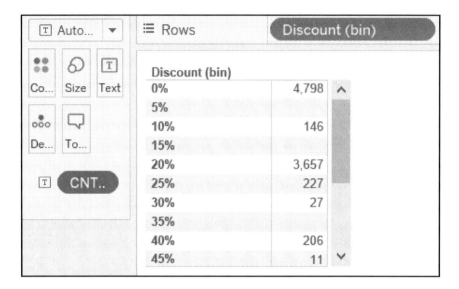

8. Complete the exercise by right-clicking on **Discount (bin)** and deselecting **Show Missing Values**.

Utilizing **Show Missing Values** for bins or dates is often helpful in a visualization, but may not be helpful in a crosstab view. This is especially true if there are many rows or columns without values.

Working with cubes

For the most part, Tableau behavior is uniform across data sources. For example, the experience of working with an Access database and an Oracle database is very similar. Of course, different data sources will have different nuances but, in general, Tableau attempts to make working with different data sources a seamless experience. However, working with cubes (that is, multidimensional data sources) is quite different. Major differences include the inability to alias, create calculated fields on dimensions, create groups or hierarchies, change aggregation types, generate extracts, and more. Tableau knowledge base articles provide many workarounds for these shortcomings.

At the time of writing, the central cube-related article is located at `http://kb.tableau.com/articles/knowledgebase/functional-differences-olap-relational`.

This article provides detailed information and is well-worth studying in detail if you work with cubes. Provided with the article is a `.twbx` file with over twenty worksheets demonstrating how to reproduce typical Tableau behavior when working in a cube environment. Similarly the other cube-related articles in the Tableau knowledge base also provide accompanying workbooks. Although this material is excellent, there is little mention of using data blending to work more effectively with cubes. This section addresses that shortcoming.

In order to complete the following cube-related exercises, you must have access to Microsoft Analysis Services with an instance of the Adventure Works cube. (Adventure Works is the sample cube that ships with Microsoft Analysis Services) Detailed instructions for installing SQL Server, Analysis Services, and the accompanying Adventure Works cube are available at MSDN. A search engine query on hh403424 will return the link to these instructions.

Exercise – using a data blend for continuous months when accessing a cube

Typically, a cube includes one or more date hierarchies. When Tableau is connected to a cube, the members of a date hierarchy that display in the **Data** pane behave like strings. So, Tableau's built-in hierarchy capabilities, which are available when working with dates in relational data sources, are not available. This limitation can be partially overcome by coding MDX queries in Tableau, but to achieve all the Tableau date capabilities, a data blend is necessary.

Exercise steps

This exercise demonstrates a technique for using data blending to achieve Tableau's full range of date capabilities when working with a cube:

1. In the workbook associated with this chapter, navigate to the worksheet entitled `Cube - Continuous Days`.
2. Connect to the **Adventure Works** data source via **Data | New Data Source | Microsoft Analysis Services**. (See the preceding notes to learn how to install Analysis Services and the Adventure Works cube.)

3. In the dimension portion of the **Data** pane, expand **Date** and locate the **Date** field.
4. Note that different versions of the Adventure Works cube have slightly different naming conventions.
5. Right-click on **Date** and select **Change Data Type | Date**.
6. Drag **Date** to the **Columns** shelf.
7. Place **Internet Sales Amount** on the **Rows** shelf:

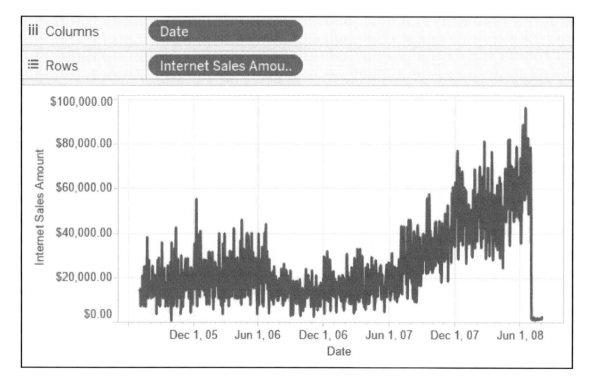

8. Select the worksheet entitled Cube - Preparing Dates.

9. Expand **Date**, then **Calendar**, and lastly, **Date.Calendar**:

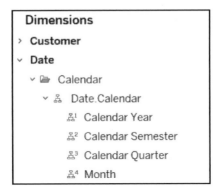

10. Drag **Calendar Year** and **Month** to the **Rows** shelf. Also, drag **Internet Sales Amount** to the **Text** shelf.

11. Note that including **Internet Sales Amount** forces every month to be displayed.

12. Select **Worksheet | Export | Crosstab to Excel**.

13. Adjust the Excel spreadsheet to look like the following screenshot. Be sure to replace the **Internet Sales Amount** column with a column named **Blended Month** that should include first-of-the-month date information for each row; for example, **6/1/2011**. Also, fill down **Calendar Year** so that every cell is populated:

	A	B	C	D
1	Calendar Year	Month	Blended Month	
2	CY 2010	December 2010	12/1/2010	
3	CY 2011	January 2011	1/1/2011	
4	CY 2011	February 2011	2/1/2011	
5	CY 2011	March 2011	3/1/2011	
6	CY 2011	April 2011	4/1/2011	
7	CY 2011	May 2011	5/1/2011	
8	CY 2011	June 2011	6/1/2011	
9	CY 2011	July 2011	7/1/2011	
10	CY 2011	August 2011	8/1/2011	

14. Save the Excel spreadsheet as `AWDates.xlsx`.

15. In Tableau, select the worksheet entitled `Cube - Continuous Months`.

16. Select the **Adventure Works** dataset and drag **Internet Sales Amount** to the **Rows** shelf.

17. Add `AWDates.xlsx` as a new dataset.

18. Select **Data | Edit Data Relationships** and set the relationships so that **Date.Date.Calendar.Calendar Year** blends with **Calendar Year** and **Date.Date.Calendar.Month** blends with **Month**, as shown in the following screenshot:

19. In the **Data** pane, select the **AWDates** data source and blend on **Calendar Year** and **Month** by clicking the gray broken chain link icons.

20. Right-click and drag **Blended Month** to the **Columns** shelf and select **Month** continuous:

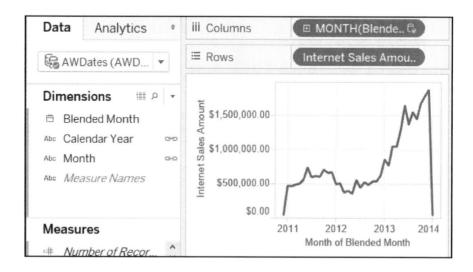

Exercise commentary

The preceding steps 1-5 demonstrate a simple way to create a view with a continuous date when connected to a cube. No MDX code was necessary. However, these same steps also reveal shortcomings of working with a cube; namely, that many of the choices normally available for dates in Tableau are not accessible. This is a problem that cannot be overcome by restructuring the cube or writing MDX code. The remaining steps in the exercise demonstrate how this problem can be overcome via data blending. Although the data blend created in the exercise only provides month level granularity, it would not be difficult to include day level granularity. The end result is a demonstration that the date capabilities normally expected in Tableau can be made available when connected to a cube. Furthermore, if the blended data source remains small, the impact on performance should be negligible.

Exercise – using a data blend for hierarchies, aliasing, and grouping when accessing a cube

MDX can be used to provide some of the functionality normally available in Tableau that is otherwise missing when connected to a cube. For example, although you cannot create groups in Tableau when accessing a cube data source, MDX can be passed to the cube via a calculated member to create groups. Instructions for how to do this are provided in the aforementioned knowledge base articles. Similarly, it is possible to use MDX to create hierarchies or to alias dimension members, but that requires knowledge of MDX that most Tableau authors do not possess. This exercise will demonstrate how to use data blending to accomplish all three:

1. Create an Excel spreadsheet named `Aliasing` with the following data:

Group	Hemispheres
Europe	Eastern Hemisphere
North America	Western Hemisphere
Pacific	Eastern Hemisphere

2. In the workbook associated with this chapter, navigate to the worksheet entitled Cube - Hierarchy.
3. If you have not already added the **Adventure Works** dataset, connect via **Data | New Data Source | Microsoft Analysis Services**. (See the previous notes to learn how to install Analysis Services and the Adventure Works cube.)
4. Select the **Adventure Works** dataset and place **Internet Sales Amount** on the **Text** shelf.
5. Add the newly created Excel spreadsheet, Aliasing, as a data source.
6. In the Aliasing source, blend on **Group** by clicking the gray broken chain link icon.
7. Create a hierarchy on **Group** and **Hemispheres** by selecting both in the **Data** pane, right-clicking, and selecting **Hierarchy | Create Hierarchy**. Name the hierarchy as desired.
8. Make **Hemispheres** the first dimension in the hierarchy by dragging it before **Group**.
9. Place **Hemispheres** and **Group** on the **Rows** shelf:

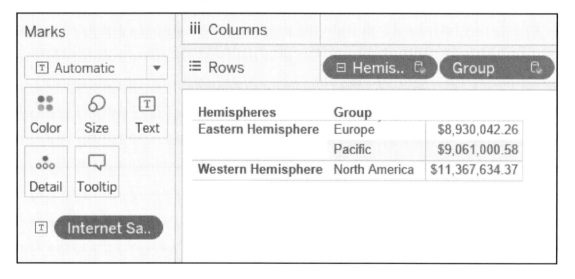

10. Navigate to the worksheet entitled Cube - Aliasing & Grouping.
11. Select the **Adventure Works** dataset and place **Internet Sales Amount** on the **Text** shelf.

12. Select the `Aliasing` dataset, right-click on **Group**, and select **Duplicate**. Name the duplicate field `Regional Groups`.

13. Right-click on **Regional Groups** and select **Aliases**. Adjust the aliasing so that **Europe** is aliased as **EMEA**, **Pacific** is aliased as **AsiaPac**, and **North America** is left unchanged.

14. Blend on **Group** by clicking the gray broken chain link icon.

15. Place **Hemispheres** and **Regional Groups** on the **Rows** shelf:

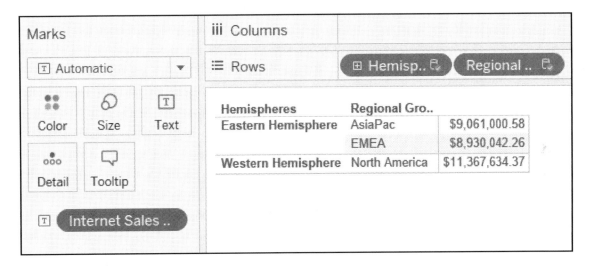

Typically, dimensions are not enabled for secondary data sources in a data blend; however, in the previous case, since the secondary data source is blended on **Group** and there is a one-to-many relationship between **Hemispheres** and **Group**, both of these fields can be used as dimensions in the view. Nonetheless, for unrestricted use of dimensions, always use the primary data source. Thus, to further extend the exercise, select the **Adventure Works** data source and drag various dimensions to the **Rows** or **Columns** shelfs, including **Country** and **Region**.

One point of interest in the previous exercise is the necessity of creating **Regional Groups** in the secondary data source by duplicating **Group**. This was required to successfully alias the dimension members. Attempting to alias members directly within **Group** breaks the data blend, as shown in the following screenshot:

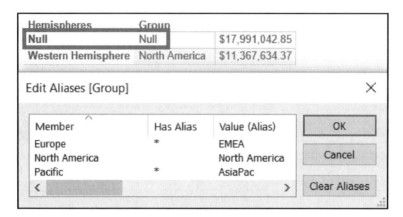

The deprecation of cubes

Are cubes here to stay? Maybe not. The advent of big data solutions and the continued evolution of **Relational Database Management Systems (RDBMS)** may make cubes obsolete. Cubes pre-aggregate data, which can make certain analytic and reporting needs very quick; however, as RDBMS and big data solutions become faster, easier to query, and more sophisticated, the pre-aggregation paradigm may become obsolete. Some argue that cubes are already obsolete. Also, cubes have serious drawbacks, including no performance advantage for non-aggregated data (which is typical at lower levels of granularity), challenges with more complex analytic needs, the difficulty of mastering the MDX language, and the fact that many BI vendors do not cater to cubes. This last point is true of Tableau. Although, as has been shown in this section, Tableau can be used with cubes, there are many challenges to overcome.

Tableau and big data

Perhaps the first challenge of big data is defining it adequately. It's a term so widely used as to be almost meaningless. For example, some may refer to data exceeding 1,048,576 rows as big data (that is, the row limit in Excel 2010 and 2013), while others would only apply the term to datasets in the multiple petabyte range. Definitions found on Wikipedia and Webopedia are so broad as to encompass both of these examples.

Big data is a broad term for data sets so large or complex that traditional data processing applications are inadequate: `https://en.wikipedia.org /wiki/Big_data`

Big data is a buzzword, or catch-phrase, meaning a massive volume of both structured and unstructured data that is so large it is difficult to process using traditional database and software techniques: `http://www.w ebopedia.com/TERM/B/big_data.html`

True, we should probably not consider data that merely exceeds Excel's row limitation as big data; nevertheless, from the perspective of the individual for whom Excel is the *"traditional data processing application"*, the preceding definitions fit.

Rather than trying to provide an adequately narrow definition to what is essentially a buzzword, this section will primarily focus on one aspect of big data; that is, **Massively Parallel Processing (MPP)**. However, before we begin that focus, let's consider a couple of housekeeping items. First, when I have been asked about Tableau and big data, the intent of the question has invariably been about Tableau performance when working with large datasets. Since a chapter of this book is dedicated to Tableau performance, this section will not address performance thoroughly. Second, for the user who works predominately or exclusively with Excel, exceeding the row limit is a real problem for which a solution may proof helpful.

Exercise – a strategy for addressing Excel's row limitation

As mentioned previously, data that is merely in excess of Excel's row limitation should not be considered big data. Nonetheless, that limitation can be an issue, and telling a Tableau author to use a database is often not helpful. A Tableau author may indeed desire to utilize a database but may not have direct access. For example, the data residing in the database may be exported via a web application and then imported into an Excel workbook that Tableau utilizes as a data source. If this process is performed weekly or monthly and each import involves 10,000+ rows, it won't be long before the Excel row limit is hit. Here is one strategy for addressing the issue. Note that the following exercise is Windows-centric. Similar tasks can be implemented in a Mac environment.

1. In the workbook associated with this chapter, navigate to the dashboard entitled `Excel Row Limit`. That dashboard includes a link to files necessary to complete this exercise.
2. Download the files.
3. Open `Spreadsheet_2` in Excel or a text editor and remove the header, that is, the first row. Save the spreadsheet as a CSV file.
4. Place copies of the two files in a new directory.
5. Open a command prompt. This can be quickly done by pressing the Windows key + *R* and then entering `cmd`.
6. In the command prompt, type the following in order to navigate to the newly created directory:

   ```
   cd [filepath to the newly created directory]
   ```

   An example filepath – `C:\Users\DavidBaldwin\Desktop\New_Directory`

7. Press *Enter* on the keyboard.
8. In command prompt, enter the following:

   ```
   for %f in (*.csv) do type "%f" >> output.csv
   ```

10. Press *Enter* on the keyboard.
11. Note that the resulting CSV file (that is, `output.csv`) will not open successfully in Excel but, as shown in the following steps, it can be used as a data source in Tableau.
12. In Tableau, press *Ctrl + D* to open a new data source.

13. In the resulting window, select **Text File**:

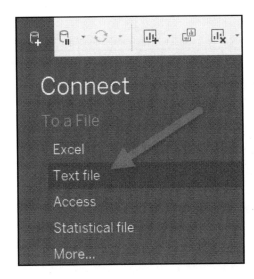

14. Connect to the `output.csv` data source.

15. Place **Number of Records** on the **Text** shelf and observe that the total equals the number of rows in `Spreadsheet_1` plus the number of rows in `Spreadsheet_2`:

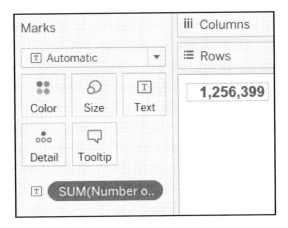

The preceding exercise essentially unites two spreadsheets. As of version 9.3, unions are available in Tableau; however, wildcard capabilities such as demonstrated by (*.csv) in the preceding exercise are not possible, though Tableau 10.1 will probably include wildcard options. Regardless, the preceding method still has certain advantages. For example, this method could be extended with a PowerShell script to automate the creation of a super file including all the necessary data on a scheduled basis. This could be useful for purposes outside of Tableau.

Massively parallel processing

Big data may be semi-structured or unstructured. MPP architecture structures big data to enable easy querying for reporting and analytic purposes. MPP systems are sometimes referred to as **shared nothing systems**. This means that data is partitioned across many servers (otherwise known as nodes) and each server processes queries locally. Let's explore MPP in more detail via a diagram:

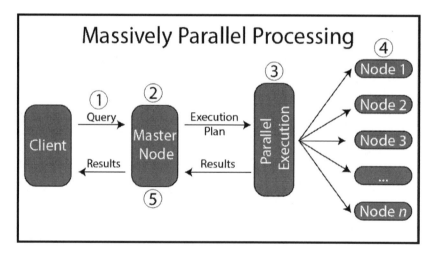

Let's discuss the five steps listed in the preceding diagram:

1. The process begins by the **Client** issuing a query that is then passed to the **Master Node**.
2. The Master Node contains information such as the data dictionary and session information, which it uses to generate an execution plan designed to retrieve the required information from each underlying **Node**.
3. **Parallel Execution** represents the implementation of the execution plan generated by the Master Node.

4. Each underlying Node executes the unique query it has received and then passes the results to the Master Node. Each Node is actually a standalone server with its own RAM, disk space, and operating system.

5. The Master Node assembles the results, which are then passed to the Client.

On the plus side, MPP systems are easily scalable. Once the initial architecture is set up, adding additional hard drive space and processing power can be as easy as adding additional servers. On the minus side, MPP systems can be quite costly to implement, requiring thousands or even tens of thousands of servers along with associated failover requirements and highly skilled, costly labor for support. As a result of the expense, many organizations choose a cloud-based solution such as Amazon Redshift or Google BigQuery. Amazon Redshift uses an MPP system, as described previously. Google BigQuery uses Tree Architecture, which is a little different but nonetheless takes advantage of MPP techniques.

Exercise – building a visualization with Google BigQuery

In order to build a visualization with Google BigQuery, you will need to first set up access to BigQuery. Accordingly, the following exercise will point you in the right direction. Once you have set up access to BigQuery, you will be able to connect to the BigQuery sample datasets. In the remainder of the exercise you will build a visualization while connected to BigQuery. Assuming you have a good Internet connection, the performance will probably exceed what you experience when working with a local copy of an extracted data source of a similar size.

Exercise steps

1. Log in to your Google account.

2. Navigate to `https://cloud.google.com/bigquery/` and follow the provided instructions to try BigQuery for free.

3. In the workbook associated with this chapter, navigate to the worksheet entitled `BigQuery`.

4. Press *Ctrl + D* to connect to a data source. In the resulting window, select `Google BigQuery` and, when prompted, provide your login information.

5. On the **Data Source** page, choose the **publicdata** project, the **samples** dataset and the **natality** table.

6. The **natality** table provides birth demographics for the United States from 1969 – 2008:

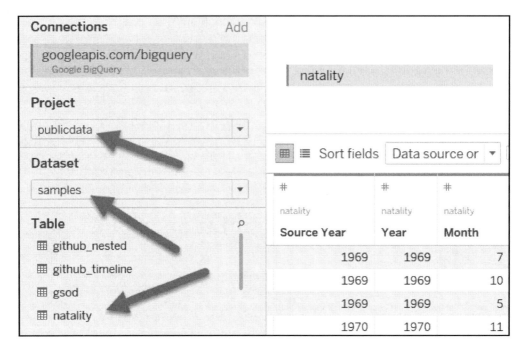

7. In the **Data** pane, double-click **Number of Records**.
8. From the **Data** pane, drag **Month** to the **Columns** shelf.
9. Set **Month** to **Discrete**.
10. Right-click on the axis and select **Edit Axis**.
11. Deselect **Include Zero**.

12. Format as desired:

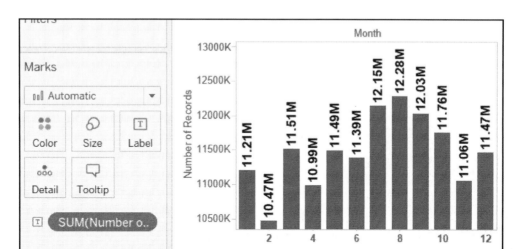

The preceding visualization displays the number of infants born in each month from 1969 – 2008.

Summary

We began this chapter with a discussion of data densification and discovered that there are two types of data densification: domain completion and domain padding. While reviewing these two types of data densification, we learned how to how each can be deployed, when each is useful, and when each can be a problem.

Next, we learned how to work with cubes. Tableau knowledge base articles were discussed, as well additional techniques using data blending to address some of the limitations that are inherent when accessing cubes as data sources.

Lastly, we explored big data. We surveyed **Massively Parallel Processing (MPP)** and walked through an example of using Tableau to connect to Google BigQuery.

Having completed three chapters of data-centric discussion, we will discuss table calculations in the next chapter. We will focus that discussion on directional and non-directional table calculation functions, as well as partitioning and addressing.

5

Table Calculations

The topic of table calculations in Tableau is so rich and deep that it alone could legitimately be the subject of an entire book. Exploring the various options that are available for each table calculation function and the various ways in which table calculations can be applied is an interesting and rewarding endeavor.

As you review the examples in this chapter, you will undoubtedly encounter techniques that you can apply in your day-to-day work; however, you may struggle to understand why some of these techniques work. Furthermore, as you read the Tableau documentation, you may be frustrated at the brevity with which certain major aspects of table calculations are covered and the complete lack of coverage of more detailed aspects. If you want to gain a deep understanding of table calculations, it is necessary to dive into forums, blogs, white papers, and videos and to experiment relentlessly. This chapter has been written with the intent of providing ways of thinking about table calculations that will prove useful in your journey of mastering this fascinating topic. Along the way, some practical examples will be considered as well.

The structure of this chapter was created with the intent of providing a simple schema for understanding table calculations. This schema (and hence the structure of the chapter) is communicated via two questions:

- What is the function?
- How is the function applied?

These two questions are inexorably connected. You cannot reliably apply something until you know what it is. And you cannot get useful results from something until you correctly apply it. The section in this chapter entitled *What is the function?* explores each unique table calculation function and how each can be considered directional or non-directional. The section entitled *How is the function applied?* explores how table calculations are applied to the view via partitioning and addressing dimensions.

I would like to draw attention to the work of three individuals who helped make this chapter possible. Joshua Milligan provided the idea of directional and non-directional as a taxonomy for considering how Tableau table calculation functions are applied. Of the dozens of blogs, forum posts, conference sessions, articles, and white papers reviewed for this chapter, Jonathan Drummy's blog post *At the Level – Unlocking the Mystery Part 1: Ordinal Calcs* was the most clear and insightful for understanding the various nuances of partitioning and addressing. Lastly, Joe Mako's unsurpassed understanding of the inner workings of Tableau and his willingness to share that insight via the Tableau forums was of constant assistance.

A definition and two questions

As discussed in `Chapter 1`, *Getting Up to Speed – a Review of the Basics*, calculated fields can be categorized thus: row level, aggregate level, and table level. For row- and aggregate-level calculations, the underlying data source engine does most (if not all) of the computational work, and Tableau merely visualizes the results. For table calculations, Tableau also relies on the underlying data source engine to execute computational tasks; however, after that work is completed and a dataset is returned, Tableau performs additional processing before rendering the results. This can be seen within the following process flow diagram, in the circled part titled **Tableau performs additional processing**. This is where table calculations are processed:

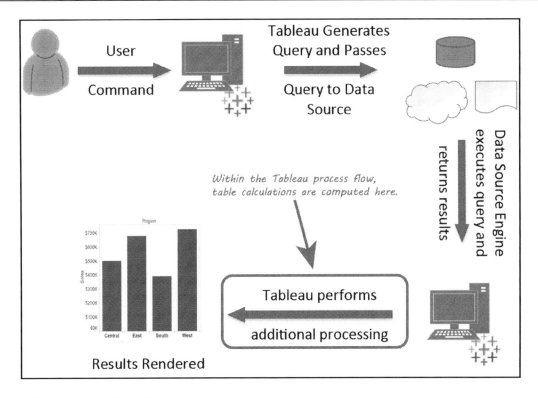

We will continue with a definition:

A table calculation is a function performed on a dataset in cache that has been generated as a result of a query from Tableau to the data source.

Let's consider a couple of points regarding the dataset in cache mentioned in the preceding definition. First, it is important to understand that this cache is not simply the returned results of a query. Tableau may adjust the returned results. For example, as discussed in the previous chapter, Tableau may expand the cache via data densification. Secondly, it's important to consider how the cache is structured. Basically, the dataset in cache is a table and, like all tables, is made up of rows and columns. This is particularly important for table calculations since a table calculation may be computed as it moves along the cache. Such a table calculation is directional. Alternatively, a table calculation may be computed based on the entire cache with no directional consideration. Table calculations such as this are non-directional. Directional and non-directional table calculations will be considered more fully in the following section.

Note that in the Tableau documentation, the **dataset in cache** is typically referred to as a **partition**. This chapter will often use both terms side by side for clarity.

What is the function?

As discussed in the introduction to this chapter, it may be helpful to enhance your understanding of table calculations via the following two questions: *What is the function?* and *How is the function applied?*

We will begin by considering how each table calculation function can be considered directional or non-directional.

Directional and non-directional

As of Tableau 10, there are 32 table calculation functions in Tableau. However, many of these are simply variations of a theme; for example, there are five Running functions, including RUNNING_SUM and RUNNING_AVG. If we narrow our consideration to unique groups of table calculations functions, we will discover that there are only 11. The following table shows these 11 functions organized in two categories:

Directional table calculation functions	Non-directional table calculation functions
LOOKUP	SCRIPT_STR functions
PREVIOUS VALUE	SIZE
RUNNING functions	TOTAL
WINDOW functions	
FIRST	
INDEX	
LAST	
RANK functions	

As mentioned previously, non-directional table calculation functions operate on the entire cache and thus are not computed based on movement through the cache. For example, the SIZE function doesn't change based on the value of a previous row in the cache. On the other hand, RUNNING_SUM does change based on previous rows in the cache and is therefore considered directional.

Exercise – exploring directional and non-directional table calculation functions

In this example, we'll see directional and non-directional table calculation functions in action:

1. Navigate to `https://public.tableau.com/profile/david.baldwin#!/` to locate and download the workbook associated with this chapter.

2. Navigate to the worksheet entitled `Directional/Non-Directional`.

3. Create the following calculated fields:

Name	Calculation	Notes
Lookup	LOOKUP(SUM([Sales]),-1)	Notice the −1 included in this calculation. This instructs Tableau to retrieve the value from the previous row.
Size	SIZE()	As Tableau help states, the SIZE function returns the number of rows in the partition. Therefore, as can be seen in the next screenshot, the size equals the total number of rows.
Window Sum	WINDOW_SUM(SUM([Sales]))	Window sum functions can operate either directionally or non-directionally. Since this example does not include the [start, end] option, it operates non-directionally.
Window Sum w/ Start&End	WINDOW_SUM(SUM([Sales]),0,1)	This example of a window function is operating directionally, as can be seen by the inclusion of the [start, end] option.

Running Sum	`RUNNING_SUM(SUM([Sales]))`	By their nature, RUNNING functions operate directionally since they consider previous rows in order to compute.

4. Place **Category** and **Ship Mode** on the **Rows** shelf.
5. Double-click on **Sales, Lookup, Size, Window Sum, Window Sum w/ Start&End**, and **Running Sum** to populate the view.
6. Compare the following screenshot with the notes in step 3 of this exercise for better understanding:

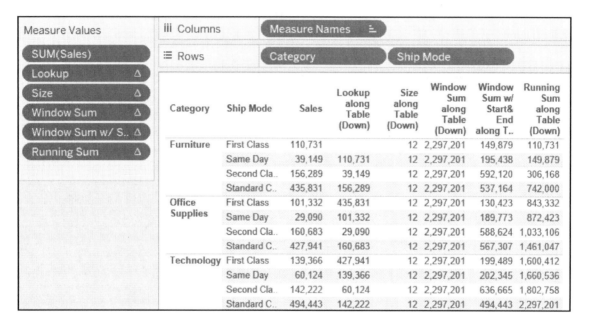

Exploring each unique table calculation function

In our answer to the question, *What is the function?*, we have considered a taxonomy comprising two categories: directional and non-directional. Now we will move on to considering the table calculation functions individually. Regretfully, space does not allow us to explore all 32 table calculations; however, to gain a working understanding it should suffice to consider all but one of the unique groups of options. The four table calculations that begin with `Script_` are covered in `Chapter 13`, *R Integration*.

Although some effort has been made to make the following exercises useful for real-world scenarios, each is focused on demonstrating table calculation functionality while considering how each interacts directionally or non-directionally with the dataset in cache (or partition).

Exercises – exploring each unique table calculation function

Here are some of the unique table calculation functions that we will use in our exercises.

LOOKUP and TOTAL

The objectives of the following worksheet are to display those customers who made purchases in the last two days of 2013 and the associated sales totals. Also included is the percentage total of those sales in the month of December. Notice in the results how LOOKUP behaves directionally, whereas TOTAL is non-directional:

1. In the workbook associated with this chapter, navigate to the worksheet entitled `Lookup/Total`.
2. Drag **Customer Name** and **Order Date** to the **Rows** shelf. Set **Order Date** to **Month/Day/Year** discrete.
3. Place **Order Date** on the **Filters** shelf and choose to view only **December 2013**.
4. Create the following calculated fields:

Name	Calculation
Lookup Intervening Time	`DATEDIFF('day',LOOKUP(Max([Order Date]),0),` `DATE("12/31/2013"))`
% Total Sales	`SUM(Sales)/TOTAL(SUM([Sales]))`

5. Right-click on **% Total Sales** and go to **Default Properties | Number format** to set the number format to percentage with two decimal places.
6. Place **Lookup Intervening Time** on the **Filters** shelf and choose a range from 0 to 1.
7. Double-click on **Sales** and **% Total Sales** to place both fields on the view.

8. Format as desired:

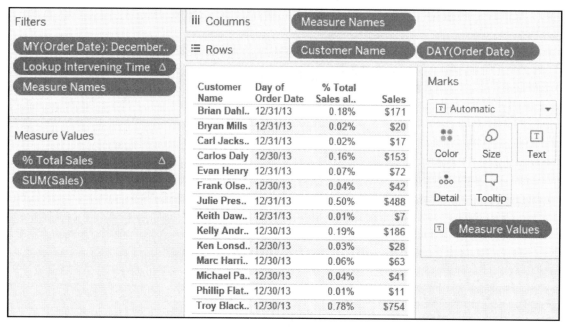

Let's consider how the previous worksheet functions:

- The filter on **Order Date** ensures that the dataset returned to Tableau only includes data from the month of December 2013.
- **% Total Sales**: SUM(Sales)/TOTAL(SUM([Sales])):
    - This calculation includes the TOTAL(SUM([Sales])) code, which returns the total sales for the entire dataset. Dividing SUM([Sales]) by this total returns the percentage of the total.
- **Lookup Intervening Time**: DATEDIFF('day',LOOKUP(Max([Order Date]),0), DATE("12/31/2013")):
    - The DATEDIFF function will return an integer reflecting the difference between the date returned by the LOOKUP function and 12/31/2013.

- Note that the LOOKUP function has an offset of zero. This results in each row returning the date associated with that row. This is different from the first exercise in this chapter, which included a LOOKUP function with an offset of −1; that caused each row in the view to return data associated with the previous row.
- At first glance, you might think that you could simplify this workbook by removing **Lookup Intervening Time** from the **Filters** shelf and adjusting the filter on **[Order Date]** to display only the last two days of December. However, if you do this, **% Total Sales** will add up to 100% across all rows in the view, which would not satisfy the workbook's objectives. Think of **Lookup Intervening Time** as not filtering but hiding all but the last two days in December. This hiding ensures that the data necessary to calculate **% Total Sales** is in the dataset in cache (partition).

PREVIOUS_VALUE

The objectives of the following worksheet are to return the aggregate value of sales for each year and set next year's sales goal. Note that two options have been provided for determining next year's sales goal in order to demonstrate how PREVIOUS_VALUE differs from LOOKUP. Also note that PREVIOUS_VALUE behaves directionally:

1. In the workbook associated with this chapter, navigate to the worksheet entitled Previous Value.
2. Create the following calculated fields:

Name	Calculation
Next Year Goal Prv_Val	PREVIOUS_VALUE(SUM([Sales])) * 1.05
Next Year Goal Lkup	LOOKUP(SUM([Sales]),0) * 1.05

3. Place **Order Date** on the **Rows** shelf.
4. Double-click on **Sales** and **Next Year Goal Prv_Val** to place each on the view.

5. Format as desired:

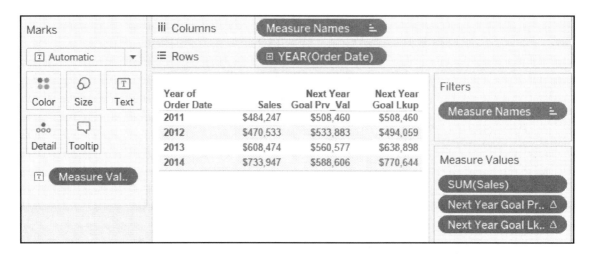

Let's consider how the previous worksheet functions:

- **Next Year Goal Prv_Val:** PREVIOUS_VALUE(SUM([Sales])) * 1.05:
    - As it is applied in this worksheet, this calculation retrieves the results from each previous row and adds 5%. In other words, the goal is a steady-state growth rate of 5% per year over all years.
- **Next Year Goal Lkup:** LOOKUP(SUM([Sales]),0) * 1.05:
    - As it is applied in this worksheet, this calculation adds 5% to the current year's sales. In other words, the goal for next year is for sales that are 5% greater than this year. Previous years are not considered.

To better understand this exercise, consider the values associated with 2014 in the preceding screenshot. **Next Year Goal Prv_Val** is calculated via the 2013 **Next Year Goal Prv_Val** field, that is, $560,577 * 1.05. On the other hand, **Next Year Goal Lkup** is calculated via the 2014 sales, that is, $733,947 * 1.05.

RUNNING

The objective of the following worksheet is to display the running minimum profit, running average profit, and running maximum profit compared with **SUM(Profit)** for each month in the dataset. This example demonstrates how RUNNING functions behave directionally:

1. In the workbook associated with this chapter, navigate to the worksheet entitled `Running`.

2. Create the following calculated fields:

Name	Calculation
Running Min	`RUNNING_MIN(SUM([Profit]))`
Running Max	`RUNNING_MAX(SUM([Profit]))`
Running Avg	`RUNNING_AVG(SUM([Profit]))`

3. Place **Order Date** on the **Columns** shelf and set to **Month/Year** continuous.
4. Place **Measure Values** on the **Rows** shelf.
5. Remove all instances of measures from the **Measure Values** shelf except **Running Min, Running Max, Running Avg,** and **Profit**.
6. Move **SUM(Profit)** from the **Measure Values** shelf to the **Rows** shelf.
7. Right-click on **SUM(Profit)** and select Dual Axis.
8. Format as desired:

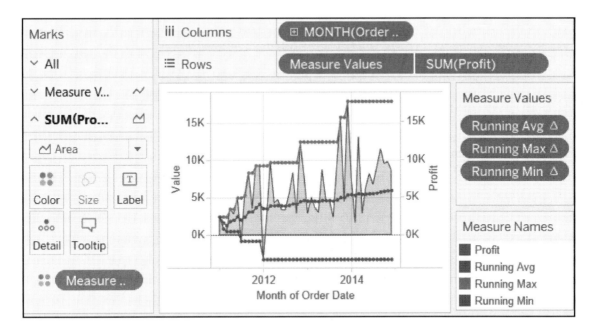

Let's consider how the preceding worksheet functions:

- **Running Min**: `RUNNING_MIN(SUM([Profit]))`:
    - As is visible in the screenshot, **Running Min** compares the current **SUM(Profit)** with the least **SUM(Profit)** recorded to that point in time. If the current **SUM(Profit)** is less than the least **SUM(Profit)** recorded to date, then the current **SUM(Profit)** replaces the least **SUM(Profit)**.
- **Running Max**: `RUNNING_MAX(SUM([Profit]))`:
    - **Running Max** operates similarly to **Running Min**, but of course, it looks for maximum values.
- **Running Avg**: `RUNNING_AVG(SUM([Profit]))`:
    - In this example, **Running Avg** calculates the average **SUM(Profit)** based on every month to the current month.

WINDOW

The objective of the following worksheet is to display a directional instance of a `WINDOW` function and a non-directional instance:

1. In the workbook associated with this chapter, navigate to the worksheet entitled `Window`.
2. Create the following calculated fields:

Name	Calculation
Win Avg Directional	`WINDOW_AVG(SUM([Profit]),-2,0)`
Win Avg Non-Directional	`WINDOW_AVG(SUM([Profit]))`

3. Place **Order Date** on the **Columns** shelf and set to **Month/Year** continuous.
4. Place **Measure Values** on the **Rows** shelf.
5. Remove all instances of measures from the **Measure Values** shelf except **Win Avg Directional**, **Win Avg Non-Directional**, and **Profit**.
6. From the **Data** pane, drag another instance of **Profit** to the **Rows** shelf.
7. Right-click on the instance of **Profit** on the **Rows** shelf and select **Quick Table Calculation | Moving Average**.
8. Right-click on the instance of **Profit** on the **Rows** shelf and select **Dual Axis**.
9. Right-click on the axis labeled **Moving Average of Profit** and select **Synchronize Axis**.

10. Format as desired:

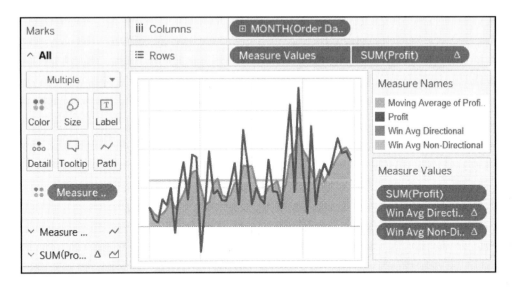

Let's consider how this worksheet functions:

- **Win Avg Directional**: `Window_AVG(SUM([Profit]),-2,0)`:
  - The start point of `-2` and end point of `0` signify that Tableau will create a point based of the average of the **SUM([Profit])** calculated on the current month and the previous two months. Changing `0` to `2` would cause the average of each point to be calculated on the previous two months, the current month, and the next two months.
  - Double-click on the instance of **Profit** on the **Rows** shelf to view the underlying code (this is the instance of **Profit** that was changed into a table calculation by right-clicking and selecting **Quick Table Calculation | Moving Average**). Note that the code is identical to the code created for **Win Avg Directional**. However, if you right-click on both pills and select **Edit Table Calculation**, you will notice that the resulting dialog boxes differ. The dialog box associated with **Profit** has more options including the ability to change the previous and next values. Changing the previous and next values for **Win Avg Direction** requires adjusting the calculated field.

- **Win Avg Non-Directional**: `WINDOW_AVG(SUM([Profit]))`:
  - The horizontal line across the view is associated with the calculated field **Win Avg Non-Directional**. Note that it is not dependent on direction. Instead, it is a single value generated by the average of all aggregated **Profit** values in the dataset in cache (partition).

FIRST and LAST

The objective of the following worksheet is to display the first and last instances of the best-selling item in the **Superstore** dataset. Notice how this example demonstrates that the FIRST and LAST functions behave directionally:

1. In the workbook associated with this chapter, navigate to the worksheet entitled First/Last.
2. Create the following calculated fields:

Name	Calculation
First	FIRST()
Last	LAST()
First or Last	FIRST() = 0 OR LAST() = 0

3. Place **Product Name** on the **Filters** shelf, select the **Top** tab, and choose **Top 1 by Sum of Sales**, as shown in the following screenshot:

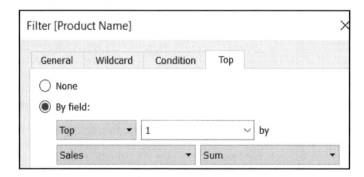

4. Place **First or Last** on the **Filters** shelf and select **True** in the resulting dialog box.
5. Drag **Product Name**, **Order Date**, and **Row ID** to the **Rows** shelf.
6. Set **Order Date** to **Month/Day/Year** discrete.
7. Double-click on **Sales**, **First**, and **Last** to place each on the view.

8. Right-click on **First, Last,** and **First or Last**; select **Compute Using | Table (Down)**.

9. Format as desired:

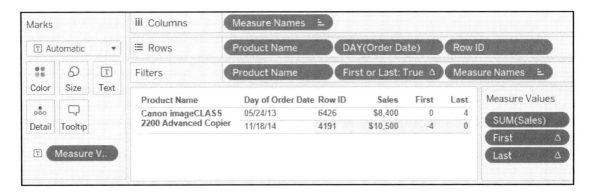

Let's consider how the preceding worksheet functions:

- **First**: FIRST():
    - FIRST() starts at 0 and counts down to the last row of the dataset in cache. In the preceding screenshot, note that the first instance of **Canon imageCLASS 2200 Advanced Copier** occurs on **05/24/13**. The fact that FIRST() ranges from 0 to -4 means that there are five instances of **Canon imageCLASS 2200 Advanced Copier** in the dataset in cache.

- **Last**: LAST():
    - LAST() starts at the last row of the dataset in cache and counts down to the 0. In the preceding screenshot, note that the last instance of **Canon imageCLASS 2200 Advanced Copier** occurs on **11/18/14**. The fact that LAST() ranges from 4 to 0 means that there are five instances of **Canon imageCLASS 2200 Advanced Copier** in the dataset in cache.

- **First**: FIRST() = 0 OR LAST() = 0:
    - This calculated field, when placed on the **Filters** shelf and set to **True**, hides all instances of matching rows except the first and last.

- The **Row ID** field is included in the view to make sure that the very first and last instances of **Canon imageCLASS 2200 Advanced Copier** are displayed. Otherwise, if there are multiple instances of **Canon imageCLASS 2200 Advanced Copier** on the first or last date, the sales numbers will reflect multiple values.

- It's important to set **Compute Using** to **Table (Down)** for each table calculation in the view. **Compute Using** is the same as **Addressing,** which will be discussed in detail in the next section of this chapter.

INDEX

The objective of the following worksheet is to list those states in the USA with over 50 postal codes represented in the underlying dataset. Notice how this example demonstrates that the INDEX function behaves directionally:

1. In the workbook associated with this chapter, navigate to the worksheet entitled Index.
2. Set the **Marks View** card to **Circle.**
3. Place **State** on the **Rows** shelf and **Postal Code** on the **Detail** shelf.
4. Create a calculated field named **Index** with the following code: INDEX()
5. Drag **Index** to the **Filters** shelf and choose to view only values that are 50 or greater.
6. Right-click on **Index** and select **Edit Table Calculation**. Select **Specific Dimensions** and check **Postal Code.**
7. Navigate to **Analysis** | **Stack Marks** | **Off:**

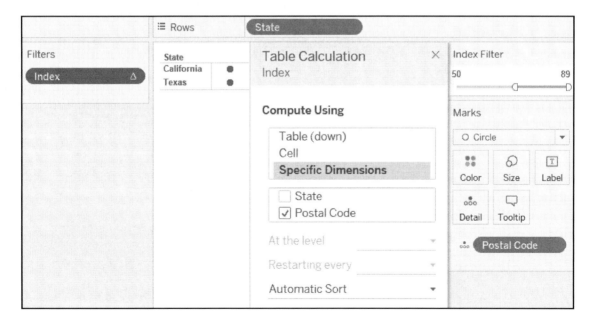

Let's consider how the preceding worksheet functions:

- **Index**: INDEX()
- An **Index** counts from 1 to n. As such, it behaves directionally. In this case, as a result of the partitioning and addressing settings, Index is counting postal codes (partitioning and addressing will be discussed in detail in the next section of this chapter). Setting the **Index** filter to display only values of 50 or more ensures that only those states with 50 or more postal codes in the partition (dataset in cache) are displayed.

RANK

The objective of the following worksheet is to display the top three selling items in each region. This example will demonstrate how RANK interacts directionally with the dataset in cache:

1. In the workbook associated with this chapter, navigate to the worksheet entitled Rank.
2. Place **Product Name** on the **Filters** shelf, select the **Top** tab, and choose **Top 3 by Sum of Sales**.
3. Place **Region** and **Product Name** on the **Rows** shelf and **Sales** on the **Columns** shelf.
4. Note that only two items display for each region. The reason for this behavior will be discussed in the following section.
5. Create a calculated field named **Rank** with the code Rank(SUM(Sales)).
6. Drag **Rank** between **Region** and **Product Name** on the **Rows** shelf.
7. Note that before you can place **Rank** between the two pills on the **Rows** shelf, you will have to cast it as discrete. One way to accomplish this is by placing **Rank** on the **Details** shelf, right-clicking on the pill, and selecting **Discrete**.
8. Right-click on **Rank** and select **Compute Using | Product Name**.
9. Remove **Product Name** from the **Filters** shelf.
10. Press *Ctrl* key and click and drag **Rank** from the **Rows** shelf to the **Filters** shelf.

11. Pressing the *Ctrl* key while dragging a pill from one shelf to another will create a copy of that pill. Failing to press the control key will, of course, simply result in moving the pill.

12. In the resulting dialog box, select **1**, **2**, and **3**.

13. Format as desired:

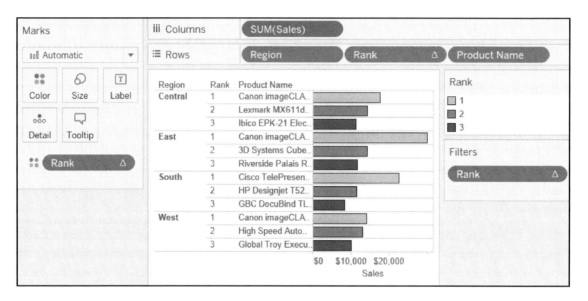

Having completed the above, let's consider the following points:

- After placing **Region** and **Product Name** on the **Rows** shelf and filtering to show only the top three product names, the resulting visualization shows only two products in each region. This is because the filter on **Product Name** showed the top three products overall, but only two were present in each region. To fix this issue, we employed the RANK table calculation function.

- **Rank:** Rank(Sum(Sales))
    - Although the preceding instructions directed writing the code for **Rank**, the same code will be automatically generated by right-clicking on an instance of **Sales** on any shelf and selecting **Quick Table Calculation | Rank**.
    - Note in the preceding screenshot that Rank is counting the **Product Names** within each region. This demonstrates that the RANK table calculation operates directionally on the dataset in cache (or partition).

SIZE

The objective of the following worksheet is to display all states with five or fewer cities in the **Superstore** dataset. This example will demonstrate how SIZE utilizes the entire partition (dataset in cache) and is thus non-directional. We will also use the FIRST table calculation function, which is directional, in order to clean up the view:

1. In the workbook associated with this chapter, navigate to the worksheet entitled Size.
2. Set **Stack Marks** under **Analysis** to **Off**.
3. Create the following calculated fields:

Name	Calculation
Size	`SIZE()` `//(Note that this calculated field was created in a previous exercise in this chapter)`

City Count	`IF FIRST() = 0 THEN [Size]`
	`ELSE NULL`
	`END`

4. Drag **State** to the **Rows** shelf, **City** to the **Detail** shelf, **City Count** to the **Text/Label** shelf, and **Size** to the **Detail** shelf.
5. Right-click on the **Size** filter and select **Compute Using | City**.
6. Move **Size** from the **Marks View** card to the **Filters** shelf.
7. In the resulting dialog box, select an **At most** value of 5.
8. On the **Marks View** card, right-click on **City Count** and select **Edit Table Calculation**.
9. Under **Nested Calculations**, select **City Count**.
10. Select **Compute Using | Specific Dimensions** and check **City**.
11. Under **Nested Calculations**, select **Size**.

12. Select **Compute Using** | **Specific Dimensions** and check **City**:

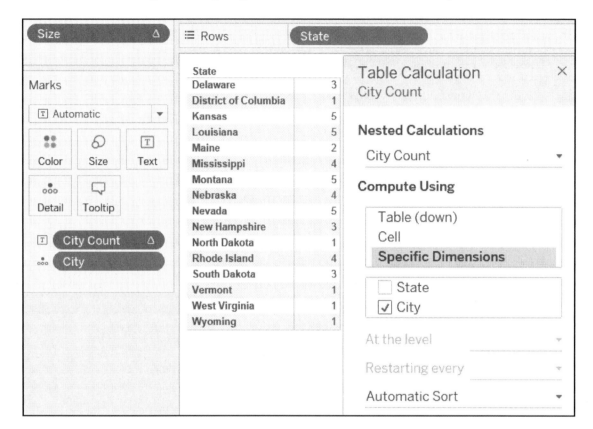

Let's consider how the preceding worksheet functions:

- **Size**: `Size()`:
  - Size generates a single number based on the partition (dataset in cache). That number can change depending on partitioning and addressing settings but does not change based on movement across the partition. As such, it behaves non-directionally.
- **City Count**: `IF FIRST() = 0 THEN LOOKUP([Size],0) ELSE NULL END`:
  - This calculated field is not strictly necessary. You could, instead, simply place **Size** on the **Text/Label** shelf. However, if you do so, you will note that the numbers in the view will look bolded. This occurs because the numbers are actually repeated and then layered on top of each other. Utilizing `FIRST() = 0` causes only one set of numbers to display.

- Perhaps the most difficult thing to grasp about this exercise is the use of partitioning and addressing. We will delay a detailed discussion of partitioning and addressing until the next section. One thing, however, deserves comment at this point. The preceding exercise had an option for **Nested Calculations**. The reason is that the **Size** calculated field was referenced within the **City Count** calculated field.

How is the function applied?

Up to this point, we have covered the first of two major questions to ask of every table calculation. That question was *What is the function?* Now we will proceed to the next question: *How is the function applied?* Let's try to understand that question via the three options shown here:

One application of INDEX()	Another application	And another

	Segment		
Category	Consumer	Corporate	Home Office
Furniture	1	2	3
Office Sup..	1	2	3
Technology	1	2	3

	Segment		
Category	Consumer	Corporate	Home Office
Furniture	1	1	1
Office Sup..	2	2	2
Technology	3	3	3

	Segment		
Category	Consumer	Corporate	Home Office
Furniture	1	2	3
Office Sup..	4	5	6
Technology	7	8	9

The INDEX function is used in each of these three screenshots; however, it is applied differently in each. The first and second screenshots both display 1, 2, and 3 but differ directionally. The third screenshot ranges from 1 to 9. How is Index being applied in each case? Answering this question can be confusing because Tableau uses different terminology. Within Tableau itself, the way a table calculation is applied may be referred to as running along, moving along, compute using, or partitioning and addressing. For our purposes we will utilize the terms partitioning and addressing which we will define here. As mentioned in the previous chapter, this is what the Tableau documentation says:

> "The dimensions that define how to group the calculation, that is, define the scope of data it is performed on, are called partitioning fields. The table calculation is performed separately within each partition.The remaining dimensions, upon which the table calculation is performed, are called addressing fields, and determine the direction of the calculation."

Before Tableau 10 the terms partitioning and addressing could be readily seen when editing a table calculation. As of Tableau 10 these terms are someone difficult to find in the interface. They are only viewable via a link that is displayed when working with a table calculation in the calculated field editor. The link is **Default Table Calculation**. If you click on that link and then in the resulting dialog box select the **Advanced** option, you will see these two terms. The important thing, however, is that the concept is alive and well in Tableau 10. It's simply represented differently. If a table calculation is utilized in the view, you can right-click on it and select **Edit Table Calculation**. Upon doing so, you will see a dialog box that will allow you to choose specific dimensions. If a dimension is checked, it is addressed. If it is unchecked, it is partitioned:

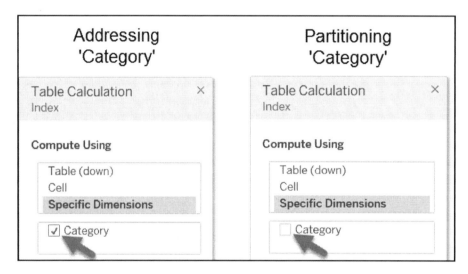

Tableau provides many out-of-the-box partitioning and addressing settings, including **Table(Down)**, **Table(Across)**, **Pane(Down)**, and **Cell**. We will reference these options occasionally but will not give these options a detailed review. This leads us to our first partitioning and addressing guideline.

Partitioning/Addressing guideline: Don't use the out-of-the-box partitioning and addressing settings provided by Tableau, including **Table(Across)**, **Pane(Down)**, and so on. Force yourself to click on **Specific Dimensions** and manually define the partitioning and addressing so that you clearly understand how every table calculation is applied.

There are a couple of caveats to the preceding guideline. First, there's an exception, that is, **Cell**. It is not possible to address individual cells in a view using partitioning and addressing. Instead it is necessary to use **Compute Using: Cell** or, within the **Table Calculation** dialog box, to select **Cell**. Surprisingly, addressing a table calculation along each cell can be useful. An example is provided in the workbook associated with this chapter.

Second, if you set partitioning and addressing for a given table calculation and then add dimensions to the view, usually Tableau will not automatically adjust the partitioning and addressing settings; they are locked down. However, when using **Table(Down)**, **Pane(Across)** and the like, Tableau will make automatic adjustments as dimensions are added to the view. This leads us to our next guideline.

 Partitioning/Addressing guideline: Place all the needed dimensions on the desired shelves before setting the partitioning and addressing for table calculations.

Following these guidelines will help ensure that you are always clear about how your table calculations are applied.

Building a playground

To proceed, we'll set up a simple playground environment to quickly and efficiently explore partitioning and addressing:

1. In the workbook associated with this chapter, navigate to the worksheet titled `Playground`.
2. Place **Category** on the **Rows** shelf and the **Index** calculation created earlier in this chapter on the **Text/Label** shelf. Note that the Index calculation is simply `Index()`.
3. Click on the drop-down menu associated with **Index** and select **Edit Table Calculation**.
4. In the resulting dialog box, click on **Specific Dimensions**.

6. Position the screen components optimally. See the following screenshot for one possible setup:

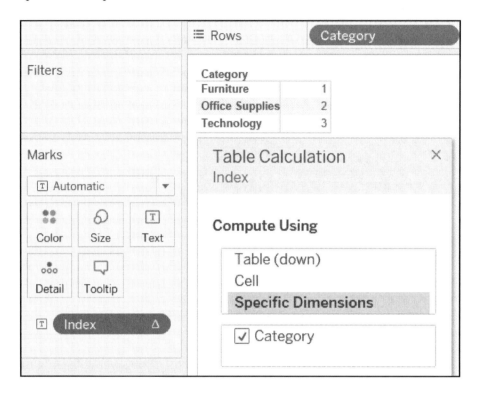

In the following pages we will utilize our playground extensively and modify it as necessary. However, for the sake of efficiency, we will need to keep the focus of the playground and the accompanying discussion narrow. The discussion will be confined to dimensions on the **Rows** and **Columns** shelves and the INDEX function on the **Text** shelf. We could explore different functions on various shelves and the different options that affords. For instance, placing a date field on the **Pages** shelf will cause a table calculation that uses the TOTAL function to display an option to **Compute total across all pages**. Regretfully, exploring every possible nuance is simply not possible due to space constraints.

Partitioning and addressing with one dimension

Let's use our playground to start exploring partitioning and addressing with the simplest possible example:

	Partitioning: Category Addressing: Null		Partitioning: Null Addressing: Category
1A	Category Furniture 1 Office Supplies 1 Technology 1	1B	Category Furniture 1 Office Supplies 2 Technology 3

In this simple example, addressing **Category** causes each member of the **Category** dimension to be counted. This demonstrates that addressing a dimension determines the direction of the calculation.

Partitioning and addressing with two dimensions

Two additional options are made available when partitioning and addressing two or more dimensions:

- **At the level**
- **Restarting every**

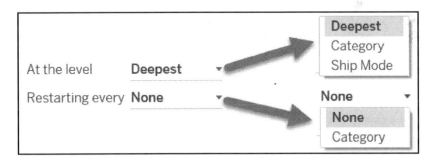

Both **At the level** and **Restarting every** allow the author to choose dimensions from a drop-down menu. **At the level** allows the author to choose what level to increment at and, as the name suggests, **Restarting every** allows the author to choose which dimensions to restart on. The many examples that follow will provide context for understanding.

Note that **At the level** has one additional choice: **Deepest**. In this case, setting **At the level** to **Deepest** is the same as selecting **Ship Mode**. This leads us to our next guideline.

Partitioning/Addressing guideline: It is not necessary to choose the bottom dimension in the **At the level** drop-down menu. It is always identical to **Deepest**.

To recreate the following iterations listed, you will need to make some changes to the playground environment. In addition to **Category** on the **Rows** shelf and **Index** on the **Text/Label** shelf also place **Ship Mode** on the **Rows** shelf. We will not cover iterations that include one or more dimensions on the **Columns** shelf since the behavior of these possibilities are much the same.

As you consider and/or reproduce the following options, note that the Addressing order is important. For options 3-5, Category is first on the addressing list. For options 6-8, **Ship Mode** is first on the list:

ID	Partitioning	Addressing	At the level	Restarting every	Results
1	Category	Ship Mode			**Category / Ship Mode** **Furniture**: First Class 1, Same Day 2, Second Class 3, Standard Class 4 **Office Supplies**: First Class 1, Same Day 2, Second Class 3, Standard Class 4 **Technology**: First Class 1, Same Day 2, Second Class 3, Standard Class 4

ID	Partitioning	Addressing	At the level	Restarting every	Results
2	Ship Mode	Category			**Category** / **Ship Mode** Furniture: First Class 1, Same Day 1, Second Class 1, Standard Class 1 Office Supplies: First Class 2, Same Day 2, Second Class 2, Standard Class 2 Technology: First Class 3, Same Day 3, Second Class 3, Standard Class 3
3		Category Ship Mode	Deepest	None	**Category** / **Ship Mode** Furniture: First Class 1, Same Day 2, Second Class 3, Standard Class 4 Office Supplies: First Class 5, Same Day 6, Second Class 7, Standard Class 8 Technology: First Class 9, Same Day 10, Second Class 11, Standard Class 12

ID	Partitioning	Addressing	At the level	Restarting every	Results
4		Category Ship Mode	Deepest	Category	**Category** **Ship Mode** **Furniture** First Class 1; Same Day 2; Second Class 3; Standard Class 4 **Office Supplies** First Class 1; Same Day 2; Second Class 3; Standard Class 4 **Technology** First Class 1; Same Day 2; Second Class 3; Standard Class 4
5		Category Ship Mode	Category	None	**Category** **Ship Mode** **Furniture** First Class 1; Same Day 2; Second Class 3; Standard Class 4 **Office Supplies** First Class 1; Same Day 2; Second Class 3; Standard Class 4 **Technology** First Class 1; Same Day 2; Second Class 3; Standard Class 4

ID	Partitioning	Addressing	At the level	Restarting every	Results
6		Ship Mode Category	Deepest	None	See table below

Category	Ship Mode	
Furniture	First Class	1
	Same Day	4
	Second Class	7
	Standard Class	10
Office Supplies	First Class	2
	Same Day	5
	Second Class	8
	Standard Class	11
Technology	First Class	3
	Same Day	6
	Second Class	9
	Standard Class	12

ID	Partitioning	Addressing	At the level	Restarting every	Results
7		Ship Mode Category	Deepest	Ship Mode	See table below

Category	Ship Mode	
Furniture	First Class	1
	Same Day	1
	Second Class	1
	Standard Class	1
Office Supplies	First Class	2
	Same Day	2
	Second Class	2
	Standard Class	2
Technology	First Class	3
	Same Day	3
	Second Class	3
	Standard Class	3

ID	Partitioning	Addressing	At the level	Restarting every	Results
8		Ship Mode Category	Ship Mode	None	(see table below)

Category	Ship Mode	
Furniture	First Class	1
	Same Day	2
	Second Class	3
	Standard Class	4
Office Supplies	First Class	1
	Same Day	2
	Second Class	3
	Standard Class	4
Technology	First Class	1
	Same Day	2
	Second Class	3
	Standard Class	4

Let's consider some of the possibilities presented in the table in more detail.

Some of the options are identical. In fact, out of the eight options listed previously, only four are unique. Let's consider options 1, 4, and 8, each of which have identical end results. Does this mean that each is truly identical? Options 1 and 4 are identical. Option 8, however, is slightly different. To understand this note the description within the table calculation dialog box for option 4:

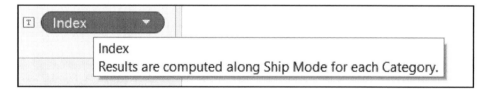

Results are computed along Ship Mode for each Category can be translated as **Partitioning Category and Addressing Ship Mode**. This translation is identical to the actual partitioning/addressing setup accomplished in option 1. Furthermore, the text in the description box for option 1 is identical to that for option 4. Therefore options 1 and 4 are identical. Option 8, however, is slightly different in that the description reads Results are computed along **Ship Mode, Category**. But does this mean there are practical differences? Personally, I do not know of any.

Option 6 may seem initially confusing. Why has the odd numbering sequence occurred?

Because the order in which the dimensions are addressed differs from the order of dimensions on the **Rows** shelf. The addressing order is **Ship Mode, Category**. The order on the **Rows** shelf is **Category, Ship Mode**. Simply reversing the position of **Category** and **Ship Mode** on the **Rows** shelf and noting the change in the number sequence should help dispel confusion:

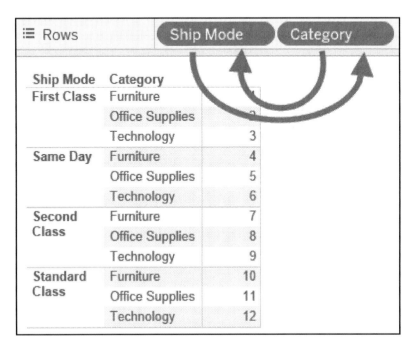

Is there any practical use for option 6? Yes. From time to time, it may be necessary to address dimensions in a different order than they are listed on a shelf. But this is not usually the case. This leads us to our next guideline.

Partitioning/Addressing guideline: When addressing multiple dimensions for a table calculation, the order of addressing will usually reflect the order of dimensions on the **Rows** and/or **Columns** shelves.

Partitioning and addressing with three dimensions

Let's add another dimension to our playground and reorder slightly. Place **Category** and **Region** on the **Rows** shelf and **Ship Mode** on the **Columns** shelf. **Index** should remain on the **Text** shelf. Also add two filters. Filter **Region** to **East**, **South**, and **West**. Filter **Ship Mode** to **First Class**, **Second Class**, and **Standard Class**.

When partitioning and addressing three dimensions, the number of possible iterations jumps to 57; however, only 14 of these are unique. The following is a listing of those unique possibilities:

ID	Partitioning	Addressing	At the level:	Restarting every	Results
1	Category Region	**Ship Mode**			*See table below*
2	Category Ship Mode	Region			*See table below*

Results for ID 1:

		Ship Mode		
Category	Region	First Class	Second Class	Standard Class
Furniture	East	1	2	3
	South	1	2	3
	West	1	2	3
Office Supplies	East	1	2	3
	South	1	2	3
	West	1	2	3
Technology	East	1	2	3
	South	1	2	3
	West	1	2	3

Results for ID 2:

		Ship Mode		
Category	Region	First Class	Second Class	Standard Class
Furniture	East	1	1	1
	South	2	2	2
	West	3	3	3
Office Supplies	East	1	1	1
	South	2	2	2
	West	3	3	3
Technology	East	1	1	1
	South	2	2	2
	West	3	3	3

ID	Partitioning	Addressing	At the level:	Restarting every	Results

ID 3 — Partitioning: Category — Addressing: Region, Ship Mode

Category	Region	Ship Mode		
		First Class	Second Class	Standard Class
Furniture	East	1	1	1
	South	1	1	1
	West	1	1	1
Office Supplies	East	2	2	2
	South	2	2	2
	West	2	2	2
Technology	East	3	3	3
	South	3	3	3
	West	3	3	3

ID 4 — Partitioning: Category — Addressing: Region, Ship Mode — At the level: Deepest — Restarting every: None

Category	Region	Ship Mode		
		First Class	Second Class	Standard Class
Furniture	East	1	2	3
	South	4	5	6
	West	7	8	9
Office Supplies	East	1	2	3
	South	4	5	6
	West	7	8	9
Technology	East	1	2	3
	South	4	5	6
	West	7	8	9

ID 5 — Partitioning: Category — Addressing: Ship Mode, Region — At the level: Deepest — Restarting every: None

Category	Region	Ship Mode		
		First Class	Second Class	Standard Class
Furniture	East	1	4	7
	South	2	5	8
	West	3	6	9
Office Supplies	East	1	4	7
	South	2	5	8
	West	3	6	9
Technology	East	1	4	7
	South	2	5	8
	West	3	6	9

ID	Partitioning	Addressing	At the level:	Restarting every	Results
6	Region	Category Ship Mode	Deepest	None	
7	Ship Mode	Category Region	Deepest	None	
8	Ship Mode	Region Category	Deepest	None	

ID 6 — Results:

Ship Mode				
Category	Region	First Class	Second Class	Standard Class
Furniture	East	1	2	3
	South	1	2	3
	West	1	2	3
Office Supplies	East	4	5	6
	South	4	5	6
	West	4	5	6
Technology	East	7	8	9
	South	7	8	9
	West	7	8	9

ID 7 — Results:

Ship Mode				
Category	Region	First Class	Second Class	Standard Class
Furniture	East	1	1	1
	South	2	2	2
	West	3	3	3
Office Supplies	East	4	4	4
	South	5	5	5
	West	6	6	6
Technology	East	7	7	7
	South	8	8	8
	West	9	9	9

ID 8 — Results:

Ship Mode				
Category	Region	First Class	Second Class	Standard Class
Furniture	East	1	1	1
	South	4	4	4
	West	7	7	7
Office Supplies	East	2	2	2
	South	5	5	5
	West	8	8	8
Technology	East	3	3	3
	South	6	6	6
	West	9	9	9

ID	Partitioning	Addressing	At the level:	Restarting every	Results
9		Category Ship Mode Region	Deepest	None	*(see table below)*

Results for ID 9:

		Ship Mode		
Category	Region	First Class	Second Class	Standard Class
Furniture	East	1	4	7
	South	2	5	8
	West	3	6	9
Office Supplies	East	10	13	16
	South	11	14	17
	West	12	15	18
Technology	East	19	22	25
	South	20	23	26
	West	21	24	27

ID	Partitioning	Addressing	At the level:	Restarting every	Results
10		Ship Mode Category Region	Deepest	None	*(see table below)*

Results for ID 10:

		Ship Mode		
Category	Region	First Class	Second Class	Standard Class
Furniture	East	1	10	19
	South	2	11	20
	West	3	12	21
Office Supplies	East	4	13	22
	South	5	14	23
	West	6	15	24
Technology	East	7	16	25
	South	8	17	26
	West	9	18	27

ID	Partitioning	Addressing	At the level:	Restarting every	Results
11		Ship Mode Category Region	Category	None	*(see table below)*

Results for ID 11:

		Ship Mode		
Category	Region	First Class	Second Class	Standard Class
Furniture	East	1	4	7
	South	1	4	7
	West	1	4	7
Office Supplies	East	2	5	8
	South	2	5	8
	West	2	5	8
Technology	East	3	6	9
	South	3	6	9
	West	3	6	9

ID	Partitioning	Addressing	At the level:	Restarting every	Results
12		Ship Mode Region Category	Deepest	None	*(table below)*

Ship Mode

Category	Region	First Class	Second Class	Standard Class
Furniture	East	1	10	19
	South	4	13	22
	West	7	16	25
Office Supplies	East	2	11	20
	South	5	14	23
	West	8	17	26
Technology	East	3	12	21
	South	6	15	24
	West	9	18	27

ID	Partitioning	Addressing	At the level:	Restarting every	Results
13		Ship Mode Region Category	Deepest	Ship Mode	*(table below)*

Ship Mode

Category	Region	First Class	Second Class	Standard Class
Furniture	East	1	1	1
	South	4	4	4
	West	7	7	7
Office Supplies	East	2	2	2
	South	5	5	5
	West	8	8	8
Technology	East	3	3	3
	South	6	6	6
	West	9	9	9

ID	Partitioning	Addressing	At the level:	Restarting every	Results
14		Region Ship Mode Category	Deepest	None	*(table below)*

Ship Mode

Category	Region	First Class	Second Class	Standard Class
Furniture	East	1	4	7
	South	10	13	16
	West	19	22	25
Office Supplies	East	2	5	8
	South	11	14	17
	West	20	23	26
Technology	East	3	6	9
	South	12	15	18
	West	21	24	27

We will not address the various instances of the preceding possibilities. Instead, the reader is encouraged to recreate these 14 possibilities in Tableau in order to solidify their understanding of partitioning and addressing. Even better, consider recreating all 57 possible iterations and working to understand how Tableau produces each end result. The process may be tedious but the resulting understanding is invaluable.

Summary

In this chapter we explored the inner workings of table calculations. We began by considering two questions, that is, *What is the function?* and *How is the function applied?*

As we explored these two questions, we surveyed each unique group of table calculation functions with the exception of the `Script_` functions, which are covered in `Chapter 13`, *R Integration*. We also learned how to apply these functions to a view via partitioning and addressing.

In the next chapter, we will explore **level-of-detail (LOD)** calculations, where we will build a sound understanding of this functionality which, though introduced in Tableau 9.0, is still unfamiliar to many Tableau authors. Along the way, we will discover how LOD calculations can easily accomplish tasks that were previously only possible through complex table calculations. It is important to note, however, that even though LOD calculations can replace table calculations in some cases, they can by no means replace every instance of table calculations. Table calculations remain an important part of everyday Tableau usage.

6
Level of Detail Calculations

Like most software products, every new version of Tableau heralds new features. In Tableau 9.0, that big new feature was **Level of Detail (LOD)** calculations. Prominent voices in the Tableau community heralded the new capability as a major breakthrough. The average, everyday Tableau author, however, may have been underwhelmed. In particular, I recall a student in one of my classes communicating, *I've learned how to use table calculations to accomplish pretty much what I want. Why do I need LOD calculations?*

With the advent of Tableau 10, it may be tempting to some to put LOD calculations on the back burner. After all, they seem unimpressive as they encompass only three expressions: FIXED, INCLUDE, and EXCLUDE. But these three expressions open a world of options by providing the ability to create calculations that target specific levels of granularity. In older versions of Tableau, data granularity for a worksheet was established by the dimensions in the view. If the view contained dimensions for **Region**, **State**, and **Postal Code** but the author wanted to create a **City**-level calculation, the **City** dimension would need to be included on the view. Furthermore, there was no mechanism for excluding or ignoring a given dimension on a view. Admittedly, the desired results could normally be obtained via some complex and sometimes convoluted use of table calculations, data blends, and the like. Fortunately, LOD calculations greatly simplify such use case scenarios and, in some cases, enable what was previously impossible.

In this chapter, we will discuss the following topics:

- Building playgrounds
- Practical application

Building playgrounds

Delivering reports as required by one's job duties may lead to a thorough knowledge of a limited set of capabilities, that is, a deep but narrow understanding. It can be difficult to set aside time (and also justify that time to the boss!) to explore the capabilities of Tableau that on the surface may seem to have no direct correlation to job duties. Playground environments can help overcome difficulties and objections by providing efficient avenues of exploration. In this chapter, we'll build two playground environments to help make the task of deep and broad understanding easier by providing an efficient avenue for exploration and understanding.

Playground 1 – FIXED and EXCLUDE

The first playground we will build will be for the purpose of exploring two of the three LOD functions: FIXED and EXCLUDE. We will use a set of parameters and associated calculated fields to efficiently explore how these functions work.

Exercise – exploring FIXED and EXCLUDE – setting up the workbook

Much of the groundwork for this exercise has already been completed in the workbook associated with this chapter. If you do not have ready access to the workbook, you should be able to construct a similar one by referencing the following information.

Inspecting the worksheet and initial setup

1. Navigate to `https://public.tableau.com/profile/david.baldwin#!/` to locate and download the workbook associated with this chapter.
2. Open the workbook associated with this chapter and navigate to the worksheet entitled `Fixed and Exclude`.
3. Navigate to `https://public.tableau.com/profile/david.baldwin#!/` to locate and download the workbook associated with this chapter:
   - Data Type: `Integer`
   - Allowable Values: `List`

- Value and Display As table is shown here:

Value	Display As	Value	Display As	Value	Display As
1	Category	6	Order ID	11	Segment
2	City	7	Postal Code	12	Ship Mode
3	Country	8	Product ID	13	State
4	Customer ID	9	Product Name	14	Sub-Category
5	Customer Name	10	Region	15	Null

4. The parameters named 2nd Dim, 3rd Dim, and 4th Dim are identical to 1st Dim.

5. Note that except for **Order Date** and **Ship Date**, every dimension in the dataset is included in the **List of values**. For the purposes of this exercise, **Category, Region, Segment, Ship Mode**, and **Sub-Category** are particularly important because those are dimensions with fewer members. Dimensions with many members are more difficult to use in this context.

6. Inspect the following parameters included in the workbook and note the `Value` and `Display As` values:

Parameter	Value	Display As
Choose Fixed Dims	1	1st
	2	2nd
	3	3rd
	4	4th
	5	Fixed: Nothing
	6	0
Choose Excluded Dims 1	1	1st
	2	2nd
	3	3rd
	4	4th
	5	0
Choose Excluded Dims 2	1	1st

	2	1st – 2nd
	3	1st – 3rd
	4	1st – 4th
	5	Exclude Nothing
	6	0

7. Inspect the calculated field named 1st Dim. (It is located in the folder named `Practical: All`.) The code is as follows:

```
Case [Parameters].[1st Dim]
    WHEN 1 THEN [Category]          WHEN 2 THEN [City]
    WHEN 3 THEN [Country]           WHEN 4 THEN [Customer ID]
    WHEN 5 THEN [Customer Name]     WHEN 6 THEN [Order ID]
    WHEN 7 THEN STR([Postal Code])  WHEN 8 THEN [Product ID]
    WHEN 9 THEN [Product Name]      WHEN 10 THEN [Region]
    WHEN 11 THEN [Segment]          WHEN 12 THEN [Ship Mode]
    WHEN 13 THEN [State]            WHEN 14 THEN [Sub-Category]
    WHEN 15 THEN ""
END
```

8. The calculated fields named 2nd Dim, 3rd Dim, and 4th Dim are identical to 1st Dim except that each references the parameter bearing its name; for example, the calculated field 2nd Dim utilizes [Parameters].[2nd Dim].

9. These Case statements, in conjunction with the associated parameters, allow the author to choose which dimensions to view from a drop-down menu in the view.

10. Inspect the following calculated fields, which enable the author to choose which LOD calculations to employ and thus to compare and contrast differences and similarities.

11. Here is the code for Case Fixed:

```
CASE [Choose Fixed Dims]
WHEN 1 THEN SUM({FIXED [1st Dim]: SUM([Sales])})
WHEN 2 THEN SUM({FIXED [2nd Dim]: SUM([Sales])})
WHEN 3 THEN SUM({FIXED [3rd Dim]: SUM([Sales])})
WHEN 4 THEN SUM({FIXED [4th Dim]: SUM([Sales])})
WHEN 5 THEN SUM({FIXED : SUM([Sales])})
WHEN 6 THEN 0
END
```

12. Here is the code for Case Exclude 1:

```
CASE [Choose Excluded Dims 1]
WHEN 1 THEN SUM({EXCLUDE [1st Dim]: SUM([Sales])})
WHEN 2 THEN SUM({EXCLUDE [2nd Dim] : SUM([Sales])})
WHEN 3 THEN SUM({EXCLUDE [3rd Dim] : SUM([Sales])})
WHEN 4 THEN SUM({EXCLUDE [4th Dim]: SUM([Sales])})
WHEN 5 THEN 0
END
```

13. Here is the code for Case Exclude 2:

```
CASE [Choose Fixed Dims]
WHEN 1 THEN SUM({EXCLUDE [1st Dim]: SUM([Sales])})
WHEN 2 THEN SUM({EXCLUDE [1st Dim],[2nd Dim] : SUM([Sales])})
WHEN 3 THEN SUM({EXCLUDE [1st Dim],[2nd Dim],[3rd Dim]:
SUM([Sales])})
WHEN 4 THEN SUM({EXCLUDE [1st Dim],[2nd Dim],[3rd Dim], [4thDim]:
SUM([Sales])})
WHEN 5 THEN SUM({EXCLUDE : SUM([Sales])})
WHEN 6 THEN 0
END
```

14. Note the context filter on **Product Name**.

15. Open the filter for inspection.

16. In the resulting dialog box, click the **Wildcard** tab and note the settings shown in the following screenshot.

17. After clicking **OK**, right-click on the filter and note that it is a context filter. As you will note, context filters are denoted in gray:

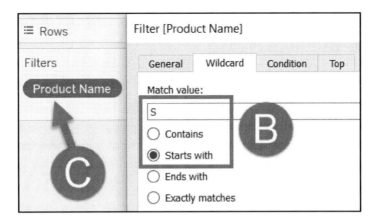

18. Place the following dimensions on the **Rows** shelf: `1st Dim`, `2nd Dim`, `3rd Dim`, and `4th Dim`.

19. Double-click on **Measure Names**. Remove measures from the **Measure Values** shelf until only the following is displayed:

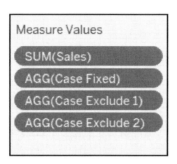

20. Right-click on each parameter and choose **Show Parameter Control**. Order the parameter controls as shown here:
    - 1st Dim
    - 2nd Dim
    - 3rd Dim
    - 4th Dim
    - Choose Fixed Dims
    - Choose Excluded Dims 1
    - Choose Excluded Dims 2

Exercise steps – exploring FIXED and EXCLUDE – understanding FIXED

Now that the playground environment is complete, let's build scenarios to better understand FIXED and EXCLUDE. We'll begin with FIXED:

1. Using the preceding worksheet, set the following parameters as listed:

Parameter	Setting
1st Dim	**Region**
2nd Dim	**Category**
3rd Dim	**Null**

4th Dim	Null
Choose Fixed Dims	2nd
Choose Exclude Dims 1	0
Choose Exclude Dims 2	0

2. Observe that the **Case Fixed** column displays the totals for each **Category** and ignores **Region**:

1st Dim	2nd Dim	Sales	Case Fixed
Central	Furniture	$10,072	47,379
	Office Supplies	$16,340	70,596
	Technology	$13,995	76,801
East	Furniture	$14,249	47,379
	Office Supplies	$21,560	70,596
	Technology	$20,646	76,801
South	Furniture	$4,494	47,379
	Office Supplies	$8,721	70,596
	Technology	$17,451	76,801
West	Furniture	$18,564	47,379
	Office Supplies	$23,975	70,596
	Technology	$24,710	76,801

3. Change the **Choose Fixed Dims** parameter to **1st** and note that **Case Fixed** now displays the totals for each **Region**:

1st Dim	2nd Dim	Sales	Case Fixed
Central	Furniture	$10,072	40,406
	Office Supplies	$16,340	40,406
	Technology	$13,995	40,406
East	Furniture	$14,249	56,455
	Office Supplies	$21,560	56,455
	Technology	$20,646	56,455
South	Furniture	$4,494	30,666
	Office Supplies	$8,721	30,666
	Technology	$17,451	30,666
West	Furniture	$18,564	67,249
	Office Supplies	$23,975	67,249
	Technology	$24,710	67,249

4. Change the **Choose Fixed Dims** parameter to **Fixed: Nothing** and note that the amount reflects the total allowed by the context filter:

1st Dim	2nd Dim	Sales	Case Fixed
Central	Furniture	$10,072	194,776
	Office Supplies	$16,340	194,776
	Technology	$13,995	194,776
East	Furniture	$14,249	194,776
	Office Supplies	$21,560	194,776
	Technology	$20,646	194,776
South	Furniture	$4,494	194,776
	Office Supplies	$8,721	194,776
	Technology	$17,451	194,776
West	Furniture	$18,564	194,776
	Office Supplies	$23,975	194,776
	Technology	$24,710	194,776

As is evident from the preceding steps, the Fixed LOD considers only the dimension(s) to which it is directed. Thus, when fixed on **Category**, **Region** is ignored. And, as demonstrated, when fixed on **Region**, **Category** is ignored. Lastly, when **Choose Fixed Dims** is set to **Fixed: Nothing,** the entire dataset not restricted by the context filter on **Product Name** is displayed.

Exercise steps – exploring FIXED and EXCLUED – understanding EXCLUDE

1. Set the parameters as shown in the following table:

Parameter	Setting
1st Dim	Region
2nd Dim	Category
3rd Dim	Segment
4th Dim	Null
Choose Fixed Dims	0

Choose Exclude Dims 1	1st
Choose Exclude Dims 2	0

2. Observe the results:

1st Dim	2nd Dim	3rd Dim	Sales	Case Exclude 1
Central	Furniture	Consumer	$5,444	26,738
		Corporate	$2,779	13,050
		Home Office	$1,849	7,592
	Office Supplies	Consumer	$9,085	31,861
		Corporate	$3,462	24,179
		Home Office	$3,793	14,556
	Technology	Consumer	$5,144	39,955
		Corporate	$3,848	23,766
		Home Office	$5,003	13,081
East	Furniture	Consumer	$6,941	26,738
		Corporate	$4,415	13,050
		Home Office	$2,893	7,592
	Office Supplies	Consumer	$11,361	31,861
		Corporate	$7,217	24,179

3. In the preceding screenshot, note that Case Exclude 1 displays the total of each **Category** and **Segment** and ignores **Region**. For example, the total of the **SegmentConsumer** within the **Category Furniture** is **$26,738**. That total is repeated for each **Region**. The relevant code that is generating these results is SUM({EXCLUDE [Region] :SUM([Sales])}).

4. Make the following changes to the parameters:

Parameter	Setting
Choose Fixed Dims	3rd
Choose Exclude Dims 1	1st
Choose Exclude Dims 2	1st – 2nd

5. Observe the results:

1st Dim	2nd Dim	3rd Dim	Sales	Case Fixed	Case Exclude 1	Case Exclude 2
Central	Furniture	Consum..	$5,444	98,554	26,738	98,554
		Corpora..	$2,779	60,994	13,050	60,994
		Home O..	$1,849	35,228	7,592	35,228
	Office Supplies	Consum..	$9,085	98,554	31,861	98,554
		Corpora..	$3,462	60,994	24,179	60,994
		Home O..	$3,793	35,228	14,556	35,228
	Technol..	Consum..	$5,144	98,554	39,955	98,554
		Corpora..	$3,848	60,994	23,766	60,994
		Home O..	$5,003	35,228	13,081	35,228
East	Furniture	Consum..	$6,941	98,554	26,738	98,554

6. Note that the preceding screenshot demonstrates that LOD calculations may be used to consider multiple dimensions in a view. In this case, **Case Exclude 2** ignores **1st Dim** and **2nd Dim**, which are associated with **Region** and **Category**. The associated code is therefore SUM({EXCLUDE [Region],[Category] :SUM([Sales])}). Note that **Case Exclude 2** and **Case Fixed** have identical results. This is because, in this case, excluding the first two dimensions is the same as fixing on the third dimension.

7. Make the following changes to the parameters:

Parameter	Setting
4th Dim	**Ship Mode**

8. Observe the results:

1st Dim	2nd Dim	3rd Dim	4th Dim	Sales	Case Fixed	Case Exclude 1	Case Exclude 2
Central	Furniture	Consumer	First Class	$740	98,554	2,961	8,843
			Second Class	$313	98,554	6,493	24,765
			Standard Class	$4,391	98,554	17,147	62,011
		Corporate	First Class	$164	60,994	779	10,622
			Second Class	$801	60,994	3,139	8,818
			Standard Class	$1,813	60,994	8,934	38,997
		Home Office	First Class	$746	35,228	1,202	3,121
			Same Day	$106	35,228	517	2,616
			Second Class	$24	35,228	2,286	6,953
			Standard Class	$973	35,228	3,586	22,537
	Office Supplies	Consumer	First Class	$251	98,554	1,854	8,843
			Same Day	$160	98,554	2,165	2,935

9. Note in the preceding screenshot that **Case Exclude 2** and **Case Fixed** no longer have identical results. This is because **Ship Mode** was introduced, and **Case Exclude 2** considers **Ship Mode**, whereas **Case Fixed** does not.

10. Experiment with other settings to further enhance your understanding of the FIXED and EXCLUDE LODs.

Exercise – exploring FIXED and EXCLUDE – understanding order of filtering

1. Set the parameters as shown in the following table:

Parameter	Setting
1st Dim	Region
2nd Dim	Category
3rd Dim	Segment
4th Dim	Null
Choose Fixed Dims	3rd
Choose Exclude Dims 1	1st
Choose Exclude Dims 2	1st – 2nd

2. Observe the results:

1st Dim	2nd Dim	3rd Dim	Sales	Case Fixed	Case Exclude 1	Case Exclude 2
Central	Furniture	Consumer	$5,444	98,554	26,738	98,554
		Corporate	$2,779	60,994	13,050	60,994
		Home Office	$1,849	35,228	7,592	35,228
	Office Supplies	Consumer	$9,085	98,554	31,861	98,554
		Corporate	$3,462	60,994	24,179	60,994
		Home Office	$3,793	35,228	14,556	35,228
	Technology	Consumer	$5,144	98,554	39,955	98,554
		Corporate	$3,848	60,994	23,766	60,994
		Home Office	$5,003	35,228	13,081	35,228
East	Furniture	Consumer	$6,941	98,554	26,738	98,554
		Corporate	$4,415	60,994	13,050	60,994
		Home Office	$2,893	35,228	7,592	35,228
	Office	Consumer	$11,361	98,554	31,861	98,554

3. Note that, as seen in the previous exercise, **Case Exclude 2** and **Case Fixed** are identical.

4. Right-click on the **Product Name** filter and select **Remove from Context**:

5. Observe the results:

1st Dim	2nd Dim	3rd Dim	Sales	Case Fixed	Case Exclude 1	Case Exclude 2
Central	Furniture	Consumer	$5,444	1,161,401	26,738	98,554
		Corporate	$2,779	706,146	13,050	60,994
		Home Office	$1,849	429,653	7,592	35,228
	Office Supplies	Consumer	$9,085	1,161,401	31,861	98,554
		Corporate	$3,462	706,146	24,179	60,994
		Home Office	$3,793	429,653	14,556	35,228
	Technology	Consumer	$5,144	1,161,401	39,955	98,554
		Corporate	$3,848	706,146	23,766	60,994
		Home Office	$5,003	429,653	13,081	35,228
East	Furniture	Consumer	$6,941	1,161,401	26,738	98,554
		Corporate	$4,415	706,146	13,050	60,994
		Home Office	$2,893	429,653	7,592	35,228
	Office	Consumer	$11,361	1,161,401	31,861	98,554

6. As you can see in the preceding screenshot, **Case Exclude 2** and **Case Fixed** are no longer identical. **Case Fixed** is no longer impacted by the **Product Name** filter because the context was removed. The reason for this will be explored in the following section.

Exercise commentary

The behavior difference observed between EXCLUDE and FIXED in the preceding exercise reflects the underlying **filter order of operation**. As shown in the following diagram, **Context Filters** will impact **Fixed**, **Exclude**, and **Include**. **Dimension Filters**, however, will only impact Exclude and Include:

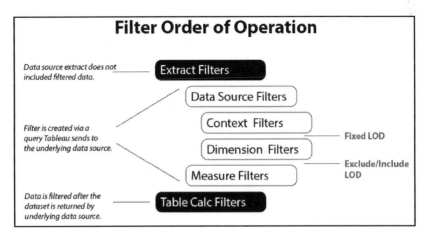

Playground #2 – INCLUDE

The second playground we will build will be for the purpose of exploring INCLUDE. Like in *Playground #1,* we'll start with setting up the workbook for effective exploration. If you do not have ready access to the workbook, you should be able to construct a similar one by referencing the following information.

Inspecting the worksheet and initial setup

1. Open the workbook associated with this chapter and navigate to the worksheet entitled Exploring Include.
2. The parameters and calculated fields named 1st Dim, 2nd Dim, 3rd Dim and 4th Dim created in the previous exercises are also utilized for this worksheet.
3. Right-click on the 1st Dim parameter and choose Duplicate.
4. Rename the duplicate Choose Included Dims.
5. Create a new calculated field named Case Include with the following code:

```
CASE [Choose Included Dims]
WHEN 1 THEN AVG({INCLUDE [Category]: SUM([Sales])})
WHEN 2 THEN AVG({INCLUDE [City]: SUM([Sales])})
WHEN 3 THEN AVG({INCLUDE [Country]: SUM([Sales])})
WHEN 4 THEN AVG({INCLUDE [Customer ID]: SUM([Sales])})
WHEN 5 THEN AVG({INCLUDE [Customer Name]: SUM([Sales])})
WHEN 6 THEN AVG({INCLUDE [Order ID]: SUM([Sales])})
WHEN 7 THEN AVG({INCLUDE [Postal Code]: SUM([Sales])})
WHEN 8 THEN AVG({INCLUDE [Product ID]: SUM([Sales])})
WHEN 9 THEN AVG({INCLUDE [Product Name]: SUM([Sales])})
WHEN 10 THEN AVG({INCLUDE [Region]: SUM([Sales])})
WHEN 11 THEN AVG({INCLUDE [Segment]: SUM([Sales])})
WHEN 12 THEN AVG({INCLUDE [Ship Mode]: SUM([Sales])})
WHEN 13 THEN AVG({INCLUDE [State]: SUM([Sales])})
WHEN 14 THEN AVG({INCLUDE [Sub-Category]: SUM([Sales])})
WHEN 15 THEN 0
END
```

6. Place the following measures and dimensions on their respective shelves:

Field(s)	Shelf
Case Include	Detail
Sum(Sales)	Columns
1st Dim, 2nd Dim, 3rd Dim, 4th Dim	Rows

7. Display each of the following parameters via right-clicking on **Show Parameter Control**:

1st Dim
2nd Dim
3rd Dim
4th Dim
Choose Included Dims

Exercise steps – exploring INCLUDE

Now that the playground environment is complete, let's build scenarios to better understand INCLUDE:

1. Set the parameters as shown in the following table:

Parameter	Setting
1st Dim	**Region**
2nd Dim	**Null**
3rd Dim	**Null**
4th Dim	**Null**
Choose Included Dims	**Region**

2. Add two reference lines with the following settings:

	Scope	Value	Label
Reference Line 1	Entire Table	**SUM(Sales)** and **Average**	**Custom	Overall Avg: <Value>**
Reference Line 2	Entire Table	**AGG(Case Include)**	**Custom	Include Dim Avg: <Value>**

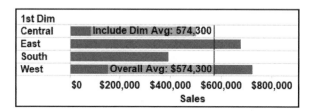

3. Note that both reference lines are equal.
4. If the reference lines are overlapping each other, edit the formatting and set the **Alignment** to **Top**. To access the formatting, click on the reference line in the view:

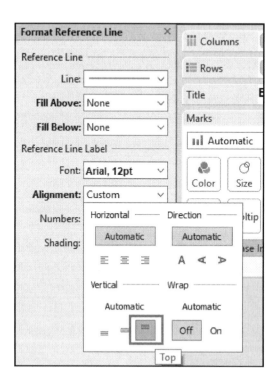

5. Set the parameters as shown in the following table:

Parameter	Setting
1st Dim	Region
2nd Dim	Category
3rd Dim	Ship Mode
4th Dim	Segment
Choose Included Dims	Region

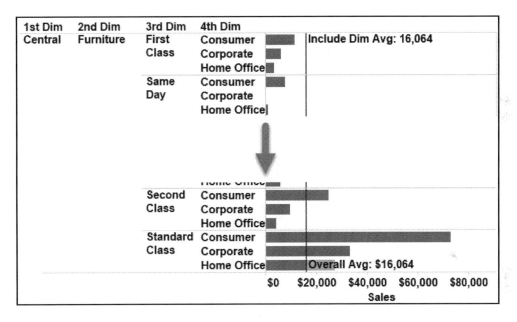

6. Note that, as before, the reference lines are equal.
7. Change the **Choose Included Dims** parameter to **Category**, **Ship Mode**, and **Segment** respectively.
8. Note that the reference lines equal one another for each of these settings. This is because **Choose Included Dims** is only introducing dimensions already represented in the view.

9. Now change the **Choose Included Dims** parameter to **Sub-Category**:

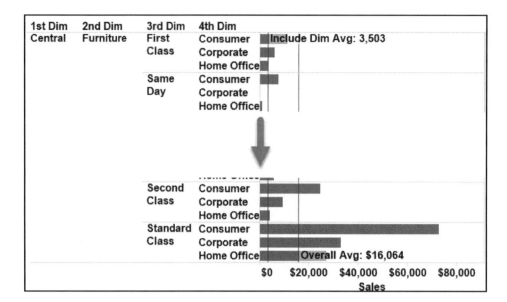

10. Note that the **Included Dim Avg** reference line now includes **Sub-Category** in the average and so differs from the **Overall Avg** reference line. Furthermore, note that the **Sub-Category** dimension is not used in the view. LOD calculations do not require a calculation to reside in the view.

Practical application

The first portion of this chapter was designed to demonstrate how LOD calculations work. The remainder will be dedicated to practical applications. Specifically, we will consider three typical challenges that were previously solved using other Tableau capabilities such as table calculations and data blending.

Exercise – practical FIXED

This exercise will look at a problem that occurs when mixing a table calculation that calculates the percentage of the total with a dimension filter. We will consider the problem, a workaround used in previous versions of Tableau, and a solution using an LOD calculation. After covering these three options, a commentary section will discuss the germane points of each.

Exercise steps – practical FIXED – the problem

1. Open the workbook associated with this chapter and navigate to the worksheet entitled `The Problem`.
2. Select the **2012_World_Pop** dataset.
3. Create a calculated field named **Percent of Total** with the following code:

   ```
   SUM([Population]) / TOTAL(SUM([Population]))
   ```

4. Right-click on **Percent of Total** and select **Default Properties | Number Format | Percentage**.
5. Place **Country** on the **Columns** shelf, **Measure Names** on the **Rows** shelf, and **Measure Values** on the **Text** Shelf.
6. Remove **Number of Records** from the **Measure Values** shelf.
7. Right-click on **Percent of Total** and set to **Compute Using | Country**.
8. Create a filter on **Country** so that only **Afghanistan** is displayed:

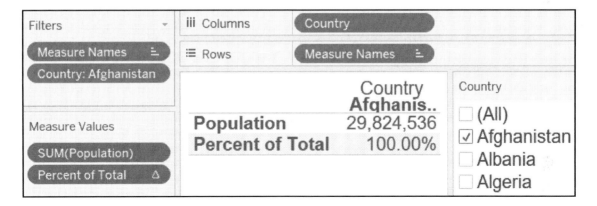

Afghanistan displays a percentage of the total of 100%. Obviously, this does not represent Afghanistan's percentage of the total population of the world.

Exercise steps – practical FIXED – table calc solution

1. Duplicate the previous worksheet (the one named `The Problem`) and entitle it `Solution: Table Calc`.
2. Create a calculated field named `[Country - Table Calc Filter]` with the following code:

   ```
   LOOKUP ( MAX ( [Country] ) ,0 )
   ```

3. Remove **Country** from the **Filter** shelf.
4. Create a filter on **[Country – Table Calc Filter]** and display only **Afghanistan**.
5. Note that **Afghanistan** displays a percent of total of **0.43%**:

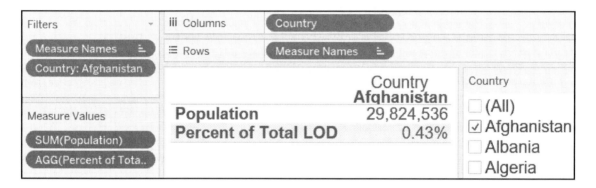

Exercise steps – practical FIXED – LOD solution

1. Duplicate the first worksheet created previously (the one named `The Problem`) and rename it `Solution LOD`.
2. Create a calculated field named **[Percent of Total LOD]** with the following code:

   ```
   SUM([Population])/SUM({ FIXED : SUM([Population])})
   ```

3. Place **[Percent of Total LOD]** on the **Measure Values** shelf and note that the displayed percentage equals **0.43%**. If 0 is displayed, change the number formatting to percentage.

4. Remove the **[Percent of Total]** table calculation that was previously created from the **Measure Values** shelf:

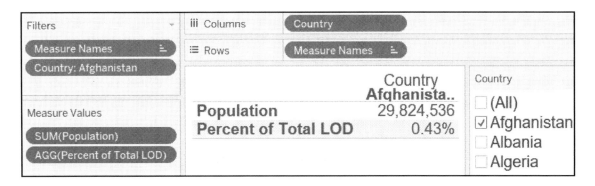

Exercise commentary

Assuming a SQL data source, let's look at a query that Tableau generates for the worksheet, The Problem. Generated queries can be viewed via **Help** | **Settings and Performance** | **Start Performance Recording**. (See Chapter 11, *Improving Performance*, for additional information regarding viewing Tableau generated queries.):

```
SELECT ['2012_World_Pop$'].[Country] AS [Country],
SUM(['2012_World_Pop$'].[Population]) AS [sum:Population:ok]
FROM [dbo].['2012_World_Pop$'] ['2012_World_Pop$']
WHERE (['2012_World_Pop$'].[Country] = 'Afghanistan')
GROUP BY ['2012_World_Pop$'].[Country]]
```

Note the WHERE clause in the query limiting the returned dataset to only those rows that have **Afghanistan** as **Country**. This WHERE clause was generated as a result of placing **Country** on the **Filters** shelf. By limiting the returned data, the processing requirements are shifted from Tableau to the underlying data source engine. In other words, the data source engine does the work of executing the query and Tableau thus works with a smaller dataset. The reasoning behind this design is that data source engines are specifically engineered to efficiently query large datasets and also typically have underlying hardware to support such activities. Furthermore, limiting the rows of data returned to Tableau can reduce inefficiencies due to latency.

Inefficiencies are further reduced because Tableau works from the cache whenever possible. Often, a user may perform various operations without generating a call to the underlying data source. However, in the preceding case, if a user was to select a different country from the filter, Tableau would generate a new query to the data source. For example, if a user interacts with the filter and deselects **Afghanistan** and selects **Albania**, a new query with a corresponding WHERE clause is generated.

Although the logic of Tableau's reliance on the data source engine is demonstrable, the problem proposed in the previous example still remains. What can a Tableau author do to calculate the percent of the whole regardless of filtering? Prior to Tableau 9.0, a common solution was to create a table calculation like we did previously for the worksheet entitled Solution: Table Calc. The code, LOOKUP(MAX([Country]),0), simply references each country in the underlying dataset and can thus be used to display the list of countries. It can also be used as a filter. The difference is that, unlike in the previous worksheet (that is, The Problem), the query generated by Tableau to the data source returns the entire dataset. We can see this in the underlying SQL:

```
SELECT ['2012_World_Pop$'].[Country] AS [Country],
MIN(['2012_World_Pop$'].[Country]) AS [TEMP(TC_)(1470307846)(0)],
SUM(['2012_World_Pop$'].[Population]) AS [TEMP(TC_)(616435453)(0)]
FROM [dbo].['2012_World_Pop$'] ['2012_World_Pop$']
GROUP BY ['2012_World_Pop$'].[Country]
```

The preceding query does not include a WHERE clause. No filtering occurs at the data source. When a table calculation is used in a filter, the filtering does not take place until the underlying data is returned. In other words, Tableau performs the filtering. This preserves percent of total percentages regardless of which country's population totals the user chooses to view.

A potential issue with this table calculation solution is that the returned dataset may be quite large, which may cause performance challenges. Latency may be experienced due to increased time required to return a large dataset and Tableau may perform more slowly because of additional processing responsibilities to filter the dataset. An LOD calculation can address these challenges. Let's take a look at the SQL queries created by the **Percent of Total LOD** calculated field in the worksheet entitled Solution: LOD:

```
SELECT [t0].[Country] AS [Country],
  [t1].[__measure__0] AS
[TEMP(Calculation_418553293854285824)(2417030171)(0)],
  [t0].[TEMP(Calculation_418553293854285824)(616435453)(0)] AS
[TEMP(Calculation_418553293854285824)(616435453)(0)]
FROM (
  SELECT ['2012_World_Pop$'].[Country] AS [Country],
    SUM(['2012_World_Pop$'].[Population]) AS
```

```
[TEMP(Calculation_418553293854285824)(616435453)(0)]
  FROM [dbo].['2012_World_Pop$'] ['2012_World_Pop$']
  WHERE (['2012_World_Pop$'].[Country] = 'Afghanistan')
  GROUP BY ['2012_World_Pop$'].[Country]
) [t0]
  CROSS JOIN (
  SELECT SUM(['2012_World_Pop$'].[Population]) AS [__measure__0]
  FROM [dbo].['2012_World_Pop$'] ['2012_World_Pop$']
  GROUP BY ()
) [t1]
```

Note CROSS JOIN in the preceding section. The LOD calculation generates a query that instructs the underlying data source engine to return data in such a way that it allows Tableau to divide the population values of one or more countries by the world population total, thus returning the correct percentage of total.

Exercise – practical INCLUDE

In this exercise we will create a worksheet that displays the following:

- Total sales per region
- The average of total sales across all regions
- The average of total sales across all states in each region

Using an LOD calculation to display this is pretty straightforward. Prior to 9.0, however, such a worksheet could be rather convoluted. Let's explore.

Exercise steps part 1 – solve by using an LOD calculation

1. Select the Practical Include worksheet.
2. Select the **Superstore** dataset.
3. Create a calculated field named Per State INCLUDE with the following code:

   ```
   {INCLUDE [State]:SUM([Sales])}
   ```

4. Drag **Region** to the **Columns** shelf, **SUM(Sales)** to the **Rows** shelf, and **AVG(Per State INCLUDE)** to the **Details** shelf. Be sure to change **Per State INCLUDE** to an average aggregation.

5. Add two reference lines by right-clicking on the sales axis and selecting **Add Reference Line**. Use the following settings:

	Scope	Value	Label
Reference line 1	Per pane	**SUM(Sales)** and **Average**	Custom: Avg per Region: \<Value\>
Reference line 2	Per cell	**AVG(Per State INCLUDE)** and **Average**	Custom: Avg Per State: \<Value\>

6. Complete the worksheet by formatting as desired:

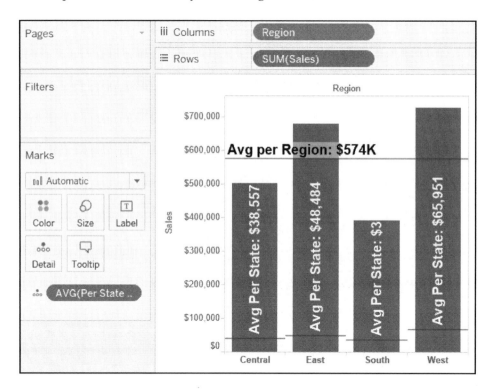

Exercise steps part 2 – solve without an LOD calculation

1. In a new worksheet, create a calculated field named `Window_AVG` with the following code:

```
WINDOW_AVG(SUM([Sales]))
```

2. Place **Region** on the **Columns** shelf, **Sales** on the **Rows** shelf, and **WindowAvg** on the **Rows** shelf.
3. Select the **Window Avg** pane in the **Marks View** card and add **State** to the **Detail** shelf.
4. Right-click on **Window Avg** and select **Compute Using | State**.
5. Select the **Window Avg** pane in the **Marks View** card and select **Gantt Bar** as the view type:

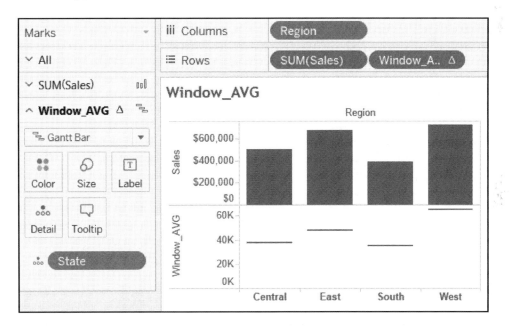

6. Adjust the color of the **Gantt Bar** to contrast with the bar chart associated with **SUM(Sales)**.

7. Right-click on the **Window Avg** pill in the **Rows** shelf and select **Dual Axis**.
8. Select the **SUM(Sales)** pane in the **Marks View** card and select **Bar Chart** as the view type.
9. Right-click on the **Window Avg** axis and select **Synchronize Axis**.
10. Right-click on the **Windows Avg** axis and deselect **Show Header**.
11. Add a reference line via right-clicking on the **Sales** axis and selecting **Add Reference Line**. Use the following settings:

Scope	Value	Label
Per Pane	**SUM(Sales)** and **Average**	Custom: Avg per Region: <Value>

12. Complete the worksheet by formatting as desired:

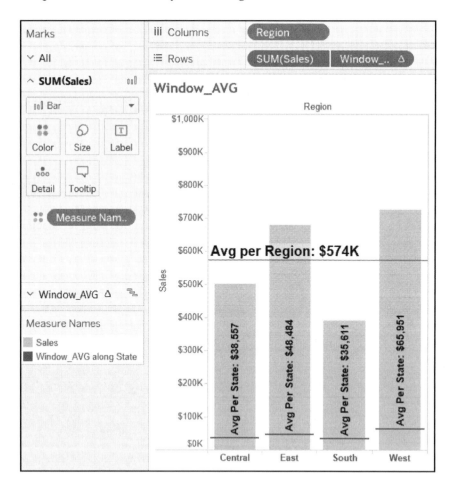

Exercise commentary

Part 1 of the preceding exercise is mostly self-explanatory. The one point to stress is that the INCLUDE statement does not require **State** to be in the view. **State** is simply declared within the calculation.

Part 2 of the exercise is more complicated and less intuitive and requires many more steps. The key thing to note is that the dimension **State** has to be on the view in order to be referenced to correctly calculate the average of each state per region. That's the nature of table calculations. In order to use **Compute Using** for any given dimension, that dimension must be in the view.

Exercise – practical EXCLUDE

In this exercise, we will create two worksheets using the **Superstore** dataset. Each will calculate the percentage of sales generated by each city in a region. In the first solution, we will use LOD calculations. In the second solution, we will use a data blend.

Exercise steps part 1 – solve by using an LOD calculation

1. Select the worksheet entitled Practical Exclude.
2. Select the **Superstore** dataset.
3. Create the following calculated fields:

Region Values	% Per Region LOD
{ EXCLUDE [City],[State]:ZN(SUM([Sales]))}	SUM([Sales])/SUM([Region Values])

4. Place **Region** and **City** on the **Rows** shelf.
5. Place **Measure Names** on the **Columns** shelf and **Measure Values** on the **Text** shelf.
6. Remove all instances of measures from the **Measure Values** shelf except **Sales**, **Region Values**, and **% Per Region LOD**.

7. In order for **% Per Region LOD** to be displayed as a percentage, the number formatting must be adjusted. Simply right-click on the calculation in the **Data** pane and select **Default Properties** | **Number Format** | **Percentage**.

8. Place an instance of **SUM(% Per Region LOD)** on the **Filter** shelf and adjust to display **At Least** 10%:

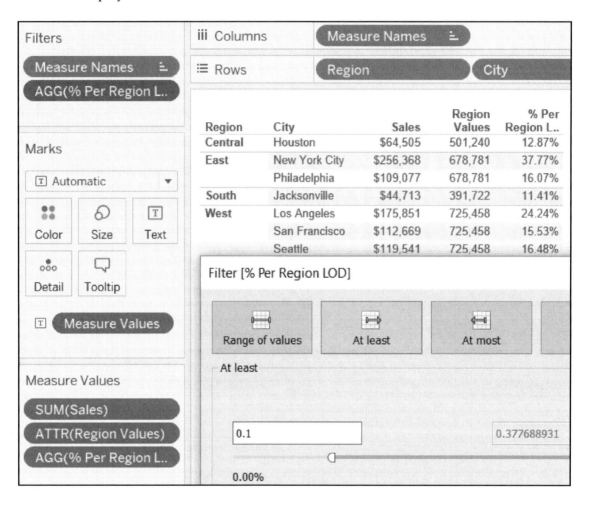

9. Place **State** on the **Rows** shelf between **Region** and **City**. Note that **Jacksonville** disappears:

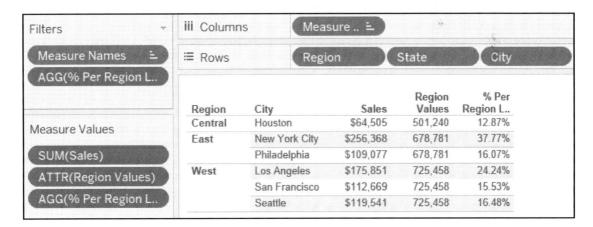

10. Right-click on **State** in the **Rows** shelf and deselect **Show Header**:

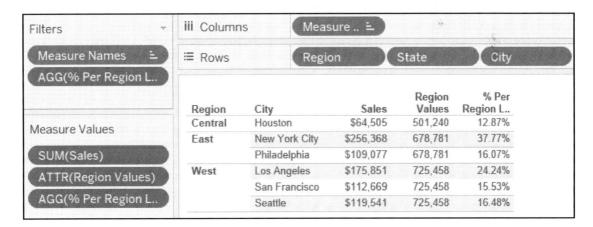

Exercise steps part 2 – solve by using blending

1. Create a new worksheet.
2. Place **Region** and **City** on the **Rows** shelf.
3. Place **Measure Names** on the **Columns** shelf and **Measure Values** on the **Text** shelf.
4. Remove all instances of measures except **Sales**, **City Values**, and **Region Values**.
5. Right-click on the **Superstore** dataset and duplicate:

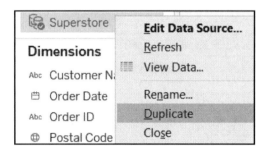

6. Name the duplicated data source **Superstore Blend**.
7. Select **Superstore Blend** and link by **Region**. Ensure that no other fields are linked:

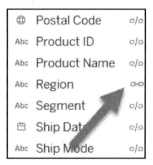

8. Double-click on **Sales** in the **Superstore Blend** data source to place **Sales** in the view.
9. Alternately link on **Region**, **State**, and **City** and observe changes. Make sure that **Region** is the only option selected when you're done.

10. In the primary data source (**Superstore**), create a calculated field named **% Blend**:

    ```
    SUM([Sales])/SUM([Superstore Blend].[Sales])
    ```

11. Place **% Blend** on the **Measure Values** shelf and adjust the formatting to display percentage.
12. Place an instance of **% Blend** on the **Filter** shelf and adjust to display **At Least 10%**.
13. Remove **City Values** and **Region Values** from the **Measure Values** shelf.
14. Rename the instance of **Sales** from the secondary data source to **Sales by Region**.
15. Note that **Jacksonville** is displaying. It should not because there are actually two different cities named **Jacksonville** in the **South Region**.
16. From the primary data source place **State** between **Region** and **City** on the **Rows** shelf.
17. If the view expands to include several more cities, check the secondary data source to insure that the blend is only on **Region**.
18. Right-click on **State** in the **Rows** shelf and deselect **Show Header**.

Exercise commentary

The first part of this exercise utilized an LOD calculation to arrive at a fairly simple solution. The only tricky part was catching the fact that two cities named **Jacksonville** exist in the **South Region**. The blended solution also worked fairly well, although it took more steps. So which solution is better? The LOD solution wins because it will probably perform better. Any solution requiring a data blend necessitates querying another data source and then blending the results from the two data sources, which impacts performance.

Summary

We began this chapter exploring why LOD calculations are so impactful and why their inclusion in Tableau was so lauded. Next, we built a couple of playgrounds to explore how the three LOD calculations, FIXED, EXCLUDE, and INCLUDE, work. Lastly, we covered three common scenarios that might utilize LOD calculations and explored alternative solutions using table calculations and data blending.

In the next chapter, we'll turn our attention to the visual side of Tableau and explore chart types that go beyond the out-of-the-box potential provided by Tableau.

7
Beyond the Basic Chart Types

Data visualization is such a new and vibrant field that new things can be discovered almost daily. Visit `https://d3js.org/` or `https://github.com/mbostock/d3/wiki/Gallery` and you will find an ever-expanding gallery of visualization types for all kinds of use case scenarios. Many of the visualization types listed on these websites are reproducible in Tableau. Due to their sheer number, it is not possible to review a substantial percentage in the space allotted in a chapter of a book. However, what can be covered are visualization types and concepts that will hopefully prove useful and stimulating.

The assumption behind this chapter is that you are familiar with basic chart types such as bar, line graph, treemap, pie, and area. Exotic chart types such as Sankey and Node-Link diagrams, though reproducible in Tableau, are not covered because such chart types are not typically useful. Instead, the focus will be on the middle ground, with the intent of relating how to improve visualization types you may already use on a regular basis as well as introducing chart types that you may be unfamiliar with but are nonetheless widely useful.

Perhaps, the most useful part of this chapter is actually not contained in the book at all but rather in the workbook associated with the chapter. Be sure to download that workbook to check out a wider range of visualization types.

This chapter will explore the following visualization types and topics:

- Improving popular visualizations:
    - Bullet graphs
    - Pies and donuts on maps
    - Pareto charts
- Custom background images:
    - Creating a grid
    - Creating polygons on a background image

There are some people whose work and insight were particularly helpful in writing this chapter. Preston Howell, my colleague at Teknion, built most of the bonus visualizations in the workbook that accompanies this chapter. Stephen Few's creation of the bullet graph provided fodder for two exercises. Joshua Milligan came up with the idea of improving on Pareto and graciously gave permission for me to share his approach here. Noah Salvaterra's techniques for building mind-bending 3D visualizations and an enigma machine were utilized in building the SVG grid generator discussed in the following sections. Lastly, Sean Boon and Amy Forstrom's presentation *Beyond Mark Types* at the 2015 Tableau Conference in Las Vegas provided ideas and helped me organize my thoughts for this chapter.

Improving popular visualizations

Most popular visualizations are popular for good reasons. Basic bar charts and line graphs are familiar, intuitive, and flexible, and are thus widely used in data visualization. Other less basic visualizations such as bullet graphs and Pareto charts may not be something you use every day but are nonetheless useful additions to the data analyst's toolbox. In this section, we will explore ideas to tweak, extend, and even overhaul a few popular chart types.

Bullet graphs

The bullet graph was invented by Stephen Few and communicated publically in 2006 through his book *Information Dashboard Design: The Effective Visual Communication of Data*. Stephen Few continues to be a strong voice in the data visualization space through his books and his blog, `http://www.perceptualedge.com/`. Bullet graphs communicate efficiently and intuitively by packing a lot of information into a small space while remaining attractive and easy to read. Understandably, they have gained much popularity and are being utilized for many purposes as can be readily seen via a web search. The following two exercises communicate the basics and how to improve on those basics. That is not to say that I have improved on the bullet graph in this chapter! The intent is merely to relay how this important visualization type can be used more effectively in Tableau.

Exercise steps for bullet graph – the basics

As suggested by the section title, in this exercise we will build a basic bullet chart:

1. Navigate to `https://public.tableau.com/profile/david.baldwin#!/` to locate and download the workbook associated with this chapter.

2. Navigate to the worksheet titled `Bullet Graph` and select the **CoffeeChain** data source.

3. Place these fields on their respective shelves:

Field	Shelf
Profit	Columns
Market	Rows
Budget Profit	Detail

4. Right-click on the axis and select **Add Reference Line**.

5. Within the top-left corner of the **Edit Reference Line, Band or Box** dialog box, select **Line**. Also set **Scope** to **Per Cell**, **Value** to **SUM(Budget Profit)**, and **Label** to **None**. Click on **OK**:

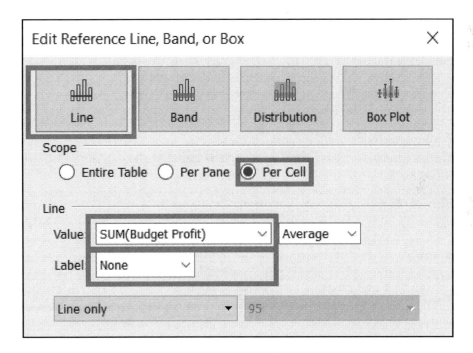

6. Once again, right-click on the axis and select **Add Reference Line**.

7. Within the dialog box, select **Distribution** and set **Scope** to **Per Cell**.

8. Under **Computation**, set **Value** to **Percentages** with **90, 95, 100** and **Percent of:** to **SUM(Budget Profit)**.

9. Set **Label** to **None**:

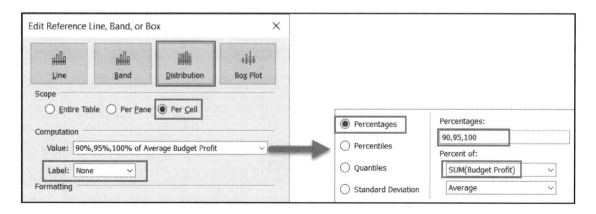

10. Create the following calculated fields:

Name	Code
Profit to Budget Profit Ratio	SUM([Profit])/SUM([Budget Profit])
Quota Met?	SUM([Profit])>=SUM([Budget Profit])

11. Right-click on **Profit to Budget Profit Ratio** and navigate to **Default Properties** | **Number Format** | **Percentage**.

12. Place **Profit to Budget Profit Ratio** on the **Label** shelf and **Quota Met?** on the **Color** shelf:

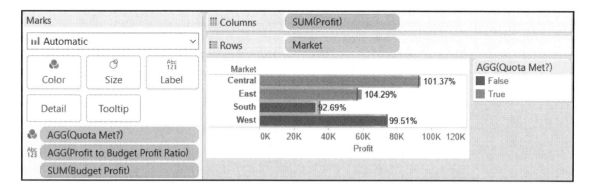

As you survey our results thus far, you will notice that there are positive aspects to this visualization. For example, the reference lines and the colored bars clearly delineate when quota was met and missed. Furthermore, the percentages communicate how close the actual profit was to the budgeted profit for each market. However, there are also some problems to address:

1. The percentage associated with the **South** market is partially obscured.
2. The background colors represented by the reference distribution are obscured.
3. The colors of the bars are not intuitive. Orange is set to **True** which signifies, in this case, the markets that made quota. However, psychologically speaking, orange is a warning color used to communicate problems and therefore would be more intuitively associated with those markets that *failed* to make quota. Furthermore, these colors are not easily distinguishable when presented in grayscale.
4. The words **False** and **True** in the legend are not immediately intuitive.

Exercise steps for bullet graph – beyond the basics

In this exercise we'll upgrade the above rendition of the bullet chart by making some improvements:

1. Continuing from the previous exercise, access the **Data** pane at the left-hand portion of the screen, right-click on **Quota Met?**, and adjust the calculation as follows:

```
IF SUM([Profit])>=SUM([Budget Profit])
THEN 'Quota Met'
ELSE 'Quota Missed'
END
```

Note that the legend is more intuitive than the previous **True** and **False** values.

2. Create a calculated field named **Greater of Profit or Budget Profit** with the following code:

```
IF SUM(Profit) > SUM([Budget Profit])
THEN SUM(Profit)
ELSE SUM([Budget Profit])
END
```

3. Place **Greater of Profit or Budget Profit** on the **Columns** shelf after **Profit**. Also right-click on the pill and select **Dual Axis**.

4. Right-click on the axis for **Greater of Profit or Budget Profit** and select **Synchronize Axis**.

5. Within the **Marks View** card, select the pane labeled **All**:
    1. Set the view type to **Bar**.
    2. Remove **Measure Names**.

6. Within the **Marks View** card, select the pane labeled **AGG(Greater of Profit or Budget Profit)**.

7. Click on the **Color** shelf and set **Transparency** to 0%.

8. Within the **Marks View** card, select the pane labeled **SUM(Profit)**.

9. Remove **AGG(Profit to Budget Profit Ratio)** from the **Marks View** card. Note that the percentage labels are no longer obscured.

10. Click on the **Color** shelf and select **Edit Colors…**. Within the resulting dialog box, complete the following steps:
    1. Double-click on **Quota Met** and set the HTML to #FFFFFF.
    2. Double-click on **Quota Missed** and set the HTML to #000000.

11. After you have clicked on **OK** for each dialog box and returned to the main screen, once again click on the **Color** shelf and select black for the border:

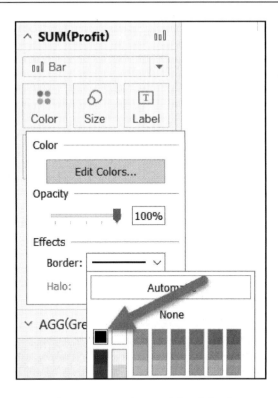

12. Click on the **Size** shelf to narrow the width of the bars.
13. Right-click on the **Profit** axis and select **Edit Reference Line | 90%,95%,100%** of **Average Budget Profit:**
    1. Click the **Fill Below** checkbox.
    2. Set the **Fill** color to **Gray**.
    3. Select the **Reverse** checkbox. Note that the background colors are now more easily distinguished:

14. Right-click on the axis labeled **Greater of Profit or Budget Profit** and deselect **Show Header**.
15. You may wish to make some additional tweaks:

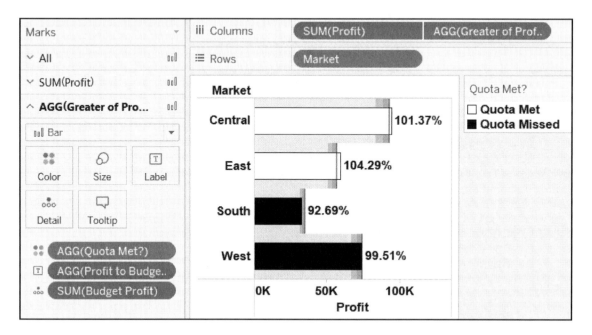

Note that each of the aforementioned problems have now been addressed:

1. The percentage numbers are no longer obscured.
2. The background colors are easier to distinguish due to having narrowed the bars.
3. The color of the bars is more intuitive. Furthermore, using black, white, and grey has circumvented any readability problems arising from color blindness or grayscale print.
4. The words **False** and **True** in the legend have been replaced with more descriptive terms: **Quota Met** and **Quota Missed**.

Making useful pies and donuts on maps

Pie charts are normally frowned upon in data visualization circles. They simply have too many drawbacks. For instance, pie charts don't utilize space well on a rectangular screen. Treemaps fit much better. Also, the number of slices that are reasonable on a pie chart is fairly limited; perhaps six to eight at best. Once again, treemaps are superior because they can be sliced at a finer level of granularity while remaining useful. Lastly, when using pie charts it can be difficult to discern which of two similarly sized slices is largest. Treemaps are no better in this regard; however, if the viewer understands that treemap sorting is from top left to bottom right, that knowledge can be used to distinguish size differences. Of course bar charts circumvent that particular problem entirely since the eye can easily distinguish widths and heights but struggles with angles (pie charts) and volume (treemaps).

Despite these drawbacks, because of their popularity pie charts will likely continue to be widely used in data visualization for years to come. For the pessimistic Tableau author, the best course of action is to grin and bear it. But for one willing to explore and push frontier boundaries, good uses for pie charts can be discovered. The following exercise is one contribution to that exploration.

Exercise – pies and donuts on maps

Occasionally, there is a need (or a perceived need) to construct pie charts atop a map. The process is not difficult (as you will see later), but there are some shortcomings that cannot be easily overcome. We will discuss those shortcomings after the exercise.

Exercise steps for pies and donuts – the basics

In this exercise we will create a dual axis chart combining pie charts and a map:

1. Within the workbook associated with this chapter, navigate to the worksheet titled `Pie Map` and select the **Superstore** data source.
2. In the **Data** pane, double-click on **State** to create a map of the United States.
3. Place **Sales** on the **Color** shelf.
4. Click on the **Color** shelf and change the palette to **Gray**.

5. Drag an additional copy of **Latitude (generated)** on the **Rows** shelf to create two rows, each of which displays a map:

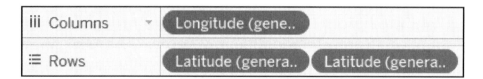

6. In the **Marks View** card you will note that there are now three panes: All, **Latitude (generated)** and **Latitude (generated)** (2). Click on **Latitude (generated)** (2) and set the view type to **Pie**.
7. Place **Category** on the **Color** shelf and **Sales** on the **Size** shelf.
8. Right-click on the second instance of **Latitude (generated)** in the **Rows** shelf and select **Dual Axis**:

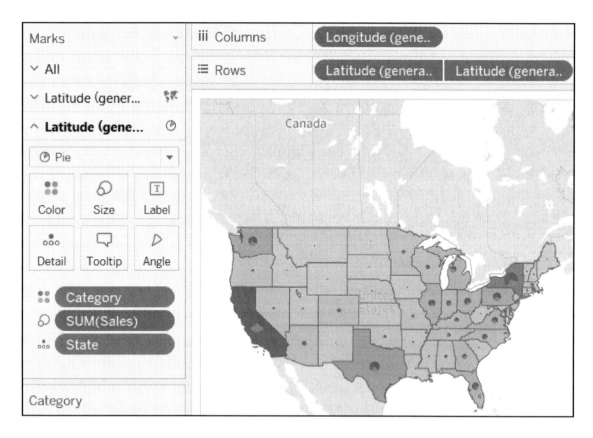

Can you see any issues in the preceding visualization? Two should be immediately apparent. First, note that the smaller pies are difficult to see. Clicking on the drop-down menu for the Size legend and selecting **Edit Sizes** could partially address this problem, but pies on smaller states such as Rhode Island will continue to be problematic. Second, many states have the same light gray background despite widely varying sales amounts.

Exercise steps for pies and donuts – beyond the basics

This exercise will address the shortcomings of the previous exercise while adding more functionality:

1. Within the workbook associated with this chapter, navigate to the worksheet titled `Altered Pie Map` and select the **Superstore** data source.
2. Create the following calculated fields:

Name	Code
Log Sales	LOG(SUM(Sales))
Category State Sales	{FIXED State, Category: SUM(Sales)}
State Max	{FIXED State : MAX([Category State Sales])}
Top Selling Category per State	MAX(If [State Max] = [Category State Sales] then Category END)

3. Within the **Marks View** card, set the view type to **Pie**.
4. Place **Log Sales** on the **Size** shelf.
5. Within the **Data** pane, select the **States** data source.
6. Click on the chain link next to **State** in the **Data** pane in order to use **State** as a linking field.
7. Drag **Column** to the **Columns** shelf and **Row** to the **Rows** shelf.
8. From the **Superstore** data source, place **Category** on the **Color** shelf and **Sales** on the **Angle** shelf.
9. Click on the **Size** shelf and adjust the size as desired.
10. At this point, you should see a rough map of the United States made up of pie charts. Next, we will further enhance the graphic by changing the pies into donuts.
11. Return to the **States** data source and place another instance of **Row** on the **Rows** shelf.
12. In the **Marks View** card, select **Row (2)**:

13. Change the view type to **Circle**.

14. From the **Superstore** dataset, place **Top Selling Category per State** on the **Color** shelf.

15. Place **Sales** on the **Label** shelf.

16. Right-click on the instance of **Sales** you just placed on the **Label** shelf and select **Format**. Make the following adjustments in the **Format** window.

17. Set the numbers formatting to **Currency (Custom)** with 0 decimal places and **Units** set to **Thousands (K)**:

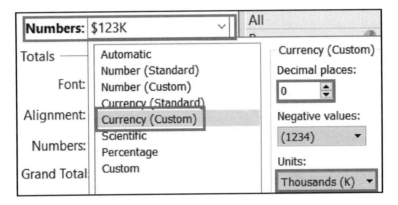

18. Set the alignment to **Middle Center,** as shown in the following screenshot, so that the numbers are centered over the circles:

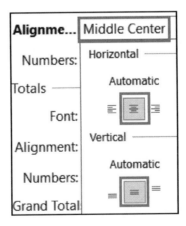

19. In the **Rows** shelf, right-click on the second instance of **Row** and select **Dual Axis**.
20. Right-click on the instance of the **Row** axis located at the far right of your screen and select **Synchronize Axis**.
21. Within the **Row** (2) instance of the **Marks View** card, click on the **Color** shelf and select **Edit Colors...**. Adjust the color settings as desired so that the color of the overlaying circle (that is, the hole of the donut) differs from underlying colors and yet retains the same hue. One way to accomplish this is by double-clicking on each color and changing the **Saturation** and **Value** numbers but leaving the Hue numbers the same.
22. Also within the **Color** shelf, set the border to the desired color.
23. Right-click on each axis and deselect **Show Header**.
24. Go to **Format** | **Lines** and set **Grid Lines** to **None**.
25. Make other formatting changes as desired:

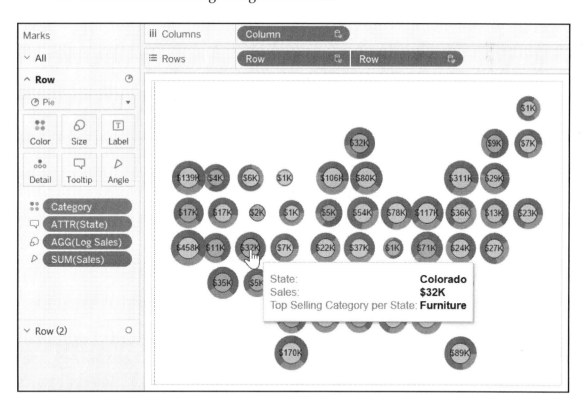

At first glance, the preceding visualization may look peculiar. It's called a **Tile Grid Map**, and although it's fairly new to the data visualization scene, it has begun to see usage at media outlets such as NPR. In the right setting, a Tile Grid Map can be advantageous. Let's consider a couple of the advantages the preceding exercise gives us. First, the grid layout in combination with the **Log Sales** calculated field creates a map immediately evident as the United States while ensuring that the sizing of the various pie charts changes only moderately from greatest to least. Thus each slice of each pie is reasonably visible; for example, District of Columbia sales are as easily visible as California sales. Second, the end user can clearly see the top selling category for each state via the color of the inner circle (that is, the hole of the donut). This was accomplished with the LOD calculations. The end result is an information-dense visualization that uses pie charts in a practical, intuitive manner.

Pareto charts

In the late 19th century, an Italian economist named Vilfredo Pareto observed that 80% of the land in Italy was owned by 20% of the people. As he looked around he observed this mathematical phenomenon in many unexpected places. For example, he noted that 80% of the peas in his garden were produced from 20% of the peapods. As a result, although Vilfredo Pareto is not a household name, the 80/20 rule has found its way into the popular vernacular. In the following exercise, we will discuss how to build a basic Pareto chart and then how to expand that chart to make it even more useful.

Of course, not every dataset is going to adhere to the 80/20 rule. Accordingly, the following exercise considers loan data from a community bank where 80% of the loan balance is not held by 20% of the bank's customers. Nonetheless, a Pareto chart can still be a very helpful analytical tool.

Exercise steps for a Pareto chart – the basics

1. Within the workbook associated with this chapter, navigate to the worksheet titled `Pareto - Basic` and select the **Bank** data source.
2. In the **Data** pane, change **Account #** to a dimension.
3. Place **Account #** on the **Columns** shelf and **Current Loan Balance** on the **Rows** shelf.
4. Click on the **Fit** drop-down menu and choose **Entire View**.

5. Right-click on the **Account #** pill and select **Sort**. Set the sort to **Descending** by the aggregated sum of the **Current Loan Balance** field.

6. Right-click on **SUM(Current Loan Balance)** located on the **Rows** shelf and select **Add Table Calculation**. Choose the settings shown in the following screenshot:

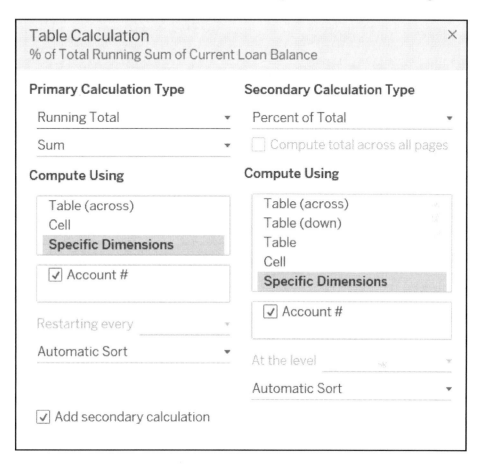

7. Drag an instance of **Account #** to the **Detail** shelf.
8. Click on the **Color** shelf and set **Border** to **None**.
9. Right-click on the instance of **Account #** that is on the **Columns** shelf and navigate to **Measure | Count (Distinct)**. Note that a single vertical line is displayed.

10. Once again, right-click on the instance of **Account** # on the **Columns** shelf and select **Add Table Calculation**. Deploy the settings listed in the following screenshot:

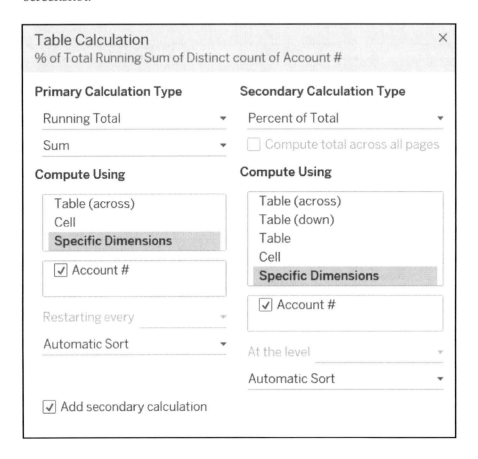

11. Click on the **Analytics** tab in the top-left corner of the screen and perform the following two steps:
    1. Drag **Constant Line** to **Table | SUM(Current Loan Balance)**.
    2. In the resulting dialog box, select **Constant** and set the value to **.8**, as shown here:

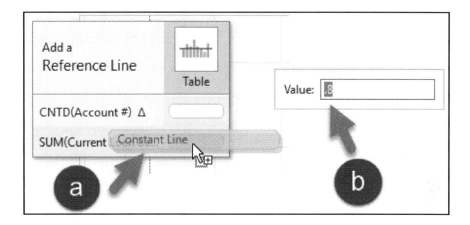

12. Repeat the previous step with the following differences:
    1. Drag **Constant Line** to **Table | CNTD(Account #) Δ**.
    2. In the resulting dialog box, select **Constant** and set the value to **.2**.

13. Drag **Current Loan Balance** to the **Rows** shelf. Place it to the right of **SUM(Current Loan Balance) Δ** that is currently on the **Rows** shelf. Note that the axis is affected by a single loan with a much larger balance than the other loans.

14. Right-click on the **Current Loan Balance** axis and select **Edit axis**.

15. In the resulting dialog box, set **Scale** to **Logarithmic** and click on **OK**. This addresses the problem of the single large loan affecting the axis, thus obscuring the view of the other loans.

16. Within the **Marks View** card, select the second instance of **SUM(Current Loan Balance)** and set the view type to **Bar**:

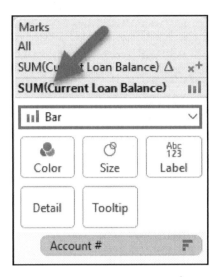

17. Right-click on **SUM(Current Loan Balance)** on the **Rows** shelf and select **Dual Axis**.

18. Right-click on the **% of Total Running Sum of Current Loan Balance** axes and select **Move Marks to Front**.

19. Change the colors, tooltip, and formatting as desired:

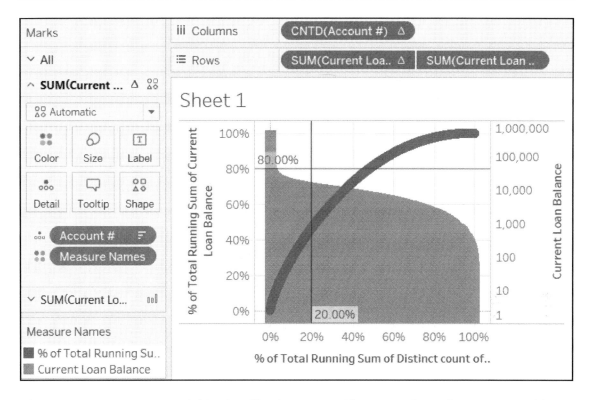

There are positive aspects of this visualization to consider. First, the end user can quickly gain an initial understanding simply by observing both portions of the graph in conjunction with the values on the axes. Furthermore the end user can hover the cursor above any part of the curve and see the resulting tooltip. Adding parameters to the two reference lines would be a quick way to add additional value, but let's see if we can go a little beyond that.

Exercise steps for a Pareto chart – beyond the basics

1. Duplicate the sheet from the previous exercise and name the duplicate `Pareto - Improved`.
2. Remove both reference lines.

3. Drag **SUM(Current Loan Balance)** Δ (that is, the table calculation) from the **Rows** shelf to the **Data** pane. When prompted, name the field **Running % of Balance**.

4. Create and display a parameter with the following settings:

Field name	Field value
Name	% of Balance
Data Type	Float
Display Format	Percentage
Allowable Values	Range
Minimum	0
Maximum	1
Step size	0.01

5. Create the following calculated fields:

Name	Code
Running % of Loans	RUNNING_SUM(COUNTD([Account #]) / TOTAL(COUNTD([Account #])))
Pareto Split	IF [Running % of Balance] < [% of Balance] THEN "Makes up X% of Balance" ELSE "Makes up rest of Balance" END
Pareto Split (label)	IF LOOKUP([Pareto Split], -1) != LOOKUP([Pareto Split], 0) THEN MID(STR([Running % of Loans] * 100), 1, 5) + "% of loans make up " + MID(STR([% of Balance] * 100), 1, 5) + "% of balance" END

6. Select the **All** portion of the **Marks View** card.

7. Drag **Pareto Split** to the **Detail** shelf.

8. Click on the drop-down menu to the left of the **Pareto Split** pill on the **Marks View** card and select **Color**:

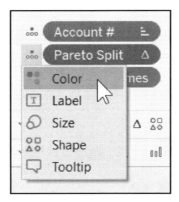

9. Select the **Running % of Balance Δ** portion of the **Marks View** card.

10. Set the **Mark** type to **Line**.

11. Drag **Pareto Split (label)** to the **Label** shelf. Note that the expected label does not display. The next two steps will address that.

12. Click on the **Label** shelf and select **Allow labels to overlap other marks**.

13. Right-click **Pareto Split (label)** on the **Marks View** card and select **Compute Using | Account #**.

14. Click on the **Analytics** tab in the top-left corner of the screen and perform the following two steps:

    1. Drag **Reference Line** to **Table | Running % of Balance Δ**.

    2. In the resulting dialog box, select **% of Balance (Parameters)** from the **Value** dropdown and set **Label** to **None**.

15. Change the colors, tooltip, and formatting as desired:

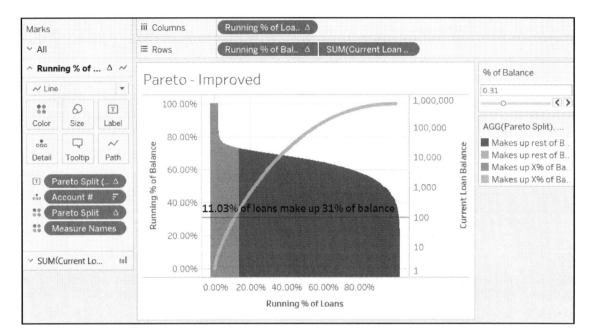

As you will note in the preceding screenshot, the end user now has a single parameter to slide that moves the horizontal reference line on the chart. As the end user moves the reference line, the text updates to display loan and balance percentages. The colors also update as the end user adjusts the parameter to vertically communicate the percentage of loans under consideration.

Custom background images

Custom background images in Tableau open a world of potential. Imagine the ability to visualize any space. Possibilities encompass sports, healthcare, engineering, architecture, interior design, and much, much more. Despite this wealth of potential, use of background images in Tableau seems to me to be underutilized. Why? Part of the reason is because of the difficulty of generating datasets that can be used with background images.

Like the Tile Grid Map discussed previously, background images require a grid layout to pinpoint X, Y coordinates. In the following section we will address how to use Tableau to create a grid that can be superimposed on an image to instantly identify locations associated with X, Y coordinates and relatively quickly produce datasets that can be accessed by Tableau for visualization purposes. Specifically, we will use Tableau to generate the XML required to construct an SVG file that can be opened with a vector graphic tool. The tool that will be referenced is **Inkscape**. Inkscape is open source and is thus available free of charge. Visit `https://inkscape.org/en/` to download the latest version.

Note that a grid with only 10 rows and columns is used in the following examples. Of course 10 rows and columns generate a grid of 100 cells. This will perform satisfactorily in Inkscape. However, if a large cell count is required, a professional graphics tool such as Adobe Illustrator may be required. I tested grids with up to 10,000 cells and found the performance in Inkscape unacceptable. The same grids performed adequately in Illustrator; that is, Illustrator remained stable and manipulating the grid was reasonably quick.

Exercise – creating a grid

The following exercise serves multiple purposes. The first purpose is, of course, to demonstrate how to use Tableau to create a grid. Additionally, this exercise requires many table calculations, which will help reinforce lessons learned in Chapter 5, *Table Calculations*. Also, this chapter provides another opportunity to use data scaffolding which was discussed in Chapter 3, *All about Data – Joins, Blends, and Data Structures*. The difference is that in Chapter 3, *All about Data – Joins, Blends, and Data Structures*, dates were used for scaffolding purposes whereas here bins are utilized. Lastly, this exercise makes use of data densification, which was discussed in Chapter 4, *All about Data – Data Densification, Cubes, and Big Data*.

Exercise – steps for creating a grid

As discussed previously, we will know use Tableau to create a grid:

1. Open a new Tableau workbook and name the first sheet Header.
2. Using Excel or a text editor, create a **Records** dataset. The following two-row table represents the **Records** dataset in its entirety:

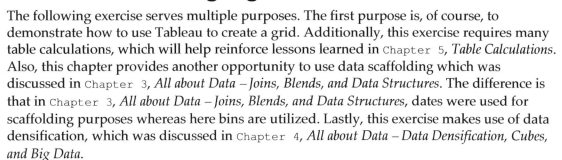

Records
1

2

3. Connect Tableau to the **Records** dataset:
   1. To be expedient, consider copying the dataset via *Ctrl* + *C* and pasting it directly in Tableau via *Ctrl* + *V*.
   2. Tableau will likely consider **Records** a measure. Drag **Records** to the dimensions portion of the **Data** pane.

4. Create two parameters. Name one **Overall Pixel Count** and the other **Rows Down/Columns Across**. The settings for both are as follows:
   1. Data type: **Integer.**
   2. Allowable values: **All.**

5. Show both parameters. Set **Rows Down/Columns Across** to 10 and **Overall Pixel Count** to 1000.

6. Create a calculated field named **Concatenate Header** with the following code. Note that entering line breaks in the **Calculated Field** dialog box may make the results difficult to extract from Tableau. In other words, remove all line breaks:

```
'<?xml version="1.0" encoding="utf-8"?> <svg version="1.1"
id="Squares" xmlns="http://www.w3.org/2000/svg"
xmlns:xlink="http://www.w3.org/1999/xlink" x="0px" y="0px"
viewBox="0 0 ' + STR( [Overall Pixel Count] ) + " " +
STR([Overall Pixel Count])+ '" style="enable-background:new 0 0
+ STR([Overall Pixel Count]) + ' ' + STR([Overall Pixel Count]) +
';" xml:space="preserve"> <style type="text/css">
.st0{fill:none;stroke:#000000;stroke-miterlimit:10;} </style>'
```

7. Place the newly created calculated field on the **Text** shelf.
8. In the toolbar, choose to fit to **Entire View** to view the results.
9. Create a new worksheet named **Location Codes**.

10. Create the following calculated fields:

Name	Code
Rows Down/Columns Across	`[Parameters].[Rows Down/Columns Across]`
Which Column?	`LAST()+1`
Which Row?	`INDEX()`
Grid Size	`[Overall Pixel Count]/LOOKUP([Which Column?],FIRST())`
X	`[Overall Pixel Count] - ([Grid Size] * ([Which Row?]))`
Y	`[Overall Pixel Count] - ([Grid Size] * ([Which Column?]-1))`
Count	`If [Records] = 1 THEN 1 ELSE [Rows Down/Columns Across] END`
Decicount	`If [Records] = 1 THEN 1 ELSE [Rows Down/Columns Across] END`
Location Codes	`Index()`
Concatenate Locations	`'<text transform="matrix(1 0 0 1 ' + STR([X]) + " " + STR([Y]) +')">' + STR( [Location Codes] ) + '</text>'`

11. Right-click on **Count** and select **Create | Bins**. In the resulting dialog box, set the size of the bin to 1.

12. Right-click on **Decicount** and select **Create | Bins**. In the resulting dialog box, set the size of the bin to 1.

13. Place **Count (bin), Decicount (bin), Location Codes, X**, and **Y** on the **Rows** shelf. Be sure to place those fields in the order listed here.

14. Right-click on each field on the **Rows** shelf and set to **Discrete**.

15. Right-click on **Count (bin)** and **Decicount (bin)** and ensure that **Show Missing Values** is selected.

16. Right-click on **Location Code** and select **Compute Using | Table (Down)**.

17. Set the **Compute Using** value for **X** to **Count (bin)**.

18. Set the **Compute Using** value for **Y** to **Decicount (bin)**.

19. Place **Concatenate Locations** on the **Text** shelf.

20. Right-click on the instance of **Concatenate Locations** you just placed on the **Text** shelf and select **Edit Table Calculations**. At the top of the resulting dialog box, note that there are four options under **Nested Calculations**: **Grid Size**, **Which Column?**, **Which Row?**, and **Location Codes**. Set the **Compute Using** definition for each as follows:

Name	Compute Using setting
Grid Size	Table (Down)
Which Column?	Discount (bin)
Which Row	Count (bin)
Location Codes	Table (Down)

21. In the toolbar, choose to fit to **Fit Width** to view the results.
22. Create a new worksheet named **Lines**.
23. Select **Analysis | Table Layout | Advanced** and set the maximum values for **Rows** and **Columns** to **16**:

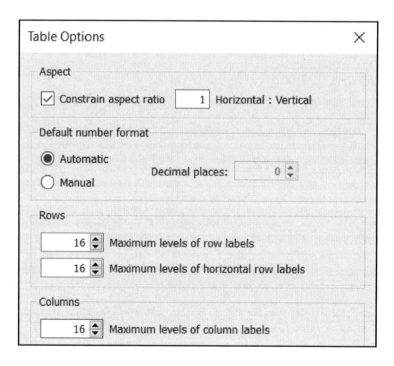

24. Create the following calculated fields:

Name	Compute Using setting
H Then V	`Index()`
HLine	`Last()`
VLine	`Index()-1`
X1	`IF [H Then V] = 1 THEN 0 ELSE` `[Overall Pixel Count] - ([Grid Size] * ([VLine])) END`
Y1	`IF [H Then V] = 2 THEN 0 ELSE` `[Overall Pixel Count] - ([Grid Size] * ([VLine])) END`
X2	`IF [H Then V] = 1 THEN [Overall Pixel Count] ELSE [Overall` `Pixel Count] - ([Grid Size] * ([VLine])) END`
Y2	`IF [H Then V] = 2 THEN [Overall Pixel Count] ELSE [Overall` `Pixel Count] - ([Grid Size] * ([VLine])) END`

25. Next, place the following eight fields on the **Rows** shelf. Note that each should be cast as discrete:

Count (bin)	Decicount (bin)	H Then V	HLine	VLine
Grid Size	X1	Y1	X2	Y2

26. Right-click on **Count(bin)** and **Decicount(bin)** and set each to **Show Missing Values.**

27. Right-click on each of the remaining fields on the **Rows** shelf and select **Edit Table Calculations**. Set the **Compute Using** definition of each field as shown in the following table. Note that some of the fields include nested table calculations. In such cases, the **Table Calculations** dialog box will include an extra option at the top entitled **Nested Calculation**, as can be seen here:

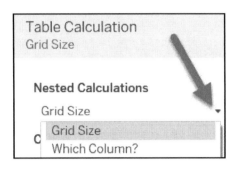

Name	Nested calculation	Compute Using setting
H then V	N/A	Count (bin)
HLine	N/A	Count (bin)
VLine	N/A	Decicount (bin)
Grid Size	Grid Size	Table (Down)
	Which Column?	Decicount (bin)
X1, Y1, X2, Y2	H Then V	Count (bin)
	Grid Size	Count (bin)
	Which Column?	Count (bin)
	VLine	Decicount (bin)

28. Filter **H Then V** to display only 1 and 2.
29. Create the following calculated field:

Name	Code
Concatenate Lines	`'<line class="st0" x1="' + STR([X1]) + '" y1="' + STR([Y1]) + '" x2="' + STR( [X2] ) + '" y2="' + STR([Y2]) + '"/>'`

30. Place **Concatenate Lines** on the **Text** shelf.

31. Export the code from the three worksheets just created. Note that this can be tricky since Tableau may try to input additional quote marks. I found the following approach to work best:
    1. Select the **Header** worksheet.
    2. Press *Ctrl + A* to select all the contents of the worksheet.
    3. Hover the cursor over the selected text in the view and pause until the tooltip command buttons appear.
    4. Select the **View Data** icon at the right-hand side of the tooltip.
    5. In the resulting **View Data** dialog box, select **Export All**.
    6. Save the CSV file using the same name as each worksheet; for example, the data exported from the **Header** worksheet will be named `Header.csv`.
    7. Repeat the preceding steps for the remaining worksheets.

32. Open an instance of Notepad (or your favourite text editor) and save it as `Grid and Location Codes.svg`.

33. Using Excel, copy the data from `Header.csv` and paste into `Grid and Location Codes.svg`. Be sure not to include the header information. Include only the XML code.

34. Using Excel, copy the required data from Location.csv and paste into `Grid and Location Codes.svg`. The required data only includes the column labeled **Concatenate Locations**. Do not include the other columns or the header. Include only the XML code.

35. Using Excel, copy the required data from `Lines.csv` and paste into `Grid and Location Codes.svg`. The required data only includes the column labelled **Concatenate Lines**. Again, do not include the other columns or the header. Include only the XML code.

36. Lastly, complete the SVG file by entering the closing tag `</svg>`.

37. Now open the SVG file in Inkscape and observe the grid. We'll cover an example of how to use the grid in the next exercise.

Exercise – steps for using a grid to generate a dataset

Skilled chess players will complete a game in about 40 moves. In chess tournaments, data is routinely captured for each game, which provides opportunities for data visualization. In this exercise, we will use data from a chess game to visualize how often each square of a chessboard is occupied:

1. Within the workbook associated with this chapter, navigate to the worksheet entitled `Chessboard`.
2. Download the pictures provided via the link in the caption. Unzip the contents to a directory of your choosing.
3. Open the SVG file created from the last exercise in Inkscape.
4. If you did not complete the previous exercise, you can copy the XML code located on the dashboard entitled `Generated SVG Code` in the solution workbook associated with this chapter. Paste that code in a text editor and save it with an SVG extension. Lastly, open the file with Inkscape.
5. Within Inkscape depress *Ctrl + A* to select all.
6. Group the selection via *Ctrl + G*.
7. From the Inkscape menu, select **Layer | Layers**. The keyboard short cut is *Shift + Ctrl + L*.
8. Within the **Layers** palette that displays on the right side of the screen, press the **+** icon to create a layer. Name the layer **Chessboard**.
9. Create another layer named **Grid:**

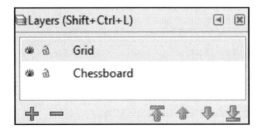

10. Click on any line or number in the view.
11. Right-click on that same line or number and select **Move to layer**. Chose the **Grid** layer.
12. Select **File | Import** and choose the **Chessboard** image included in the zip file previously downloaded.

13. Make sure that the image is placed on the **Chessboard** layer so that the location code numbers are not obscured.

14. Position the chessboard image such that location code 81 is centered over the top left hand square of the chessboard. Note that since the chessboard is only comprised of 64 squares, it will not encompass all 100 squares the grid provides.

At this point, you can generate a dataset based on how often each location is occupied. For example you might note that for one game, position 81 was occupied for 40 moves, in which case the player may simply have never moved that rook. However, in another game the position may be occupied for only 10 moves, perhaps indicating the player performed a castle early in the game.

For the next exercise, we will take a look at a dataset generated from a chess game and discover how to visualize the results based on the work done in the previous exercises.

Exercise – visualizing a chess game

1. Within the workbook associated with this chapter, navigate to the worksheet entitled **Chessboard** and select the **Chessboard** data source.

 In order to follow the next step, you will need to download the assets associated with this chapter. To do so, simply click on the link in the caption of the worksheet.

2. Right-click on the **Chessboard** data source and select **Edit Data Source** in order to examine the dataset.

3. In the dialog box asking **Where is the data file?**, steer to the Chessboard.xlsx provided with the assets associated with this chapter.

4. The table named **Board Grid** contains each location code and the X, Y coordinates associated with each location code. This dataset was taken from the **Location Codes** worksheet created earlier in this chapter.

5. The table named **Squares Occupied** contains the fields **Location Code** and **Moves Occupied**.

6. **Board Grid** and **Squares Occupied** are connected via a left join on **Location Code**:

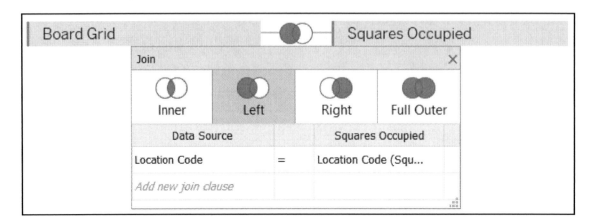

7. On the **Chessboard** worksheet, select **Map** | **Background Images** | **Chessboard**.
8. In the resulting dialog box, click on **Add Image** to add a background image.
9. Fill out the **Add Background Image** dialog box as shown in the following table:

Field	Content
Name	Chessboard
File or URL	Click **Browse** to choose a path to the **Chessboard** image previously downloaded.
X Field	X
Left	0
Right	1000
Y Field	Y
Bottom	1000
Top	0

10. Place these fields on their respective shelves:

Field	Shelf
X	Columns
Y	Rows
Moves Occupied	Color
Moves Occupied	Size
Location Code	Detail

11. Right-click on the X and Y axes and set both to **Fixed** with **Fixed start** of 0 and **Fixed end** of 875:

12. Edit the Y axis and set it to **Reversed**. Do not reverse the X axis.

 This last step was performed because the data has been structured to mirror the X, Y coordinate setup. This is the default in most graphic tools; that is, the top-left corner is where X and Y both equal 0.

13. Adjust the color, size, shapes, and so on as desired:

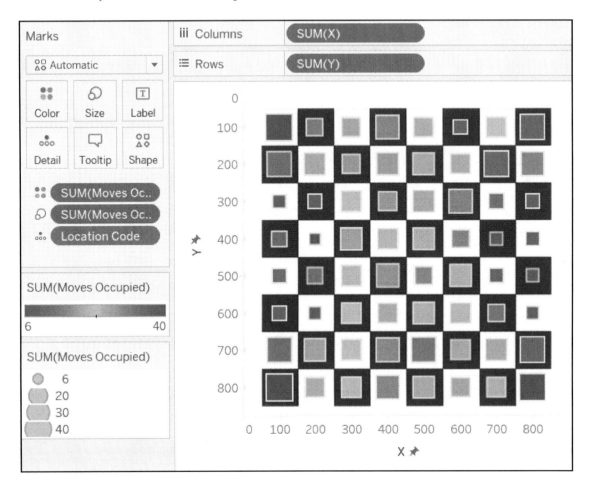

The preceding image uses large blue squares to designate spaces on the chessboard that were most frequently occupied. The small orange squares designate squares less frequently occupied.

Exercise – creating polygons on a background image

Utilizing shapes on specific points of a visualization was sufficient for the previous exercise, but sometimes it may be advantageous to use polygons to outline shapes. Polygons are natively used in Tableau in geocoding when using country, state, and other geocoded data; however, there are geocoded elements (such as cities) that are not natively available in Tableau. In the next chapter, we will discuss techniques for drawing polygons on a map. In the following section, we will discuss how to utilize polygons on a background image.

Exercise – steps for creating polygons on a background image

1. Within the workbook associated with this chapter, navigate to the worksheet titled `Dashboard – Polygon` and select the **DartBoard_W_Polygons** data source.
2. If you have not already done so when completing the previous exercise, download the pictures provided via the link in the caption. Unzip the contents to a directory of your choosing.
3. Select **Map | Background Images | Dartboard_W_Polygons**. In the **Background Images** dialog box, select **Add Image**. Fill out the dialog box as shown in the following table:

Dialog box field	Contents
Name	Dartboard_Blank
File or URL	Click **Browse** and navigate to the directory where you unzipped the compressed file just downloaded. Select `Dartboard_Blank.png`.
X Field	X
X Field Left	0
X Field Right	646
Y Field	Y
Y Field Bottom	0
Y Field Top	655

4. Create a parameter with the following information:

Dialog box field	Contents
Name	Select player
Data type	Integer
Allowable Values	List
List of Values	Value | Display As 1 | Matthew 2 | David 3 | Total Hits

5. Display the parameter created in the previous step by right-clicking on it at the bottom of the **Data** pane and selecting **Show Parameter Control**.

6. Create the following calculated fields:

Name	Code
Total Hits	`[David]+[Matthew]`

Case	`CASE [Select Player]`
	`WHEN 1 THEN SUM([Matthew])`
	`WHEN 2 THEN SUM([David])`
	`WHEN 3 THEN SUM([Total Hits])`
	`END`

7. Set the **Marks View** card to **Polygon**.

8. Survey the **Data** pane to ensure that **Point** and **Shape** are both dimensions. The other fields are measures.

9. Place these fields on their respective shelves:

Field	Shelf
X	Columns
Y	Rows
Point	Path
Shape	Detail
Case	Color

10. Right-click on each axis and set the range from 0 to 650:

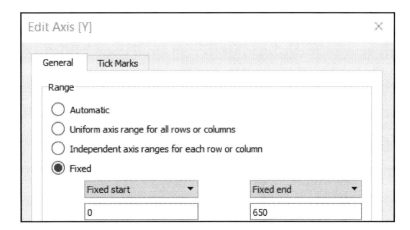

11. Click on the **Color** shelf and select **Edit Colors…**. Adjust the color as desired. Represented here is one possibility:

You likely found completing this exercise in Tableau relatively easy. The challenge is in getting the data right, particularly the polygon points. A useful (and free) tool for generating polygon data can be found at `http://powertoolsfortableau.com/tools/drawing-tool`. This is one of many tools created by InterWorks that are helpful for addressing common Tableau challenges.

You may have noticed that the curved sections of the polygons in this exercise aren't quite perfect. That's simply the nature of working with points on a Cartesian grid in Tableau. Vector graphic applications such as Inkscape and Illustrator have Bézier drawing tools with which you can create a very precise dartboard. It's not possible in Tableau to draw Bézier curves using X and Y coordinates atop a background map. However, if your graphing needs require precisely drawn curves, check out the *Circular and Hive Plot Network Graphing* article by Chris DeMartini at DataBlick for techniques utilizing math that very closely approximates Bézier curves in Tableau.

Summary

We began this chapter by considering how to tweak popular visualization types. Specifically, we fine-tuned a bullet graph, considered a very different approach for using pie charts in mapping, and ended by tweaking a Pareto chart. Next, we turned our attention to custom background images, where we considered how to build a grid using XML to generate an SVG file to expedite generating the data necessary to use with background images. We completed the chapter by building polygons on a background image.

In the next chapter, we will turn our attention to mapping, where we will consider how to extend Tableau's native mapping capabilities without ever leaving the interface, as well as how to extend Tableau's mapping capabilities with other technology.

8
Mapping

When conducting Tableau classes and workshops for people seeing Tableau for the first time, I've found demonstrating mapping to always be a big hit, sometimes literally resulting in murmurs of appreciation and surprise. People have told me on multiple occasions that Tableau's mapping capability was the key feature that caused them to take notice and consider the Tableau offering more seriously. Tableau's out-of-the-box mapping capabilities are quite powerful and flexible. You may be surprised at how much you can accomplish without ever leaving the user interface. But these out-of-the-box capabilities are just the tip of the iceberg. With proper guidance (which I will attempt to provide in this chapter), you can expand beyond the native mapping functionality and explore techniques that will greatly enhance your workbooks' functionality and aesthetics.

I would like to draw attention to the work of four individuals who helped make this chapter possible. Joshua Milligan provided the initial idea of mapping routes in Australia and then worked with me to extend the exercise to include distances via the *Great Circle Distance Formula – Allan Walker* and *Around the World in 80 Clicks –Craig Bloodworth* presentations at the 2014 Tableau conference provided excellent insight into the TMS file. Lastly, Richard Leeke's map utility tools provide free and relatively painless ways to extend Tableau's mapping capabilities. His **shapetotab** tool is utilized in this chapter to create custom polygons for Tableau.

In this chapter we will discuss the following topics:

- Extending Tableau mapping capabilities without leaving Tableau
- Extending Tableau mapping with other technology:
    - Connecting to a WMS server
    - Exploring the TMS file
    - Exploring Mapbox
    - Accessing different maps via a dashboard
    - Creating custom polygons

Extending Tableau mapping capabilities without leaving Tableau

In everyday life, a map can be helpful for understanding the world around us. For instance, maps are often used on websites, television, or in printed media to present demographic information. In such instances, the mapping requirement is static since the immediate goal does not require movement. Often, however, a map is needed to navigate from point A to point B. This kind of mapping requirement is more complicated because it encompasses static needs (what restaurant is nearby?) but must also deliver additional information such as routes and distances (how can I get to that restaurant?). These dynamic mapping needs assume that movement is required to fulfil a demand. Similarly, some businesses only have what might be referred to as static mapping requirements. For example, a retail chain might create a visualization that includes a map to better understand sales performance in a given region. In such cases, movement between locations is not a direct need. Many businesses, however, need to understand routes and mileages, that is, how to get from point A to point B and the distances involved. These dynamic mapping requirements can vary greatly, but most such needs share at least two things in common, namely, routes and distances.

Exercise – displaying routes and calculating distances

In this exercise, we will consider flight routes and associated distances in Australia. Specifically, we will cover how to extract longitude and latitude numbers from Tableau and use that information in conjunction with trigonometry to calculate mileage between various points. Along the way, we will utilize data blending, table calculations, mapping, and LOD calculations in a robust exercise that touches on many advanced features:

1. Navigate to `https://public.tableau.com/profile/david.baldwin#!/` to locate and download the workbook associated with this chapter.
2. Open the workbook and navigate to the worksheet entitled `Map`.
3. Select the **Transit Data** data source in the **Data** pane and place **City** on the **Detail** shelf. Note that the city **Melbourne** in **Florida** are the only city that is displayed:

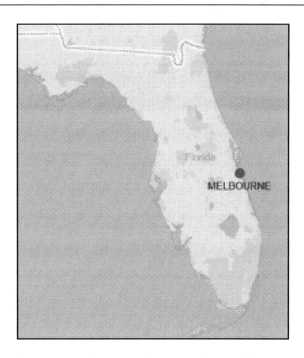

 Caveat: If you are in the United States, then Melbourne, Florida will be displayed. If you are in another country, you may get different results.

4. Create a calculated field with the following information:

Name	Code
Australia	`'Australia'`

5. In the **Data** pane right-click on **Australia** and select **Geographic Role** | **Country/Region**.

6. Place **Australia** on the **Detail** shelf. Note that **Australia** is now displayed on the map:

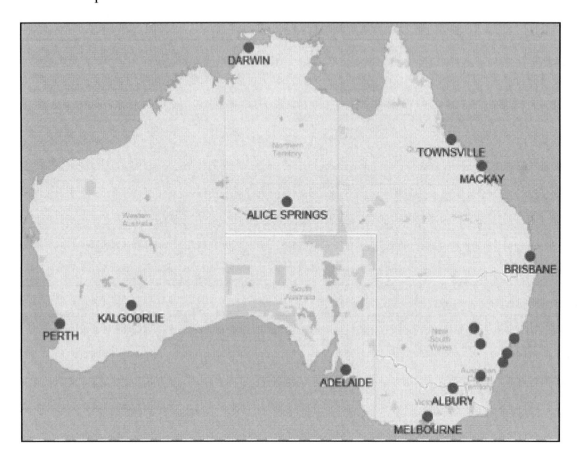

7. Navigate to the worksheet entitled `Miles` and place these fields on their respective shelves:

Field	Shelf
Trip ID	Rows
City	Rows
Latitude (generated)	Text
Longitude (generated)	Text
Australia	Detail

8. Your screen should like the image displayed previously. Note that the crosstab is rather cluttered. Ideally, **Latitude** and **Longitude** should be displayed in separate columns. Unfortunately, we can't do this with generated **Latitude** and **Longitude** because, although they are listed on the **Measures** portion of the **Data** pane, Tableau doesn't treat them as measures. In order to complete the exercise, we will need to be able to access the **Latitude** and **Longitude** coordinates from a separate data source. To do this, we will extract the coordinates and create a data blend.

9. Click on the **Map** worksheet tab.

10. Right-click on the visualization and select **View Data**:

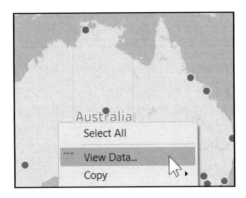

11. Copy all the data in the resulting dialog box:

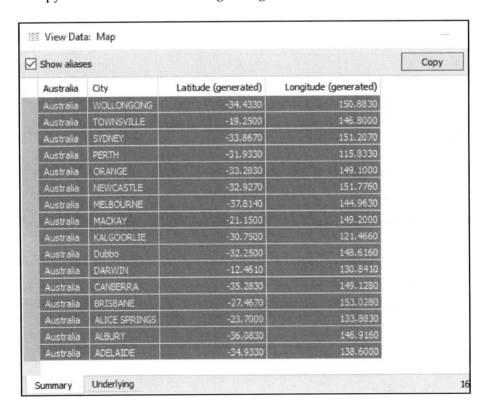

12. Close the dialog box and press *Ctrl + V* to create a new dataset in Tableau.

13. Rename the resulting dataset **Lat Long.** Also name the worksheet **Lat Long**:

14. In the **Lat Long** worksheet, rename **Latitude (generated)** and **Longitude (generated)** to **Lat** and **Long**.

15. Return to the `Miles` worksheet and within the **Transit Data** data source, create these calculated fields:

Name	Code
Lat	AVG([Lat Long].[Lat])
Long	AVG([Lat Long].[Long])

16. Remove **Latitude (generated)** and **Longitude (generated)** from the **Marks View** card.

17. Place **Measure Names** on the **Columns** shelf and **Measure Values** on the **Text/Label** shelf. Now we have the ability to treat **Latitude** and **Longitude** as true measures.

18. Remove all measures from the **Measure Values** shelf except **Lat** and **Long**.

19. Create the following calculated fields:

Name	Code
Lookup Lat	Lookup(Lat,-1)
Lookup Long	Lookup(Long,-1)

20. Place the two newly created calculated fields on the **Measure Values** shelf:

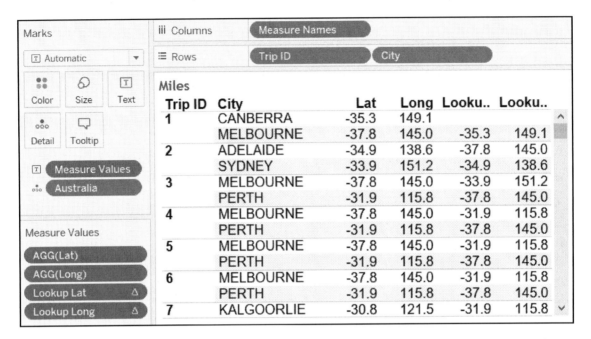

21. Create a calculated field named **Great Circle Distance Formula** with the following code:

```
3959 * ACOS
(
  SIN(RADIANS([Lat])) * SIN(RADIANS([Lookup Lat])) +
  COS(RADIANS([Lat])) * COS(RADIANS([Lookup Lat])) *
  COS(RADIANS([Lookup Long]) - RADIANS([Long]))
)
```

 For kilometers, change 3959 to 6378.

22. Place the newly created calculated field on the **Measure Values** shelf.

23. Change the calculation so that it computes using **City**:

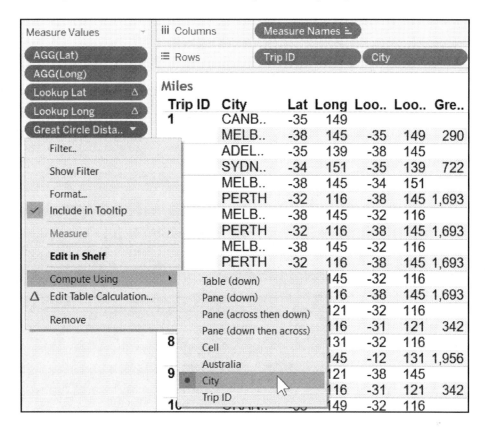

24. Adjust the following calculations accordingly:

Name	Code
Lookup Lat	IFNULL(LOOKUP(Lat,-1), LOOKUP(Lat,1))
Lookup Long	IFNULL(LOOKUP(Long,-1), LOOKUP(Long,1))

25. Select the Map worksheet and set the **Marks View** card to **Line**.
26. Place **Trip ID** on the **Detail** Shelf.

27. Drag **City** to the bottom of the **Marks View** card:

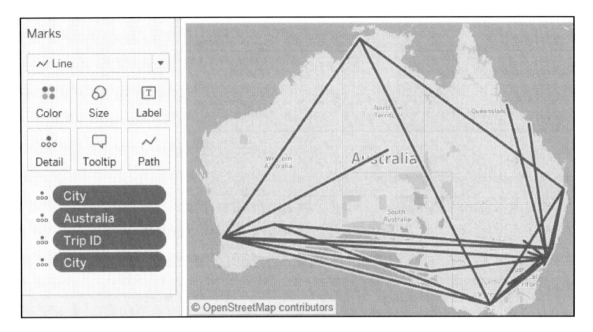

28. Place **Great Circle Distance formula** on the **Tooltip** shelf.

29. Set **Great Circle Distance formula** to **Compute Using City**.

30. Create the following calculated fields:

Name	Code
Source City	`{ FIXED [Trip ID]:MIN(IF [Dest/Orig]='Source' THEN City END)}`
Destination City	`{ FIXED [Trip ID]:MIN(IF [Dest/Orig]='Destination' THEN City END)}`

31. Use the newly created calculated fields to format as desired. In particular, notice in the following screenshot that **Source City** is on the **Color** shelf and **Destination City** is on the **Tooltip** shelf:

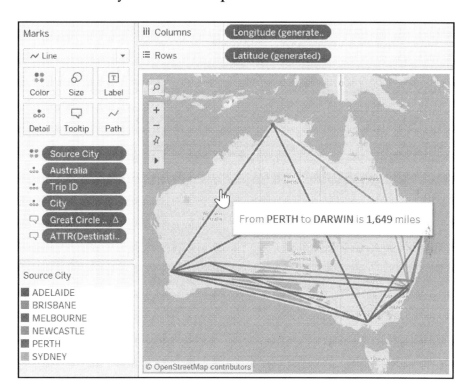

Extending Tableau mapping with other technology

Next, we will consider how to extend Tableau's mapping capabilities with other tools. Tableau developers were careful to create a mapping interface that is readily extensible. Some areas of this extensibility, such as connecting to a WMS server, are available directly from the interface. Other areas require delving into the rarely explored TMS file. And still others require the author to provide latitude and longitude points – perhaps millions of points to create complicated polygons on a map or background image. We will explore each of these following options.

Exercise – connecting to a WMS server

The easiest way to bring a custom map into Tableau is directly from the desktop. The requirement is simply a properly formatted URL pointing to a **Web Mapping Service (WMS)** server. A good place to find a list of such URLs is `http://directory.spatineo.com`, which provides information for about 45,000 mapping services at the time of writing.

The following exercise was inspired by *Jeffrey A. Shaffer's* article at `http://www.dataplusscience.com`, *Building weather radar in Tableau in under 1 minute*:

1. Open the workbook associated with this chapter and navigate to the worksheet entitled `WMS Server via Desktop`.
2. Select the `Superstore` data source.
3. Place **State** on the **Detail** shelf.
4. Copy the following URL: `http://nowcoast.noaa.gov/arcgis/services/nowcoast/radar_meteo_imagery_nexrad_time/MapServer/WMSServer?`
5. In Tableau, navigate to **Map | Background Maps | Map Services**.
6. Select **Add**, choose **WMS Servers**, and paste the URL:

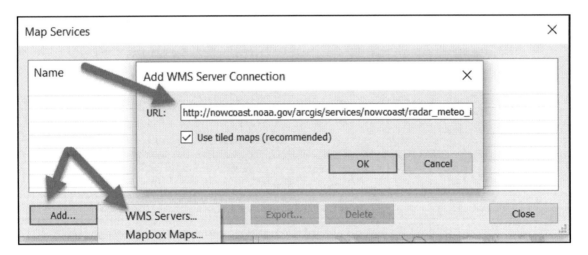

7. In the **Marks View** card, set the view type to **Filled Map**.

8. Click on the **Color** shelf to turn on borders and set the transparency to 0%:

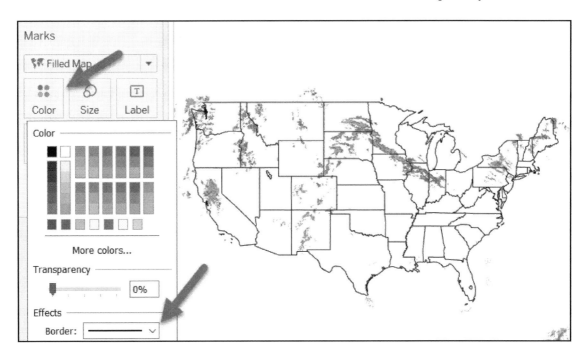

Tableau Desktop can connect to any WMS server that supports the WMS 1.0.0, 1.1.0, or 1.1.1 standard. If you need to connect to a map server using a different protocol such as a tile server, you can do so by creating a TMS file. We'll take a look at the structure of a TMS file in the next section.

A note on tiling and zooming before proceeding. Since high-resolution maps may be many gigabytes, it's impractical to require downloading an entire map in order to zoom in on one small area. Tiles solve for this problem by enabling multiple zoom levels. A zoom level of 0 results in a single tile (often a 256 pixel by 256 pixel PNG image) that displays the entire map. As the zoom levels increase, the number of map tiles increase exponentially. Also, a proportionally smaller section of the map is displayed; that is, as the zoom level increases, the area of the entire map that displays decreases and the total number of tiles required to fill the display remains constant. This helps control the amount of data downloaded at any given time.

Exploring the TMS file

By default, TMS files are located on the C drive in `Documents\My Tableau Repository\Mapsources`. After installing Tableau Desktop, this directory is blank; however, the directory may be populated with any number of TMS files. Note that in order for a TMS file to become available after placing it in the `Mapsources` directory, Tableau must be restarted.

A good way to explore the various TMS options is via the `Tableau.tms` file located in the `Program Files` directory. The default location for the Tableau.tms file is `C:\Program Files\Tableau\Tableau x.x\Mapsources`.

The TMS file structure

The following TMS example is an abbreviated version of the `Tableau.tms` file:

```
<?xml version = '1.0' encoding = 'utf-8'?>
<mapsource inline ='true' version = '8.2'>
<connection class = 'OpenStreetMap' max-scale-level = '16.0' max-stretch =
'1.0' min-shrink = '1.0' port = '80' server = ' maps.tableausoftware.com'
url-format = ' tile/d/{L}/ol/{Z}/{X}/{Y}{D}.png?apikey = {K}&amp;size={P}'
  Username = 'tabmapbeta'/>
  <layers>
<layer display-name = 'Base' name = 'base' show-ui = 'true'            type
= 'features' request-string = '/' />
<layer current-id='...' display-  name = 'Population' group = 'US
Population' name = '...' prepend- date = 'true' show-ui = 'true' type =
'data'/>
  </layers>
  <map-styles>
     <map-style display-name = 'Light' name = '...'>
     <map-layer-style name = '...' request-string = '...'/>
     </map-style>
  <map-styles>
  <mapsource-defaults version='8.2'>
     <style>
       <style-rule element='map-layer'>
<format attr='enabled' id='tab_coastline' value='false' />
       </style-rule>
       <style-rule element='map'>
         <format attr='washout' value='0.0' />
       </style-rule>
     </style>
  </mapsource-defaults>
```

Let's consider various features of the preceding TMS file:

`inline`: This required attribute must include `True` or `False`. Typically, `True` is desirable since this will embed the TMS information in the TWB file. Thus, the map referenced by the TMS file will continue to work when uploaded to Tableau Server. Selecting `False` will cause the TMS information to not be included with the TWB file, which will then require the author to upload a separate TMS file to Tableau Server in order for the map to display.

`class`: This required attribute communicates the server type. The term `OpenStreetMap` seen in the preceding code is simply communicating that a tile server is being accessed. Another term is **OGC-WMS**, which communicates that the server under consideration is using the **Open Geospatial Consortium** WMS standard.

`max-scale-level`: This optional attribute can be used to set the maximum zoom allowable. Note that the Tableau.tms file utilizes the maps.tableausoftware.com server, which supports a maximum scale level of 16. Other map servers support different levels of magnification that may exceed 16 levels.

`max-stretch/shrink`: These optional attributes allow Tableau to stretch or shrink map tiles. If the values are set to 1.0, no stretching or shrinking occurs; instead, each tile is sized exactly as dictated by the zoom level.

`port`: This optional attribute communicates which port to access. Port 80 is the typical port for HTTP servers. If omitted, port 80 is assumed.

`server`: This required attribute must include the URL to the map server.

`url-format`: This optional attribute includes additional URL fragments that the map server may require. `{Z}`,`{X}`, and `{Y}` are of particular interest. These URL fragments, also known as `Slippy Map Tilenames`, direct Tableau to the appropriate directories:

- {Z} indicates the zoom level. Zoom levels range from 0 – 20+. Tableau documentation states that the maximum zoom level is 16 but, as noted earlier, this limit can be surpassed if the map server supports a higher zoom level.
- {X} indicates a column of map tiles
- {Y} indicates a specific map tile

`layers`: This required tag must include layer display-name and may include layer `current-id` attribute.

The `layer display-name` attribute controls what is displayed in Tableau within **Map |
Map Layers**. Note that if the `show-ui` tag is set to `true` (as shown in the preceding code), at
least one of the map layers must be selected before the map will be displayed.

The `layer current-id` attribute enables access to data layers provided by the map server
within the **Map Layers** window:

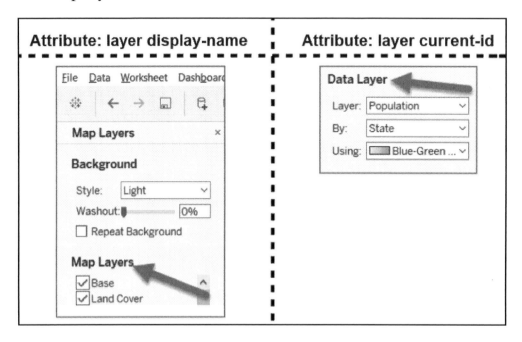

`map-styles`: This optional tag determines the options in Tableau within **Map |
Map Layers | Background**.

`mapsource-defaults`: This optional tag determines default values for various attributes, such as which Map Layers are displayed and washout. Washout can have a value ranging from 0 – 1, with 1 equal to 100%:

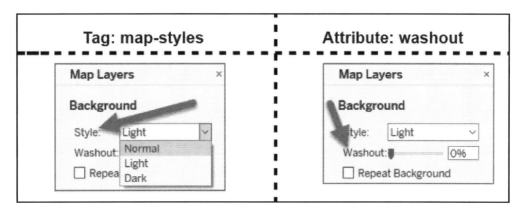

Accessing popular map servers

A TMS file may point to any one of numerous publically available map servers, commercial map servers, or an in-house map server. Setting up a map server in-house is, of course, beyond the scope of this book; however, it's important to note that this can be done if security needs dictate. In this section, we will confine ourselves to discussing three mapping services you may wish to consider for your mapping needs: ArcGIS, Stamen, and Mapbox.

ArcGIS

ArcGIS is a **Geographic Information System** (**GIS**). As the name suggests, a GIS is intended for working with geographic information; however, ArcGIS also supports other types of map, such as street maps. Although the ArcGIS infrastructure includes various commercial packages, the platform enables the creation of maps that can be accessed without charge. As a result, many ArcGIS maps are freely available for Tableau.

You can access several ArcGIS maps via `http://www.arcgis.com/home/gallery.html`. Once you've constructed a basic TMS file, you can access many of the maps provided in the ArcGIS gallery simply by making a small adjustment to the `url-format` attribute, as shown here:

```
url-format: /ArcGIS/rest/services/{map name
here}/MapServer/tile/{Z}/{Y}/{X}
```

Here's the basic information needed to create a TMS file that points to the ArcGIS World Street Map:

- **Server:** `http://services.arcgisonline.com/arcgis/rest/services`
- `url-format:`
  `ArcGIS/rest/services/World_Street_Map/MapServer/tile/{Z}/{Y}/{X}`
  `}`

Can you create a TMS file using this basic information? You should be able to do so by referencing the preceding TMS File Structure section. Regardless, the code for a barebones TMS file is provided for ArcGIS World Street Map in the dashboarding exercise presented later in this chapter.

Stamen

Stamen is a design firm that works on a broad variety of projects. As stated on their website, `http://stamen.com/`, *Stamen's client work and the research projects we pursue present us with as broad a variety of design challenges as we could hope for: from providing live views of social networks as they happen to covering live bicycle races over the internet, from building collaborative applications for car designers to describing the lifetime output of an all-but-uncategorizable artist/architect.*

Stamen has various maps available at `http://maps.stamen.com`. The toner map is particular good for Tableau. Since it's strictly black and white, you can create visualizations on top of the toner map using a wide variety of color schemes without clashing with the map colors.

Here's the basic information needed for creating a TMS file that points to the Stamen Toner map:

- **Server:** `http://a.tile.stamen.com`
- **URL Format:** `/toner/{Z}/{X}/{Y}.png`

Can you create a TMS file using this basic information? You should be able to do so by referencing the TMS file structure section. Regardless, the code for a barebones TMS file is provided for Stamen Toner in the dashboarding exercise presented later in this chapter.

Exploring Mapbox

Mapbox provides a mapping service with an accompanying web application that enables users to customize maps. This customizability encompasses fonts, colors, background images, and more. Mapbox provides basic services free of charge but, of course, more maps and greater bandwidth needs will require an upgrade with an accompanying fee. The following exercises show you how to connect to Mapbox but do not include instructions for customizing maps through Mapbox. Be sure to visit Mapbox.com to learn how to build your own custom maps.

Exercise – Mapbox classic

For this exercise we will use Mapbox classic to quickly choose between the various out-of-the-box mapping capabilities that Mapbox offers:

1. Navigate to `https://www.mapbox.com/` and create an account.
2. After completing sign up and logging into Mapbox, click on the **Studio** link located at the top of the page.
3. On the right side of the page, copy the **Access Token**:

4. In the workbook associated with this chapter, navigate to the `MapBox Classic` worksheet.
5. Select **Map | Background Maps | Map Services** to bring up the **Map Services** dialog box.

6. Click **Add** and choose **Mapbox Maps**.
7. Click on **Classic**.
8. Name the map.
9. Paste in the **API access token**.
10. Select a **Mapbox preset style**:

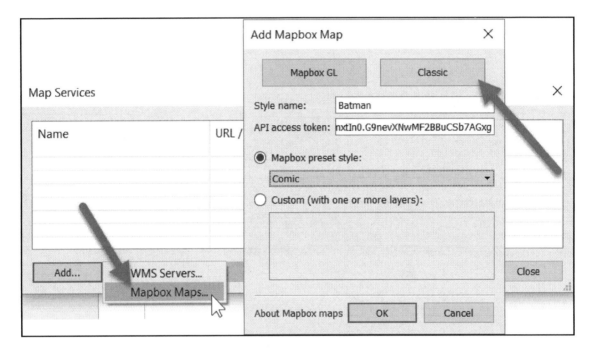

11. After closing the preceding dialog boxes, select the **Superstore** data source and double-click on **State** to see the **Mapbox Maps**.

Exercise – Mapbox GL

Mapbox GL is an upgrade from Mapbox Classic. It enables map creation via the web and renders more attractive maps. Note that this exercise assumes that you have already created a Mapbox account as outlined in the preceding exercise:

1. Log in to https://www.mapbox.com/ and click on the Studio link located at the top of the page.

2. Scroll to the bottom of the page, and in the **Develop** section, select **Mapbox Satellite Streets**:

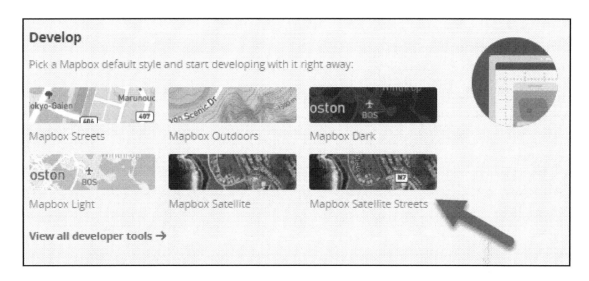

3. On the resulting web page, under **Use style in GIS apps**, select Tableau and click the **Copy** icon:

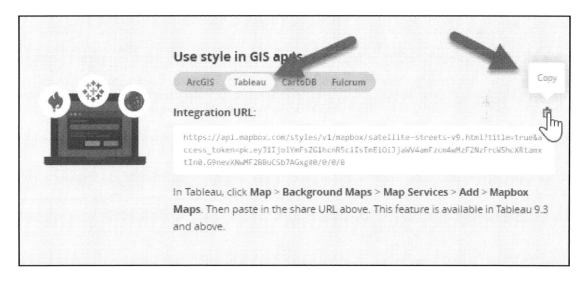

4. In the workbook associated with this chapter, navigate to the `MapBox GL` worksheet.

5. Select **Map** | **Background Maps** | **Map Services** to bring up the **Map Services** dialog box.

6. Click **Add** and choose **Mapbox Maps**.

7. Click on **Mapbox GL**.

8. Name the map.

9. Paste in the URL that was copied from Mapbox.

10. Tableau will fill out the remaining portion of the dialog box:

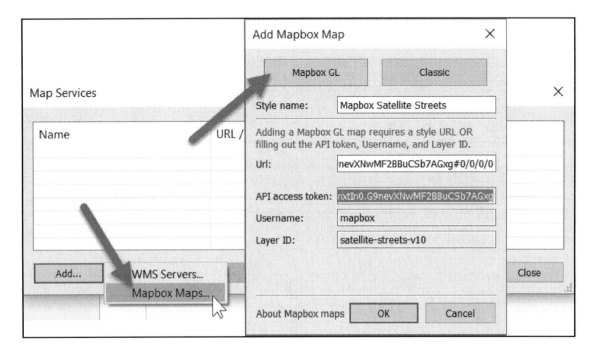

11. After closing the preceding dialog boxes, select the **Superstore** data source and double-click on **State** to see the Mapbox map.

Accessing different maps via a dashboard

Here, we will create a dashboard that allows an end user to choose between the various maps discussed previously. The exercise assumes the completion of exercises in the previous section, *Extending Tableau mapping with other technology*.

Exercise – swapping maps

The technique used for this exercise is known as *Sheet Swapping*. The necessary steps, of course, are recorded here; however, a deeper dive into this technique is presented in Chapter 10, *Visualization Best Practices and Dashboard Design*:

1. The Mapbox Classic and Mapbox GL worksheets are assumed to have been completed via the Mapbox-centric exercises presented earlier in this chapter.

2. Access the TMS files for ArcGIS World Street Map and Stamen Toner that you created earlier in this chapter. If you did not create the TMS files, you can use the XML presented here. Simply copy this code into a text editor for both files and then save those files with a TMS extension. Note that this code is very abbreviated but functional. You may wish to add options as we discussed earlier in this chapter.

If you choose to copy the following code, be aware that Tableau requires straight quotes. Curly or slanted quotes will probably not work.

ArcGIS World Street Map code for TMS file	```<?xml version="1.0" encoding="utf-8"?>```
	 ```<mapsource inline="true" version="8.2">```
	 ``` <connection class="OpenStreetMap" server='http://services.arcgisonline.com'```
	 ```url-format='/ArcGIS/rest/services/World_Street_Map/MapServer/tile/{Z}/{Y}/{X}'/>```
	 ``` <layers>```
	 ``` <layer display-name="World_Street_Map" name="World_Street_Map" show-```
	 ```ui="false" type="features" />```
	 ``` </layers>```
	 ```</mapsource>```

Stamen Toner code for TMS file	```<?xml version="1.0" encoding="utf-8"?>```
	 ```<mapsource inline="true" version="8.2">```
	 ``` <connection class="OpenStreetMap" server='http://a.tile.stamen.com' url-```
	 ```format='/toner/{Z}/{X}/{Y}.png'/>```
	 ``` <layers>```
	 ``` <layer display-name="toner" name="toner" show-ui="false" type="features"```
	 ```/>```
	 ``` </layers>```
	 ```</mapsource>```

3. Place the newly created TMS files in My Tableau Repository\Mapsources and then restart Tableau.

4. Open the workbook associated with this chapter. Select the ArcGIS worksheet.

5. Select the Superstore data source and place **State** on the **Detail** shelf.
6. Navigate to **Map | Background Maps** and select the ArcGIS map.
7. Navigate to the `Stamen Toner` worksheet and repeat the preceding two steps except, of course, choosing the `StamenToner` map.
8. Create a parameter for **ArcGIS**, **StamenToner**, **Mapbox Classic**, and **Mapbox GL**, as shown in the following screenshot:

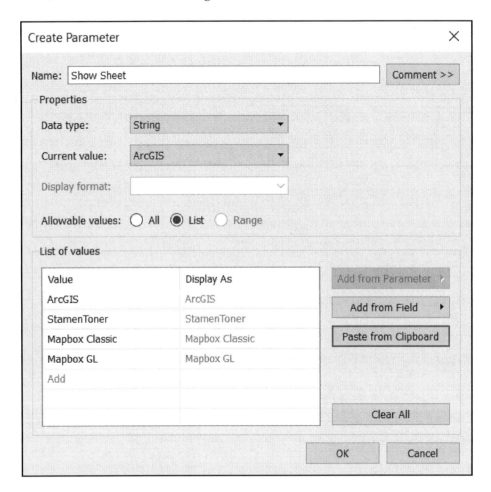

9. In the **Superstore** data source, create a calculated field named **Show Sheet Filter** with the code `[Show Sheet]`.

10. Select the `ArcGIS` worksheet.

11. Drag the **Show Sheet Filter** calculated field to the **Filters** shelf and select **ArcGIS** in the resulting dialog box.

12. Right-click on the parameter in the **Data** pane and select **Show Parameter Control**.

13. Interact with the **Show Sheet** parameter on the view and select **StamenToner**. Notice that the view goes blank:

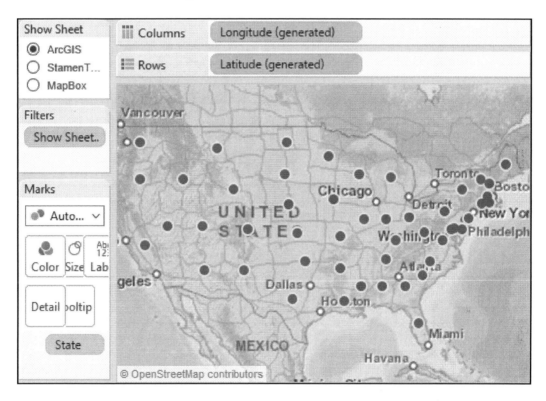

14. On the `Mapbox Classic` worksheet, show the parameter control.

15. On the **Show Sheet** parameter, select **Mapbox Classic**.

16. Drag the **Show Sheet Filter** calculated field to the **Filters** shelf and select **Mapbox GL**.

17. Repeat the last three steps for the **StamenToner** and **Mapbox GL** worksheets. Of course, be sure to set the parameter and filter to use the appropriate names for both worksheets.
18. Create a dashboard.
19. Place a horizontal container on the dashboard.
20. Drag the `ArcGIS` worksheet into the horizontal container.
21. Note that the worksheet is not displayed.
22. If the **Show Sheet** parameter is not displayed, click on the drop-down menu associated with the worksheet and choose **Show Sheet**:

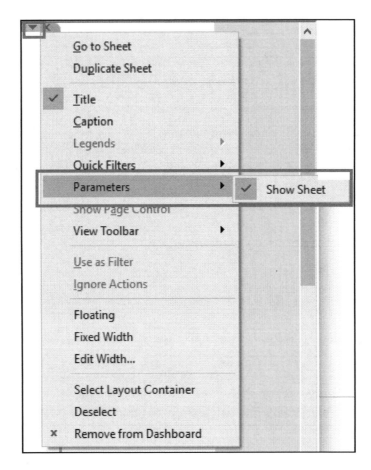

23. In the parameter drop-down menu, choose **ArcGIS**. The ArcGIS worksheet should display in the dashboard.

24. In the **Show Sheet** parameter, select **StamenToner**. Note that the dashboard goes blank.
25. Drag **StamenToner** onto the dashboard following ArcGIS. The **StamenToner** worksheet is now displayed.
26. In the **Show Sheet** parameter, select **Mapbox Classic**. The dashboard displays nothing.
27. Drag **Mapbox Classic** onto the dashboard following **StamenToner**. The **Mapbox Classic** worksheet now displays.
28. In the **Show Sheet** parameter, select **Mapbox GL**. The dashboard displays nothing.
29. Drag **Mapbox GL** onto the dashboard following **Mapbox Classic**. The **Mapbox GL** worksheet is now displayed.
30. Right-click on each of the worksheet titles and select **Hide Title**.

Creating custom polygons

Geographic areas for which Tableau natively provides polygons include country, state/province, county, and postcode/ZIP code. This means, for example, that a filled map can easily be created for the countries of the world. Simply copy a list of the world's countries and paste that list into Tableau. Next, set the **View Type** in Tableau to **Filled Map** and place the **Country** list on the **Detail** shelf. Tableau will automatically draw polygons for each of those countries.

There are other geo types for which Tableau will not automatically provide polygons. These include telephone area code and city. For these geo types, Tableau will draw a symbol map but not a filled map. Furthermore, specialty mapping needs may arise that require polygons to be drawn for areas that are not typically included on maps. For example, an organization may define sales regions that don't follow usual map boundaries.

Lastly, mapping needs may arise for custom images. A Tableau author may import an image of a basketball court or football pitch into Tableau and draw polygons to represent particular parts of the playing area.

To create a filled map for each of the previous examples for which Tableau does not natively provide polygons, custom polygons must be created. In this section, we will start with the basics by drawing a simple square around the mythical **Republic of Null Island** located at the intersection of the prime meridian and the equator. Next, we will progress to a more robust example that requires drawing polygons for every city in Texas.

Exercise – drawing a square around Null Island

There is an option in Tableau that allows an author to **Show Data at Default Position** for unknown locations. Selecting this option will cause Tableau to set latitude and longitude coordinates of 0 (zero) for all unknown locations, thus creating a symbol on the world map 1,600 kilometers off the western coast of Africa. Tableau developers affectionately refer to this area as **The Republic of Null Island** and even created a website dedicated to this mythical isle. In this exercise, we will draw a square around Null Island.

Exercise steps

1. Recreate the following dataset in Excel:

Point	Latitude	Longitude
0	-1	-1
1	-1	1
2	1	1
3	1	-1
4	-1	-1

2. Copy and paste the dataset into Tableau.
3. Clear the sheet by clicking on the **Clear Sheet** icon:

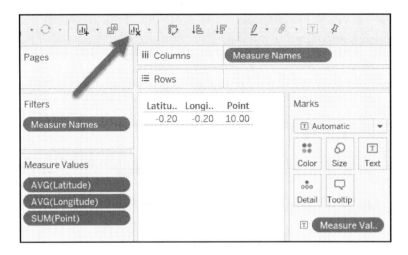

4. Convert **Point** to a dimension. This can be accomplished by either right-clicking on **Point** and selecting **Convert to** dimension or by dragging it to the dimensions portion of the **Data** pane.

5. Select the **StamenToner** map from the previous exercise or a map of your choice.

6. Double-click on **Latitude** and **Longitude**. It doesn't matter which order; Tableau will automatically place **Longitude** on the **Columns** shelf and **Latitude** on the **Rows** shelf.

7. Change the **View Type** to **Line**.

8. Drop **Point** on the **Path** shelf. You should see the following results:

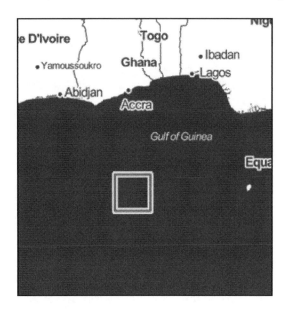

9. Now create another dataset like this:

Point	Latitude	Longitude
0	-1	-1
1	1	1
2	-1	1
3	1	-1
4	-1	-1

10. Follow the previous steps from 2 to 8 and observe the resulting image:

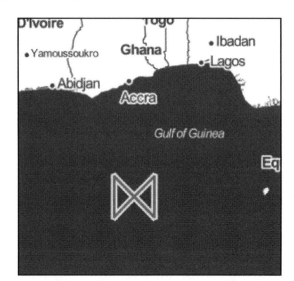

The preceding curious but incorrect image occurred because of incorrect point ordering. As a rule of thumb, when determining point order, select an order that would make sense if you were physically drawing the polygon. If you cannot draw the desired polygon on a sheet of paper using a given point order, neither can Tableau.

Converting shape files for tableau

A GIS file utilizes a standard format to encode geographic data. There are many GIS applications using various flavors of this format. One popular version (or flavor) is the shapefile format developed by Esri. At the time of writing, Tableau cannot directly read a shapefile, but one enterprising Tableau author has created an application to translate shapefile data into the CSV format, which can be accessed by Tableau. Richard Leeke's tool, **shapetotab,** is fairly easy to install and use and is free.

An alternative to **shapetotab** is QGIS, an open source GIS software package. Google *Tableau QGIS* to find step-by-step instructions for using QGIS in Tableau online help.

Exercise – polygons for Texas

As mentioned previously, Tableau does not natively provide polygons for cities. If you create a symbol map for cities and then attempt to change the view type to **Filled Map**, Tableau will display the message **Filled maps are not available for City geographic role**. In this exercise we will use **shapetotab** to overcome this limitation by utilizing **shapetotab** to convert a publically available shapefile into two CSV files, which can then be brought into Tableau to create custom polygons. Note that installation instructions for **shapetotab** are not included here. Those instructions are included with the **shapetotab** download package. Also note that the following instructions are Windows-centric.

Exercise steps

1. Google *Tableau Map Utility Downloads* to locate and download **shapetotab** from the Tableau Community website.
2. Unzip **shapetotab** to a desired directory on your computer.
3. Install and configure **shapetotab** by referencing the PDF file that was included with the download.
4. Navigate to the following URL and download the `City Limits` zip file. It's located in the section entitled `Statewide`: `http://www.txsiteselection.com/gis-data-download.aspx`.
5. After unzipping the `City Limits` file, open a command prompt and use the `cd` command to navigate to the download directory: `cd 'C:\Users\David Baldwin\Downloads\citylimits'`
6. Run the following command:

   ```
   shapetotab citylimits.shp
   ```

7. It may take several seconds for **shapetotab** to complete the operation. Once the operation has completed, you will note two new files, `citylimits_Features.csv` and `citylimits_Points.csv`. Take a moment to open and inspect these two files.
8. If this command does not work, you may not have installed **shapetotab** correctly.
9. In the workbook associated with this chapter, navigate to the `Texas_Cities` worksheet and select **Data** | **New Data Source** | **Text File**.

7. Navigate to the appropriate directory and create a join between **citylimits_Features.csv** and **citylimits_Points.csv**. It does not matter whether you choose an inner or left join:

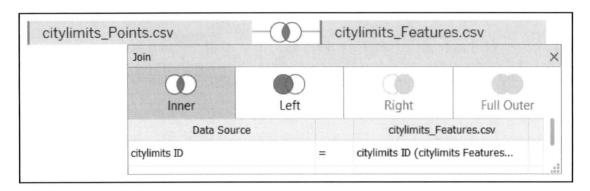

11. If you are outside of the United States, it may be necessary to change the language settings to US English in Excel or in Windows to make the join work.

12. In Tableau navigate to the `Texas_Cities` worksheet and set the **View Type** to **Polygon**.

13. Convert **Point Order** and **Objectid** to dimensions.

14. Place the following fields on their respective shelves:

Field	Shelf
Longitude	Columns
Latitude	Rows
Point Order	Path
Objectid	Detail
Name	Color
Pop 2000	Tootip

15. Lastly, create a quick filter on the field **Pop 2000** in order to explore the population of various cities:

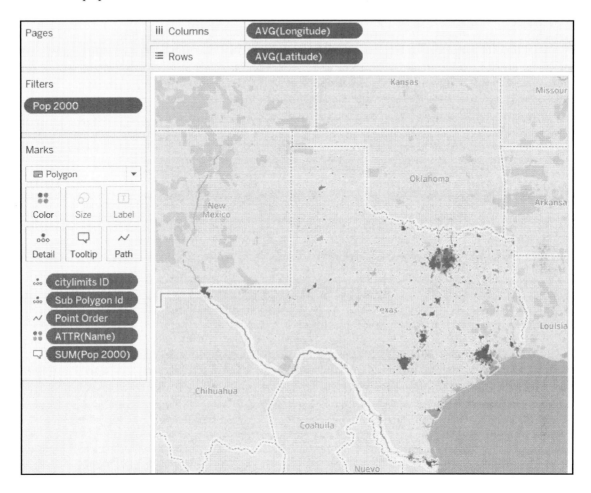

Exercise commentary

The creation of custom polygons doesn't provide much analytic value until you can begin to associate those polygons with measures. In the last step of the preceding exercise, we created a quick filter on the measure **Pop 2000**. This allowed us to begin to explore data analytically. Frequently, the next step would be to blend in a secondary data source. For instance, you could blend in the **Superstore** dataset on city; that is, create a data blend between the field **Name** in the **citylimits** dataset and **City** in the **Superstore** dataset. Once the blend is accomplished, you could visualize sales or profit or some other measure using the polygons. Thus, in this exercise we have overcome the limitation of no natively available city-level polygons in Tableau.

Summary

In this chapter, we explored how to extend Tableau mapping capabilities without leaving the interface by capturing Tableau-generated latitude and longitude data and then feeding that data back into the interface via data blending. Next, we explored various ways to extend Tableau mapping using other technology. We connected to a WMS server, explored the structure of a TMS file and then created our own TMS files and then we explored the Mapbox offering. Lastly, we covered how to draw polygons and also how to translate a shapefile into a `.csv` format usable by Tableau.

In the next chapter, we will explore using Tableau for presentations. Specifically, we will explore how to get the best images out of Tableau, how to effectively and efficiently use Tableau with PowerPoint, and how to use Tableau directly for presentations with no reliance on third-party tools.

9
Tableau for Presentations

I was surprised to discover one week that one of my students was a neonatal pediatric surgeon. This is outside the typical demographic of Tableau aficionados! At the root of the doctor's reasons for attending the class was the need to tell a story. Over her years of practice, she had observed a correlation between the use of certain cardiac medications and future neurodevelopment. But of course, it was not enough to merely personally observe the correlation. The goal of facilitating change in the medical and pharmaceutical communities required hard, demonstrable proof. Someone had introduced the doctor to Tableau, which for her was a *eureka moment*. Here she had found a tool that would allow her to present her findings. Naturally, there was much work to do to gather and structure data for effective reporting, but with such a compelling story with the potential to alter many lives, the good doctor was motivated. I look forward to reading her findings in a future issue of the *New England Journal of Medicine*.

All Tableau authors are, essentially. storytellers. Analyzing data is more than just puzzle solving. It is a search for a story that will make a difference. Topics can range from Airbnb to Zinka and may be pleasantly diverting or life-changing, but they all serve a common need: telling a story. This chapter is dedicated to helping you stock your toolkit of knowledge with ideas and methods for using Tableau to make presentations that engage, delight, and make a difference.

This chapter will explore the following presentation-centric topics:

- Getting the best images out of Tableau
- From Tableau to PowerPoint
- Embedding Tableau in PowerPoint
- Animating Tableau
- Story Points and dashboards for presentations

For the content of this chapter, I'm particularly indebted to *Robert Mundigl* and *Cathy Bridges*. A student introduced me to Robert's work on embedding Tableau in PowerPoint, which influenced the following information on interactive PowerPoint presentations. Cathy Bridges responded to a blog post I made on `http://vizpainter.com/` with clever ideas on automating PowerPoint presentations. Her thoughts influenced the section on automating a weekly PowerPoint presentation.

Getting the best images out of Tableau

In this section, we will review the options for porting an image from Tableau into other applications and discuss the pros and cons of each method. We'll begin by surveying various screenshot applications, and then we will consider the methods available directly in Tableau.

A brief survey of screen capture tools

Perhaps the easiest way to capture an image in Tableau is to use a screen capture tool. Of the screen capture tools available, SnagIt, by TechSmith, may be considered the market leader. Personally, I'm a long-time user and a big fan of SnagIt. Almost all the images in this book were captured using this tool. The default settings of SnagIt allow the user to press the print screen key and then drag a marquee over an area for capture. Other options include capturing the entire screen, capturing specific windows, and even creating short screen capture videos. Once the capture is made, SnagIt opens a feature-rich editor in which the user can create annotations and perform other image editing tasks. A trial download is available at `https://www.techsmith.com/`.

Next, we'll consider other screen capture tools that won't impact your pocketbook:

- **Snipping Tool** is installed by default with Windows and, although a very simple tool with few bells and whistles, is easy to use and effective.

- **Greenshot** is an open source screen capture tool with many features similar to SnagIt. Visit `http://getgreenshot.org/` to download the application and learn more.

- **Microsoft Office OneNote** includes a screen capture feature. If you have OneNote installed with Windows 7 or earlier, simply press *Windows + S* to activate the screen capture. If you are on Windows 8 or 10, press *Windows + N* and then the *S* key for activation.

- **Grab** is a screen capture utility natively available on OS X. Grab is located in the `Utilities` folder under `Applications`.

Tableau's native export capabilities

One of the shortcomings of screen capture tools is that they are limited to raster images. Raster images are often sufficient for documentation or a PowerPoint presentation but are subject to pixilation if enlarged. Vector images, on the other hand, do not pixelate when enlarged and may therefore provide sharper image quality. Natively, Tableau includes both raster and vector export options. These options are discussed in the following section.

The five export types

Tableau can export images in five formats, each of which is described here:

File format	Access	Pros and cons
JPEG	**Worksheet | Export | Image**	JPEG is a raster image format that is good for high-resolution images such as photographs but does not work very well for low-color images such as those typically deployed in Tableau. Export an image from Tableau in the JPEG format and then zoom in close. Note that the white space (especially white space surrounding text) includes stray pixels of various colors. These are known as artifacts or noise. Although these pixels are not visible unless zoomed in, the overall impact on an exported image is that it can look blurry. Thus, there is rarely, if ever, a reason to export to JPEG from Tableau.
PNG	**Worksheet | Export | Image**	Like JPEG images, PNG images are raster. The advantage of the PNG format is that it works well with both high-color images, such as photographs, and low-color images, such as those typically used in Tableau. Export an image from Tableau in PNG format and zoom in to observe that, although pixelation occurs, the white space is comprised of only white. Unlike JPEG images, no artifacts or noise appears. PNG should be considered the format of choice when using a raster image.
BMP	**Worksheet | Export | Image**	BMP is a raster image format that looks quite nice but is uncompressed and can thus result in large image files. Today, the BMP format is considered antiquated and should typically be avoided.

| EMF | **Worksheet \| Export \| Image** | Since the EMF format is vector (as opposed to raster), it will not pixelate. Export an image from Tableau in EMF format and zoom in close to observe. There are drawbacks, however, to using EMF . Some images (especially fonts) will look jagged when used in Microsoft Office. Thus, to effectively use an EMF image, a vector graphic tool such as Adobe Illustrator may be needed. If the intent is to alter an image with a vector graphic tool once it's exported from Tableau, an EMF format may be warranted. However, since the post-Tableau alteration possibilities are much the same for PDF and, as will be discussed later, since PDF files have additional advantages, EMF should not typically be considered. |
| PDF | **File \| Print to PDF** | PDF files handle a wide variety of graphic types, including vector and raster. When files are exported from Tableau using the PDF option, Tableau uses the vector type when possible. Export a worksheet using the PDF option and zoom in using Adobe Reader (or another PDF-centric application) to observe that the image will not pixelate. Adobe Reader handles images differently than Microsoft Office. The jagged results that can be seen when using EMF files in an Office document (as per the previous discussion of the EMF file type) do not occur with Adobe Reader. Furthermore, the **Print to PDF** feature has the added advantage of allowing exportation of the entire workbook to one PDF file. As will be shown later in this chapter, this can be quite useful. |

From Tableau to PowerPoint

PowerPoint is ubiquitous. Some may argue that other presentation tools such as Prezi are superior, but for many organizations (probably the vast majority), PowerPoint remains the software of choice. As such, it's important to integrate Tableau and PowerPoint efficiently and effectively. The following exercises explore various techniques for doing so.

Exercise – create a template

For this first PowerPoint-centric exercise, a template that will be utilized in future exercises is created. It will include common PowerPoint elements such as a header and a footer. The size of the template will be 1200 x 900, which adheres to the 4:3 aspect ratio typically used for PowerPoint presentations. Of course, other sizes may be targeted, but aspect ratio should always be kept in mind:

1. Navigate to `https://public.tableau.com/profile/david.baldwin#!/` to locate and download the workbook associated with this chapter.

2. Create a new worksheet and select the `Superstore` dataset.

3. Create the assets.

4. Create the header asset:
    1. Name the worksheet `Header`.
    2. Place **Sales** on the **Color** shelf.
    3. Click on the **Color** shelf and then on **Edit Colors...**.
    4. In the resulting dialog box, click on the color box located at the right-hand side. In the resulting secondary dialog box that appears, set the HTML hex color value to **#000000**:

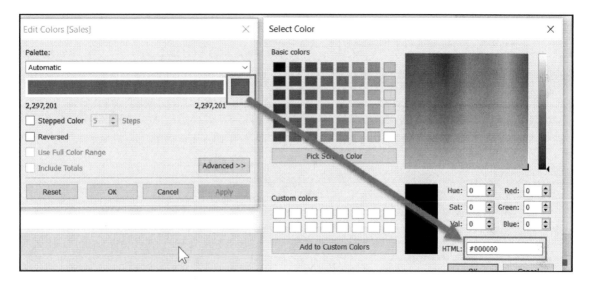

5. Create the first footer asset:
    1. Duplicate the `Header` worksheet and name the duplicate `Footer1`.
    2. Set the hex color value to **#34959e**. If needed, refer to the instructions used to create the `Header` worksheet as a guide.

6. Create the second footer asset:
    1. Duplicate the `Footer1` worksheet and name the duplicate `Footer2`.
    2. Set the hex color value to **#4cdbe8**. If needed, use the instructions used to create the `Header` worksheet as a guide.

7. Create the margins for the template:

    1. Create a new dashboard called `Template`.

    2. Within the **Dashboard** pane, set the size to 1200 x 900. Note that 1200 x 900 is a 4:3 aspect ratio.

    3. Display the dashboard title by going to **Dashboard | Show Title**.

    4. Double-click on the title. In the resulting dialog box, left justify the text if needed.

    5. In the **Dashboard** pane, make sure that **Tiled** is selected.

    6. From the **Dashboard** pane, drag **Blank** from the **Objects** panel and place it on the left-hand side of the dashboard. Be careful to place it so that it stretches from the top to the bottom of the dashboard, as shown in the following screenshot :

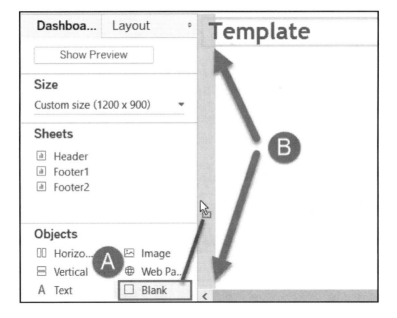

8. Repeat the previous step for the right-hand side and the bottom of the dashboard. When creating the bottom margin, be sure to position the object so that it stretches from the far right to the far left of the dashboard.

9. Size the left and right blank objects to create appropriate margins. This can be accomplished by dragging the inner edge of each blank object (that is, the edges facing the center) as far to the right or left as possible:

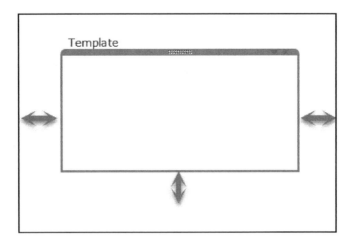

10. Create the bottom margin by clicking on the top edge of the bottom blank object and dragging it toward the title. When completed, the bottom blank object should occupy about one quarter of the vertical space.

11. Deploy the assets:

   1. In the **Objects** portion of the **Dashboard** pane, click on **Floating**.
   2. Drag the `Header`, `Footer1`, and `Footer2` assets onto to the dashboard.
   3. If a **Sales** legend appears, delete it.
   4. Right-click on the title of each asset and select **Hide title**.
   5. In the **Layout** pane, enter the following values for each asset:

		Size					Size						Size		
Header	w	960	h	3	**Footer 1**	w	1212	h	70	**Footer 2**	w	1212	h	11
		Position					Position						Position		
	x	40	y	45		x	-6	y	828		x	-6	y	817

6. Set each asset to **Entire View** by clicking in the toolbar on the fit dropdown next to the word **Standard** and selecting **Entire view**. The result should be a line just under the title stretching across four-fifths of the dashboard and two bars at the bottom stretching across the entire dashboard.

7. Click on the container located underneath the title **Template**.

8. Drag the bottom edge of the container so that it is level with the top edge of **Footer2**.

9. If you have not already done so, download the assets associated with this chapter. A link is provided in the workbook.

10. Drag an **Image** container from the **Objects** portion of the **Dashboard** pane onto the dashboard. When prompted, select the `bw_globe.png` image supplied with this chapter. Note the globe logo that appears.

11. Drag another **Image** container from the **Objects** portion of the **Dashboard** pane onto the dashboard. When prompted, select the `Mastering-Tableau.png` image supplied with this chapter. Note that the text represented by the `PNG` image is white, so it will be necessary to drag it over a colored section of the dashboard in order to see it.

12. Position the containers via the **Layout** pane, as shown in the following table:

		Size					**Size**		
Globe logo	w	68	h	62	**Text logo**	w	252	h	46
		Position					**Position**		
	x	43	y	833		x	910	y	843

Exercise – create two dashboards

This exercise will utilize the template just created to make two dashboards. Basic instructions are provided and the specifics are left to individual preference:

1. Right-click on the tab entitled `Template` created in the previous exercise and select `Duplicate sheet`.

2. Repeat the previous step.

3. Rename the first duplicate sheet `Superstore Loss Leaders`. Rename the second duplicate sheet `Map Loss Leaders`.

4. Populate the `Superstore Loss Leaders` dashboard with these worksheets: `Loss Leaders Regions`, `Loss Leaders Cities`, `Loss Leaders Zip`, and `Filter`. **Arrange as desired.**

5. Populate the `Map Loss Leaders` dashboard with these worksheets: `Map`, `Loss Leaders Cities`, `Loss Leaders Zip`, and `Filter`. **Arrange as desired.**

6. Consider hiding some of the titles for the worksheets. For instance, the title for `Filter` is not necessary, nor is the title for `Map Loss Leaders`.

7. On each dashboard, select the `Filter` worksheet and click on the **Use as Filter** icon.

8. On each dashboard, select both **Bookcases** and **Tables** from the `Filter` worksheet. Note that a worksheet with an associated action is used in place of a quick filter because the light outline used for checkboxes may not successfully make a transition to PowerPoint.

9. Right-click on `Superstore Loss Leaders` and `Map Loss Leaders` respectively and select **Hide all sheets.**

10. Go to **File | Print to PDF.**

11. In the resulting dialog box, select the options shown in the following screenshot:

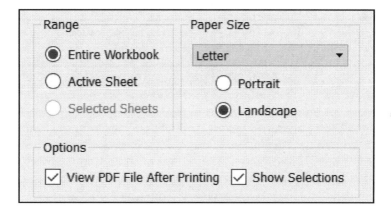

10. Click on **OK** to generate a PDF and save the results.

11. Complete the exercise by saving the Tableau workbook as `PowerPoint Approaches.twbx`.

Before moving to the next step of creating a PowerPoint presentation from the dashboards we've just created, there are a few things to note about the provided worksheets. Consider `Loss Leader Regions`. Note that axis lines and gridlines are missing. Also note that the lines between rows for `Loss Leader Cities` are relatively thick and colored dark gray. Lastly, consider `Loss Leader Zip`. The axis lines denoting 0 are solid instead of the dotted. Tableau uses dotted lines by default.

The reason the various adjustments were made to the default lines used by Tableau is much the same as why quick filters were not used in either dashboard; that is, lightly colored lines may not successfully make a transition to PowerPoint. If it is absolutely essential that dotted and lightly colored lines be displayed in a PowerPoint presentation, a more image-based approach may be necessary. Image-centric options are considered later, but first we'll consider how to generate a PowerPoint presentation that maintains as much editable text as possible.

Exercise – create a PowerPoint presentation

Various tools can be used to generate a PowerPoint presentation from a PDF file. Popular choices include Adobe Acrobat Pro DC and Nitro. These applications are powerful but also relatively expensive. Also note that the results achieved by these tools may not be any better than the results of the free online services suggested in the following section. In other words, be sure to download trial versions before purchasing.

The first of the services to be used, **PDFResizer,** is used to crop PDF files. Natively, Tableau creates a PDF with margins, which does not lead to visually appealing results in PowerPoint. **PDFResizer** removes unwanted margins. The second service, **PDF to PowerPoint**, generates the PowerPoint from the PDF. The advantage of this service is that editable text is maintained in PowerPoint. The disadvantage is that the formatting may not translate as desired. Thus, additional tweaking may be needed in the Tableau workbook or in the generated PowerPoint presentation to achieve the desired results. The third service, **PDF to PNG**, generates PNG files. Since each PNG file represents an entire dashboard, each could be quickly placed on a PowerPoint slide to produce a presentation. The advantage to this approach is that the look of the dashboard is maintained exactly. Unfortunately, editable text is not maintained:

1. Navigate to `https://pdfresizer.com/crop`.
2. Upload the PDF file created in the previous exercise.
3. On the web page, use the cursor to draw a marquee around the image displayed from the PDF. Be sure to include a margin at the top but no margin at the bottom or sides.

4. Crop and download the resulting PDF.

Press *Ctrl* and use the mouse wheel to zoom in and more carefully set the crop.

5. Inspect the downloaded PDF to ensure that the results are as desired. Pay particular attention to the margins and make sure that no white space appears on either side or the bottom.
6. Navigate to `https://www.pdftoppt.com/`.
7. Upload the PDF generated by **PDFResizer** and convert to PowerPoint. An e-mail will be sent a few minutes after conversion.
8. Navigate to `http://pdf2png.com/`.
9. Upload the PDF file generated by **PDFResizer** and convert to PNG. The results are immediately available for download.

Exercise – automating a weekly PowerPoint presentation

The preceding exercises demonstrated two methods for generating a PowerPoint presentation. The methods were identical until the final steps. One approach resulted in a PowerPoint presentation with editable text. The other approach resulted in PNG images, where each image represents a single slide. This exercise will consider a hybrid approach.

Because of the shortcomings of creating a PowerPoint presentation that includes editable text but has inconsistent formatting, or a PowerPoint presentation that is simply a raster image of the dashboard, a hybrid approach that combines the best of both methods may provide more consistency and better versatility.

1. Open the workbook created before, titled `PowerPoint Approaches.twbx`.
2. Navigate to **Map Loss Leaders** and right-click on **Map** in the **Dashboard** pane. Deselect **Hide Sheet**.
3. Navigate to the **Map** worksheet.
4. Remove any pills on the **Filters** shelf.
5. Right-click on **Sub-Category** in the **Data** pane and select **Show filter**.

6. Go to **Worksheet** | **Export** | **Image....**.

7. Click on **OK**; in the resulting dialog box choose to save the image as `Map.png`.

8. Open the PowerPoint presentation generated in the preceding exercise by the **PDF to PowerPoint** website.

9. Navigate to the first slide, titled **Template**.

10. Select the **Insert** ribbon and choose **Pictures**.

11. Navigate to the PNG image you just exported.

12. In the **Insert** dialog box, choose the drop-down menu next to **Insert** and select **Insert and Link** as shown in the following screenshot. Note that this step is important because it will allow pictures to be swapped out easily as will be demonstrated:

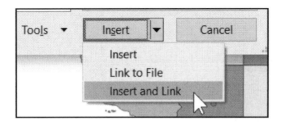

13. Save the PowerPoint presentation as `Auto Update.pptx`.

14. Close PowerPoint.

15. In Tableau, modify the `Map` worksheet by changing the filter.

16. Overwrite the previously exported `Map.png` image via **Worksheet** | **Export** | **Image....**.

17. Open `Auto Update.pptx` and note that the new image of the map is displayed.

Frequently when teaching Tableau classes, I encounter people responsible for providing PowerPoint presentations on a weekly or monthly basis. The presentations include charts and graphs that are updated along with a few annotations but the overall layout remains unchanged. The technique covered in the immediately preceding exercise can make that process much quicker. Although Tableau Desktop only allows the author to update one image at a time, Tableau Server can be configured to export multiple images simultaneously, thus making the process even more efficient.

Embedding Tableau in PowerPoint

It is possible to embed Tableau directly in a PowerPoint presentation. Or, to be more accurate, it's possible to embed a web browser through which an instance of Tableau Server may be accessed. There are various methods for accomplishing this, including the Web Viewer app, a third party add-in called LiveWeb, and VBA code.

The Web Viewer app is available at `https://store.office.com`. Although it works well for Tableau Public, the default Tableau Server settings disallow access via Web View. LiveWeb works well but requires an additional installation. The third method, using VBA, is perhaps the most workable method and will be discussed next.

Exercise – create an interactive PowerPoint presentation

The following steps utilize PowerPoint 2013 on Windows. Other versions of PowerPoint may require a slightly different approach, but any differences should be relatively easy to figure out. Also, the exercise assumes that the Developer toolbar is activated. If the Developer toolbar is not activated for your instance of PowerPoint, a quick search on *developer tab PowerPoint* will provide instructions:

1. Create a new PowerPoint file with a single blank slide.
2. Select the **Developer** tab in the ribbon and click on the **Command Button** icon located in the **Controls** group:

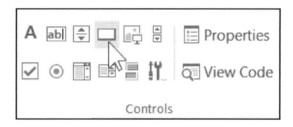

3. In the bottom-left portion of the slide, create a **Command Button** by clicking and dragging.
4. Right-click on the **Command Button** just created and select **Property Sheet**.
5. Within the property sheet, locate **Caption** and set the text to **Launch Workbook**. The command button should now be labeled **Launch Workbook**:

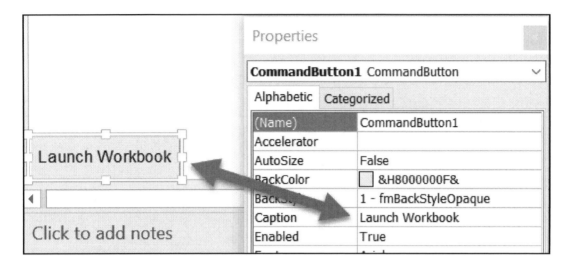

6. Within the **Controls** group in the **Developer** ribbon, select **More Controls**:

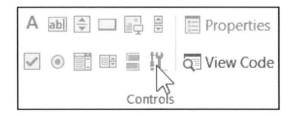

7. Within the resulting dialog box, choose **Microsoft Web Browser** and click on **OK**. If a warning dialog box displays stating that **The ActiveX control cannot be inserted**, continue reading. This problem will be discussed and resolved in the following section:

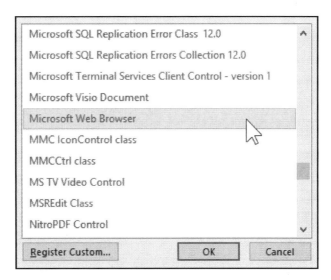

8. Drag a marquee over most of the slide, allowing only enough room for the **Launch Workbook** command button previously created.

9. If you receive the error message displayed in the following screenshot, proceed to steps from 10 to 18. If not, skip to step 19. Note that steps 10 to 18 provide instructions regarding adjusting registry settings. Adjusting registry settings can be tricky business! Proceed at your own risk!

10. Save the file and close PowerPoint.

11. Press the *Windows button* and *R*.

12. Within the **Run** dialog box, type **Regedit**.

13. In the Registry Editor, locate the following ClassID: `8856F961-340A-11D0-A96B-00C04FD705A2`. This ClassID will be located differently based on different installation methods for Office. The following three locations are likely candidates:

    1. `HKEY_LOCAL_MACHINE\SOFTWARE\Microsoft\Office\15.0\Common\COM Compatibility\`

    2. `HKEY_LOCAL_MACHINE\SOFTWARE\Microsoft\Office\15.0\ClickToRun\REGISTRY\MACHINE\Software\Wow6432Node\Microsoft\Office\15.0\Common\COM Compatibility\`

    3. `HKEY_LOCAL_MACHINE\SOFTWARE\Wow6432Node\Microsoft\Office\15.0\Common\COM Compatibility`

14. Click on the ClassID and note the type `REG_DWORD` in the right-hand panel.

15. Right-click on `REG_DWORD` and select **Modify**.

16. Change the textbox labelled **Value data** to 0 and click on **OK**:

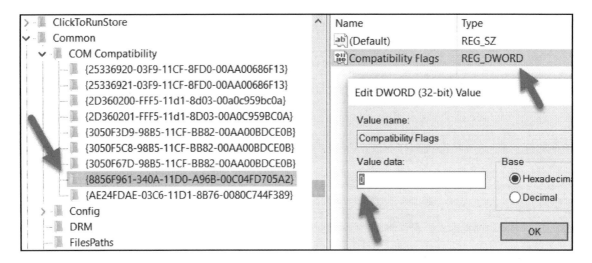

17. Start PowerPoint and open the preceding saved file.

18. Now you should be able to add the **Microsoft Web Browser** control as described previously.

19. Right-click on the **Launch Workbook** command button and select **View Code**.

20. Within the VBA console that appears, delete any existing code and enter the following:

```
Private Sub CommandButton1_Click()
'Begin Comment:  The above line of code gives
instructions regarding what action to take when clicking
 on the command button.
End Comment. WebBrowser1.Navigate
("https://public.tableau.com/profile/david.baldwin#!
/vizhome/1_Starter/SampleWorksheet")
'Begin Comment:  WebBrowser1 is the name of the
Microsoft WebBrowser control that the command button
controls. End Comment.
'Begin Comment:  The URL can be replaced with a
URL of your   choosing.
 End Comment.
'Begin Comment:  '"Navigate" is the Property/Method that
accepts the URL.  End Comment.
End Sub
```

21. Close the VBA console.

22. Press *F5* and click on the **Launch Workbook** command button. An instance of a Tableau workbook should now be displayed in PowerPoint.

Note that the preceding VBA code includes comments. The statements `Begin Comment` and `End Comment` are included for clarity but are not required.

Robert Mundigl explores various techniques for embedding Tableau in PowerPoint similar to the previous example on his blog at `http://www.clearlyandsimply.com/`. Perform a search on the blog for PowerPoint to explore these methods. Robert's creative ideas include a technique for accessing multiple workbooks on a single PowerPoint slide and a technique for embedding the Tableau Desktop authoring environment in PowerPoint for on-the-fly authoring without leaving the presentation interface.

Animating Tableau

Including animation in a presentation can be very effective for engaging the audience. *Hans Rosling* accomplishes this admirably with his popular YouTube video *200 Countries, 200 Years, 4 Minutes*. In this video, Rosling uses data visualization to track wealth and life expectancy over time. His combination of data visualization with insightful commentary and a passion for his message makes Rosling's video a must-see for anyone interested in making appealing presentations using data.

Animation is easy to implement in Tableau but has a curious shortcoming. It is available via Tableau Reader but not Tableau Server. A worksheet with animation that is uploaded to Tableau Server will provide the end user with an option to click through each frame of the animation or access any given frame via a dropdown, but there is no option to play from beginning to end. With HTML5, a play option would probably not be difficult for Tableau developers to implement. So why hasn't this been done? The following answer is speculative but perhaps defensible.

Animation is great for presentations but not well suited for analysis. To put it another way, an animation can certainly make for engaging communication but does not work well for deeper dives into the data. Tableau Server is more geared toward analysis than making presentations in group settings. This bent toward analysis can be seen in the fact that Tableau Server allows direct viewing and exportation of underlying data. Note that Tableau Reader does not offer this capability. Also, Tableau Server can connect, of course, to external data sources, whereas Tableau Reader is limited to self-contained `.twbx` files with no external connections. In a presentation setting, this is actually an advantage for Tableau Reader since relying on an Internet connection when speaking to groups adds an extra element of risk. Therefore, Tableau Reader is more geared toward presentation than analysis and is thus better suited for animation than Tableau Server.

Exercise – creating an animation with Tableau

The following exercise tracks ACT testing scores from 1991 to 2015. Complete the exercise to learn how to create an animation in Tableau and also discover if standardized testing results in the United States have improved over time:

1. Open the workbook associated with this chapter and navigate to the worksheet entitled `ACT 1991 – 2015`.
2. Select the **ACT** data source.

3. Place **Year** on the **Columns** shelf, **Score Value** on the **Rows** shelf, and **Score Type** on the **Color** shelf.
4. Right-click on the **Score Value** axis and select **Edit Axis.**
5. In the resulting dialog box, deselect **Include zero.**
6. Place **Year** on the **Pages** shelf.
7. In the **Current Page** panel that appears on the worksheet, check **Show history** and click on the dropdown. Note that neither the **Show** options nor the **Trails** options are available.
8. In the **Marks View** card, click on the dropdown to change the view type from **Automatic** to **Circle.**
9. Click on the **Show history** dropdown again and note that both the **Show** options and the **Trails** options are now available.
10. Under **Marks to show history for**, select **All.**
11. Under **Show**, select **Both.**
12. Ensure that **Fade** is deselected.
13. Click on the **Format** dropdown under **Trails** and select the dotted line option:

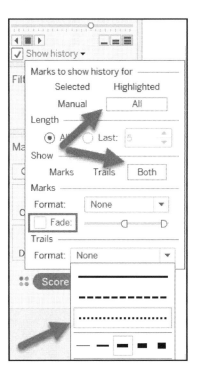

14. Interface with the **Current** page panel to play the animation.

Sometimes the question arises: *How can I create a dashed line in Tableau?* One method is demonstrated in the preceding exercise. By setting the view type to **Circle** and adjusting the **Show history** options, a dashed line was created. If a dashed line without animation is required, simply hide the **Current** page panel (that is, the video control panel).

To briefly extend the theme of creating dashed lines in Tableau, the shortcoming of using the **Pages** shelf is that only one line type is available per visualization. To discover how to create multiple lines with varying dash types, check out `https://boraberan.wordpress.c om/2015/11/22/quick-tip-creating-your-own-dashed-line-styles-in-tableau/`, where Bora Beran has pioneered a method using calculated fields to insert NULLs to achieve differing line effects.

Exercise – using an animation to export many images

There are at least two reasons why it may be necessary to export many images from a timeline. First, it may be analytically advantageous to see separate images for each time snapshot, for example, a separate image for each day of a month. Second, it may be necessary to create an animation outside of Tableau, perhaps in PowerPoint. The next two exercises cover both scenarios:

1. Open the workbook associated with this chapter and navigate to the worksheet entitled `ACT 1991 - 2015`. Note that the following steps assume that the previous exercise was completed.
2. Select **File** | **Page Setup...**

3. At the bottom of the resulting dialog box, under the **Pages** shelf, select **Show all pages**:

4. Select **File | Print to PDF**.
5. In the resulting dialog box, set **Range** to **Active Sheet**. Also set the orientation to **Landscape**.
6. Click on **OK** and save the PDF as `Animation.pdf` to a location of your choice.
7. Navigate to `https://www.pdftoppt.com/`.
8. Upload `Animation.pdf` and convert it to PowerPoint. An e-mail will be sent a few minutes after conversion.
9. Download the file via the link provided in the e-mail.
10. Open the file in PowerPoint.
11. Within PowerPoint, select **File | Save As**.
12. Within the **Save as type** dropdown, select PNG:

13. When prompted, choose to export all slides.
14. Save the PowerPoint presentation. Note that when PowerPoint finishes saving, a dialog box will state that each slide in the presentation has been saved as a separate file.
15. Open and inspect the saved PNG files as desired.

Exercise – using an animation in Tableau to create an animation in PowerPoint

This exercise demonstrates how to port an animation from Tableau to PowerPoint:

1. Access the PowerPoint presentation downloaded from `https://www.pdftoppt.com/` in the previous exercise.
2. In the **View** ribbon, select **Slide Sorter** under the **Presentation Views** group.
3. Select all slides in the PowerPoint presentation except for the last one.
4. On the **Transition** ribbon under the **Timing** group, set to advance the slide after 0.10 seconds:

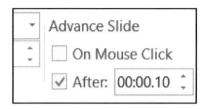

5. Press *F5* to see the animation.

To further improve the animation in PowerPoint, consider these additional steps:

- Upload the PDF to `https://pdfresizer.com/crop` and crop the size as desired. **PDFResizer** was covered earlier in this chapter.
- If the animation is too slow in PowerPoint, it is likely because all text and drawing elements are maintained. For example, the background grid is made up of individual lines. Rendering all text and drawing elements is resource intensive. Consider creating a separate PowerPoint presentation using the PNG images created in the previous exercise. This will lead to a quicker, more smoothly running animation.

Story Points dashboards for presentations

Story points are Tableau's answer to PowerPoint. As such, each shares fundamental similarities. A PowerPoint presentation provides a linear approach to communication. So do story points in Tableau. A PowerPoint presentation provides slides, each of which is a blank canvas that provides a user with infinite possibilities to communicate ideas. A story in Tableau provides story points for the same purpose.

Although there are fundamental similarities, it is important to understand that Tableau story points and PowerPoint presentations often do not fulfill the same role. Each has advantages over the other and thus a list of pros and cons should be considered:

Pros/Cons of PowerPoint	Pros/Cons of Tableau story points
Can be quick and easy to create	Can be more difficult to create
Easily fits different resolutions	Requires forethought regarding resolution size
Difficult to automate based on changes to underlying data	Automatically updates as underlying data changes
Difficult to create a presentation that allows for departure from linear thought	Easily allows nonlinear exploration in the middle of a presentation

So how does one decide between using PowerPoint and Tableau when making presentations? Perhaps this list will help:

When to use PowerPoint	When to use Tableau story points
A presentation where the audience has little opportunity for immediate feedback	A presentation where immediate feedback is likely and exploratory questions may be asked
A one-time presentation comprised of clearly delineated points	A reusable presentation with updates mostly based on changes to underlying data
A presentation where the monitor resolution size may not be known in advance	A presentation where the monitor resolution size is known or assumed

The basics of creating and using story points are straightforward; nor, at the time of writing, is there much beyond the basics. Since the focus of this book is on more advanced Tableau ideas and concepts, those basics will not be considered here. If you need to quickly understand the basics of story points, I recommend watching the 6-minute video titled *Story Points* located at `http://www.tableau.com/learn/tutorials/on-demand/story-points`.

Presentation resources

Using Story Points effectively in Tableau is perhaps more of an artistic consideration than technical. Although this book attempts to consistently consider best practices for data visualization and to encourage attractive and user-friendly worksheets and dashboards, a discussion of effective presentation techniques is out of scope. If you would like to improve your ability to create effective presentations, consider the following resources:

- Presentation Zen:
    - Garr Reynolds is a best-selling author and a repeat speaker at Tableau Conferences. His books and website (`http://www.presentationzen.com/`) provide provocative ideas for effective presentations.

- Tableau Public:
    - Learning by example is invaluable. Fine examples of Story Points can be found on Tableau Public. To learn from one of the most engaging, navigate to `https://public.tableau.com/s/` and search for `KPMG's Global Automotive Executive Survey 2016`.

- Blogs:
    - At the time of writing, the blogosphere seems a bit light on Tableau Story Points, especially from the perspective of making quality presentations. One of the more interesting posts discussing Tableau Story Points in combination with good presentation methodology can be found on Matt Frances' blog `http://wannabedatarockstar.blogspot.in/`. The post is titled *5 Tips For Better Tableau Story Points*.

Exercise – using Tableau dashboards to create a PowerPoint-like presentation

As discussed before, story points are Tableau's answer to PowerPoint. However, there is one aspect of story points that Tableau authors sometimes consider a negative, that is, the ever-present **Navigator bar**:

Some aspects of the Navigator bar can be formatted, such as font, shading, alignment, and sizing; however, it cannot be hidden or deleted. One workaround is to create linked dashboards as shown in the following exercise. Be sure to read Chapter 10, *Visualization Best Practices and Dashboard Design*, to learn other valuable dashboarding tips and tricks.

Note that the following steps assume that previous exercises in this chapter have been completed, specifically the exercises titled Create a Template, Create Two Dashboards, and Creating an Animation with Tableau:

1. Open the workbook associated with this chapter.
2. Duplicate the **Template** dashboard and name the duplicate **Animated Dashboard**.
3. Place ACT 1991 – 2015 on **Animated Dashboard** and format as desired.
4. Create a worksheet named Frt Arrow.
5. Create an ad hoc calculation by double-clicking in the bottom portion of the **Marks View** card. Enter the code Index().
6. In the **Marks View** card dropdown, set the visualization type to **Shape**.
7. Click on the **Shape** shelf and select **More shapes**.
8. In the resulting dialog box, click on the **Select Shape Palette** dropdown and select the palette called **Arrows**.

9. Choose the circular black front arrow:

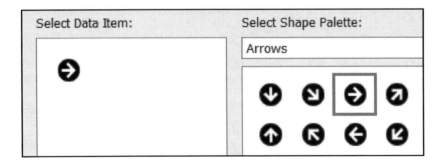

10. Set the fit of the worksheet to **Entire View**.

11. Click on the **Size** shelf to adjust the size of the arrow so that it uses the entire view. Be sure not to make the sizing so large that clipping occurs.

12. Select **Format | Borders**.

13. Within the **Format Borders** window, set **Row Divider** and **Column Divider** to **None**. This will ensure that no borders display around the arrows when they are placed on the dashboard:

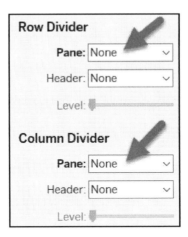

14. Select **Format | Shading**.

15. Within the **Format Shading** window, under **Default**, click on the dropdown for **Worksheet** and select **More colors...**:

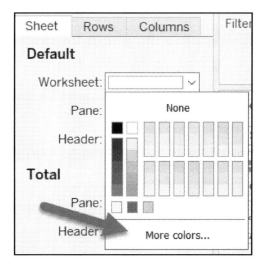

16. Within the resulting dialog box, set the shading to #34959e. This will cause the background color around the arrow to match the background color on the dashboard.

17. Select **Worksheet | Tooltip...** and deselect the **Show Tooltips** option.

18. Duplicate the `Frt Arrow` worksheet and name the duplicate `Bk Arrow`.

19. Click on the **Shape** shelf to swap the front arrow for the back arrow:

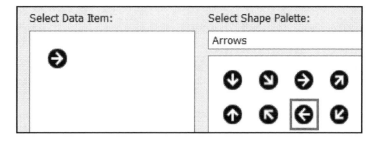

20. Open the dashboard entitled **Map Loss Leaders**.

21. Within the **Objects** section of the **Dashboard** pane, click on the **Floating** button.

22. Place `Frt Arrow` and `Bk Arrow` on the dashboard.

23. Hide the titles for both `Frt Arrow` and `Bk Arrow`.

24. Select the **Layout** Pane and set the positioning as follows:

		Size					Size		
Frt Arrow	w	60	h	30	**Bk Arrow**	w	60	h	30
		Position					**Position**		
	x	1145	y	835		x	1145	y	865

25. Right-click on the **Mastering Tableau** image and select **Floating Order | Bring to Front**. The results should look like the following screenshot:

26. Select **Dashboard | Actions** and click on the **Add Action** button to create the filter actions pictured in the following screenshot. Pay special attention to selecting the **Source** and **Target** sheets correctly:

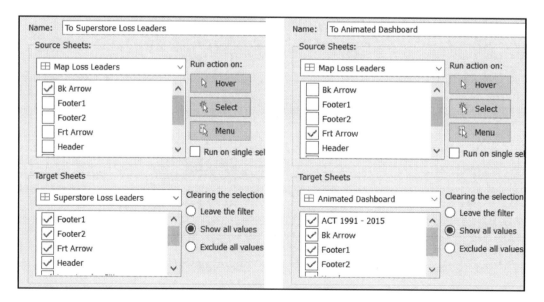

27. Open the **Superstore Loss Leaders** dashboard and place the `Frt Arrow` worksheet (but not `Bk Arrow`) on the dashboard.

28. Hide the title for `Frt Arrow`.

29. Set the positioning to be the same as the `Frt Arrow` positioning previously listed, that is, w: 60 h: 30 x: 1145 y: 835.

30. Set the float order of the **Mastering Tableau** image to **Front**.

31. Select **Dashboard | Actions** and click on the **Add Action** button to create the filter action described in the following table:

Field	Selection
Name	To Map Loss Leaders
Source Sheets (dropdown)	Superstore Loss Leaders
Source Sheets (checkbox)	Frt Arrow
Target Sheets (dropdown)	Map Loss Leaders
Target Sheets (checkboxes)	All
Run action on:	Select
Clearing the selection will	Show all values

32. Open **Animated Dashboard** and place the `Bk Arrow` worksheet (but not `Frt Arrow`) on the dashboard.

33. Hide the title for `Bk Arrow`.

34. Set the positioning to be the same as the `Bk Arrow` positioning listed in step 17, that is, w: 60 h: 30 x: 1145 y: 865.

35. Set the float order of the **Mastering Tableau** image to **Front**.

36. Select **Dashboard | Actions** and click on the **Add Action** button to create the filter action described in the following table:

Field	Selection
Name	To Map Loss Leaders
Source Sheets (dropdown)	Animated Dashboard
Source Sheets (checkbox)	Bk Arrow
Target Sheets (dropdown)	Map Loss Leaders
Target Sheets (checkboxes)	All

Run action on:	Select
Clearing the selection will	Show all values

37. In the toolbar, click on the **Presentation Mode** icon or press *F7* to enter presentation mode and test the buttons.

Summary

We began this chapter by exploring various screen capture tools as well as Tableau's native export capabilities. Next, we turned our consideration to PowerPoint, where we explored various methods for creating PowerPoint presentations from Tableau workbooks and even explored how to embed a live instance of Tableau in PowerPoint. Then we considered Tableau animation. Lastly, we explored how to use Story Points and dashboards for presentations.

In the next chapter, we will turn our attention to dashboarding, where we will push beyond the normal boundaries of the typical dashboard but not lose focus of practical application.

10
Visualization Best Practices and Dashboard Design

My first solo Tableau training engagement was in Manhattan. At that time, my understanding of the tool was okay but my understanding of data visualization theory was not. One of the students in that class was quite well-versed in data visualization theory and actually knew Edward Tufte (the godfather of data visualization) personally. It wasn't long before he found me out! I stumbled along as best as I could but it was obvious that I had a huge hole in my knowledge that needed to be filled. Perhaps I received more of an education from the student than he did from me!

Since that fateful week in Manhattan, I've read Edward Tufte, Stephen Few, and other thought leaders in the data visualization space. This knowledge has been very fruitful. For instance, quite recently, a colleague told me that one of his clients thought a particular dashboard had too many bar charts and he wanted some variation. I shared the following two quotes:

> *"Show data variation, not design variation."*
> -*Edward Tufte in The Visual Display of Quantitative Information*

> *"Variety might be the spice of life, but, if it is introduced on a dashboard for its own sake, the display suffers."*
> -*Stephen Few in Information Dashboard Design*

Those quotes proved helpful for my colleague. Hopefully, the following information will prove helpful to you.

This chapter was particularly influenced by the giants in data visualization and dashboard design, that is, Edward Tufte and Stephen Few. Additionally I would also like to draw attention to Alberto Cairo–a relatively new voice providing new insight. Each of these authors should be considered a must-read for anyone working in data visualization.

This chapter will address three main categories with the intent of empowering the reader with design knowledge and Tableau-centric techniques for creating effective dashboards. Specifically, the following will be discussed:

- Visualization design theory
- Dashboard design
- Sheet selection

Visualization design theory

Any discussion on designing dashboards should begin with information about constructing well-designed content. The quality of the dashboard layout and the utilization of technical tips and tricks do not matter if the content is sub-par. In other words, we should consider the worksheets displayed on dashboards and ensure that those worksheets are well designed. Therefore, our discussion will begin with a consideration of visualization design principles. Regarding these principles, it's tempting to declare a set of rules:

- To plot change over time, use a line graph
- To show breakdowns of the whole, use a treemap
- To compare discrete elements, use a bar chart
- To visualize correlation, use a scatter plot

But of course even a cursory review of the preceding list brings to mind many variations and alternatives! Thus, in this chapter, we will consider various rules while always keeping in mind that rules (at least rules such as these) are meant to be broken.

Formatting rules

The following formatting rules encompass fonts, lines, and bands. Fonts are, of course, an obvious formatting consideration. Lines and bands, however, may not be something you typically think of when formatting, especially when considering formatting from the perspective of Microsoft Word. But if we broaden formatting considerations to think of Adobe Illustrator, InDesign, and other graphic design tools, then lines and bands are certainly considered. This illustrates that data visualization is closely related to graphic design and that formatting considers much more than just textual layout.

Rule – keep the font choice simple

Typically, using one or two fonts on a dashboard is advisable. More fonts can create a confusing environment and interfere with readability. Fonts chosen for titles should be thick and solid, while the body fonts should be easy to read. As of Tableau 10.0, choosing appropriate fonts is simple because of the new **Tableau Font Family**. Go to **Format | Font** to display the **Format Font** window to see and choose these new fonts:

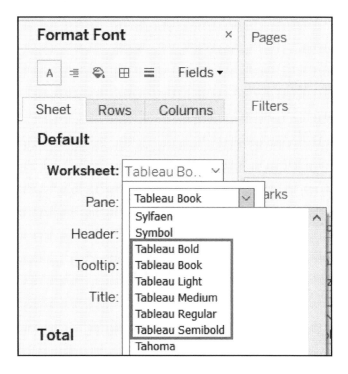

Assuming your dashboard is primarily intended for the screen, sans serif fonts are best. On the rare occasions a dashboard is primarily intended for print, you may consider serif fonts; particularly if the print resolution is high.

Rule – Trend line > Fever line > Reference line > Drop line > Zero line > Grid line

The preceding pseudo formula is intended to communicate line visibility. For example, trend line visibility should be greater than fever line visibility. Visibility is usually enhanced by increasing line thickness but may be enhanced via color saturation or by choosing a dotted or dashed line over a solid line.

The trend line, if present, is usually the most visible line on the graph. Trend lines are displayed via the **Analytics** pane and can be adjusted via **Format** | **Lines**.

The fever line (for example, the line used on a time-series chart) should not be so heavy as to obscure twists and turns in the data. Although a fever line may be displayed as dotted or dashed by utilizing the **Pages** shelf, this is usually not advisable because it may obscure visibility. The thickness of a fever line can be adjusted by clicking on the **Size** shelf in the **Marks View** card.

Reference lines are usually less prevalent than either fever or trend lines and can be formatted by going to **Format** | **Reference lines**.

Drop lines are not frequently used. To deploy drop lines, right-click on a blank portion of the view and go to **Drop lines** | **Show drop lines**. Next, click on a point in the view to display a drop line. To format drop lines, go to **Format** | **Droplines**. Drop lines are relevant only if at least one axis is utilized in the visualization.

Zero lines (sometimes referred to as base lines) are displayed only if zero or negative values are included in the view or positive numerical values are relatively close to zero. Format zero lines by going to **Format** | **Lines**.

Grid lines should be the most muted lines on the view and may be dispensed with altogether. Format grid lines by going to **Format** | **Lines**.

Rule – band in groups of three to five

Visualizations comprising a tall table of text or horizontal bars should segment dimension members in groups of three to five.

Exercise – banding

This exercise demonstrates how to create banding for crosstab views in Tableau:

1. Navigate to `https://public.tableau.com/profile/david.baldwin#!/` to locate and download the workbook associated with this chapter.
2. Navigate to the worksheet titled `Banding`.
3. Select the **Superstore** data source and place **Product Name** on the **Rows** shelf.
4. Double-click on **Discount, Profit, Quantity**, and **Sales**.
5. Navigate to **Format | Shading** and set **Band Size** under **Row Banding** so that three to five lines of text are encompassed by each band. Be sure to set an appropriate color for both **Pane** and **Header**:

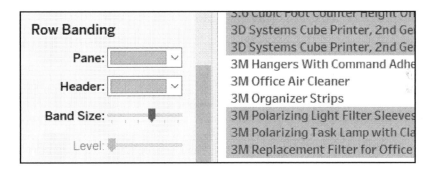

Note that after completing the preceding five steps, Tableau defaulted to banding every other row. This default formatting is fine for a short table but is quite busy for a tall table. The *band in groups of three to five* rule is influenced by Dona W. Wong, who, in her book *The Wall Street Journal Guide to Information Graphics*, recommends separating long tables or bar charts with thin rules to separate the bars in groups of three to five to help the readers read across.

Color rules

It seems slightly ironic to discuss color rules in a black-and-white publication such as *Mastering Tableau* (of course, that may not be true if you are reading this book on an electronic device)! Nonetheless, even in a monochromatic setting, a discussion of color is relevant. For example, exclusive use of black text communicates differently than using variations of gray. The following survey of color rules should be helpful to ensure that you use colors effectively in a variety of settings.

Rule – keep colors simple and limited

Stick to the basic hues and provide only a few (perhaps three to five) hue variations. Alberto Cairo, in his book *The Functional Art: An Introduction to Information Graphics and Visualization*, provides insights into why this is important.

> *The limited capacity of our visual working memory helps explain why it's not advisable to use more than four or five colors or pictograms to identify different phenomena on maps and charts.*

Rule – respect the psychological implication of colors

In Western society, there is a color vocabulary so pervasive, it's second nature. Exit signs marking stairwell locations are red. Traffic cones are orange. Baby boys are traditionally dressed in blue while baby girls wear pink. Similarly, in Tableau reds and oranges should usually be associated with negative performance while blues and greens should be associated with positive performance. Using colors counterintuitively can cause confusion.

Rule – be colorblind-friendly

Color blindness is usually manifested as an inability to distinguish red and green or blue and yellow. Red/green and blue/yellow are on opposite sides of the color wheel. Consequently, the challenges these color combinations present for colorblind individuals can be easily recreated with image editing software such as Photoshop. If you are not colorblind, convert an image with these color combinations to grayscale and observe. The challenge presented to the 8.0% of the males and 0.5% of the females who are color blind becomes immediately obvious!

Rule – use pure colors sparingly

The resulting colors from the following exercise should be a very vibrant red, green, and blue. Depending on the monitor, you may even find it difficult to stare directly at the colors. These are known as *pure colors* and should be used sparingly; perhaps only to highlight particularly important items.

Exercise – using pure colors

This exercise provides basic instructions for using pure colors in Tableau:

1. Open the workbook associated with this chapter and navigate to the worksheet entitled `Pure Colors`.

2. Select the **Superstore** data source and place **Category** on both the **Rows** shelf and the **Color** shelf.

3. Set the **Fit** to **Entire View**.

4. Click on the **Color** shelf and choose **Edit Colors…**.

5. In the **Edit Colors** dialog box, double-click on the color icons to the left of each dimension member; that is, **Furniture**, **Office Supplies**, and **Technology**:

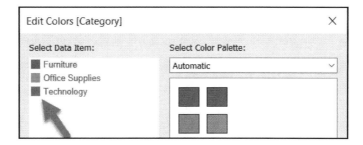

6. Within the resulting dialog box, set furniture to an HTML value of #0000ff, **Office Supplies** to #ff0000, and **Technology** to #00ff00.

Rule – color variations over symbol variation

Deciphering different symbols takes more mental energy for the end user than distinguishing color. Therefore, color variation should be used over symbol variation. This rule can actually be observed in Tableau defaults. Create a scatter plot and place a dimension with many members on the **Color** shelf and **Shape** shelf respectively. Note that by default, the view will display 20 unique colors but only 10 unique shapes. Older versions of Tableau (such as Tableau 9.0) display warnings that include text such as *the recommended maximum for this shelf is 10*:

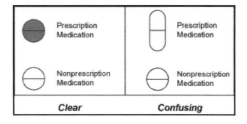

Visualization type rules

Since there's a chapter dedicated to visualization types (Chapter 7, *Beyond the Basic Chart Types*) and since much of this book explores various visualizations, we won't spend much time here delving into a lengthy list of visualization type rules. However, it does seem appropriate to review at least a couple of rules. In the following exercise, we will consider keeping shapes simple and effectively using pie charts.

Rule – keep shapes simple

Too many shape details impede comprehension. This is because shape details draw the user's focus away from the data. Consider the following exercise on using two different shopping cart images.

Exercise – shapes

In this exercise we will compare and contrast the use of simple shapes and complex shapes in Tableau:

1. Open the workbook associated with this chapter and navigate to the worksheet entitled Simple Shopping Cart.
2. Note that the visualization is a scatterplot showing the top 10 selling Sub-Categories in terms of total sales and profits.
3. On your computer, navigate to the Shapes directory located in the My Tableau Repository. On my computer, the path is C:\Users\David Baldwin\Documents\My Tableau Repository\Shapes.
4. Within the Shapes directory, create a folder named My Shapes.
5. Reference the link included in the comment section of the worksheet to download the assets associated with this chapter.
6. In the downloaded material, find the images titled Shopping_Cart and Shopping_Cart_3D and copy those images into the My Shapes directory created previously.
7. Within Tableau, access the Simple Shopping Cart worksheet.
8. Click on the **Shape** shelf and then select **More Shapes**.
9. Within the **Edit Shape** dialog box, click on the **Reload Shapes** button.
10. Select the **My Shapes** palette and set the shape to the simple shopping cart.

11. After closing the dialog box, click on the Size shelf and adjust as desired. Also adjust other aspects of the visualization as desired.

12. Navigate to the `3D Shopping Cart` worksheet and then repeat steps 8 to 11. Instead of using the simple shopping cart, use the 3D shopping cart:

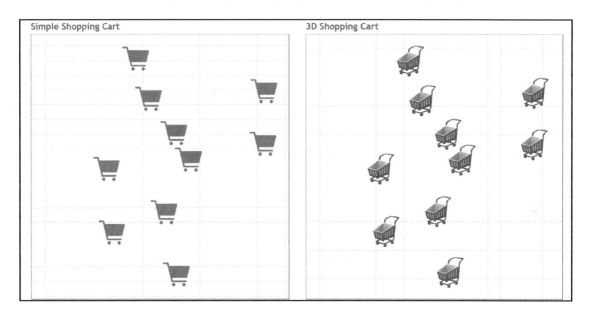

Compare the two visualizations. Which version of the shopping cart is more attractive? Probably, the cart with the 3D look was your choice. Why not choose the more attractive image? Making visualizations attractive is only of secondary concern. The primary goal is to display the data as clearly and efficiently as possible. A simple shape is grasped more quickly and intuitively than a complex shape. Besides, the cuteness of the 3D image will quickly wear off.

Rule – use pie charts sparingly

Edward Tufte makes an acrid (and somewhat humorous) comment against the use of pie charts in his book *The Visual Display of Quantitative Information*.

> *"A table is nearly always better than a dumb pie chart; the only worse design than a pie chart is several of them. Given their low density and failure to order numbers along a visual dimension, pie charts should never be used."*

The present sentiment in data visualization circles is largely sympathetic to Tufte's criticism. There may, however, be some circumstances where a pie chart is optimal. Consider the following visualization:

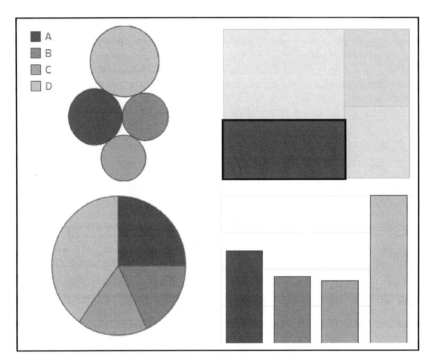

Which of the four visualizations best demonstrates that **A** accounts for 25% of the whole? Clearly it is the pie chart! Therefore, perhaps it is fairer to refer to pie charts as limited and to use them sparingly as opposed to considering them inherently evil.

Compromises

In this section, we will transition from more or less strict rules to compromises. Often, building visualizations is a balancing act. It's common to encounter contradictory directions from books, blogs, consultants, and within organizations. One person may insist on utilizing every pixel of space while another urges simplicity and whitespace. One counsels a guided approach while another recommends building wide open dashboards that allow end users to discover their own path. Avant gardes may crave esoteric visualizations while those of a more conservative bent prefer to stay with the conventional. Now we will explore a few of the more common competing requests and suggest compromises.

Make the dashboard simple versus make the dashboard robust

Recently a colleague showed me a complex dashboard he had just completed. Although he was pleased that he had managed to get it working well, he felt the need to apologize by saying, "I know it's dense and complex but it's what the client wanted." Occam's Razor encourages the simplest possible solution for any problem. For my colleague's dashboard, the simplest solution was rather complex. This is OK! Complexity in Tableau dashboarding need not be shunned. But a clear understanding of some basic guidelines can help the author intelligently determine how to compromise between demands for simplicity and demands for robustness.

More frequent data updates necessitate simpler design.

Some Tableau dashboards may be near-real-time. Third-party technology may be utilized to force a browser displaying a dashboard via Tableau Server to refresh every few minutes to ensure the absolute latest data displays. In such cases, the design should be quite simple. The end user must be able to see at a glance all pertinent data and should not use that dashboard for extensive analysis. Conversely, a dashboard that is refreshed monthly can support high complexity and thus may be used for deep exploration.

Greater end user expertise supports greater dashboard complexity.

Know thy users. If they want easy, at-a-glance visualizations, keep the dashboards simple. If they like deep dives, design accordingly.

Smaller audiences require more precise design.

If only a few people monitor a given dashboard, it may require a highly customized approach. In such cases, specifications may be detailed, complex, and difficult to execute and maintain because the small user base has expectations that may not be natively easy to produce in Tableau.

Screen resolution and visualization complexity are proportional.

Users with low-resolution devices will need to interact fairly simply with a dashboard. Thus the design of such a dashboard will probably be correspondingly uncomplicated. Conversely, high-resolution devices support greater complexity.

Greater distance from the screen requires larger dashboard elements.

If the dashboard is designed for conference room viewing, the elements on the dashboard may need to be fairly large to meet the viewing needs of those far from the screen. Thus the dashboard will likely be relatively simple. Conversely, a dashboard to be viewed primarily on end users desktops can be more complex.

Although these points are all about simple versus complex, do not equate simple with easy. A simple and elegantly designed dashboard can be more difficult to create than a complex dashboard. In the words of Steve Jobs:

"Simple can be harder than complex: You have to work hard to get your thinking clean to make it simple. But it's worth it in the end because once you get there, you can move mountains."

Presenting dense information versus presenting sparse information

Normally, a line graph should have a maximum of four to five lines. However, there are times when you may wish to display many lines. A compromise can be achieved by presenting many lines and empowering the end user to highlight as desired. The following line graph displays the percentage of Internet usage by country from 2000 to 2012. Those countries with the largest increases have been highlighted. Assuming that **Highlight Selected Items** has been activated within the **Color** legend, the end user can select items (countries in this case) from the legend to highlight as desired. Or, even better, a worksheet can be created listing all countries and used in conjunction with a highlight action on a dashboard to focus attention on selected items on the line graph:

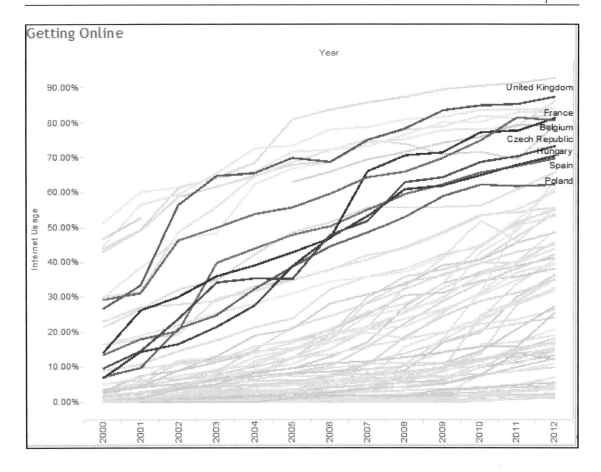

Telling a story versus allowing a story to be discovered

Albert Cairo, in his excellent book *The Functional Art: An Introduction to Information Graphics and Visualization*, includes a section where he interviews prominent data visualization and information graphics professionals. Two of these interviews are remarkable for their opposing views.

> *"I feel that many visualization designers try to transform the user into an editor. They create these amazing interactive tools with tons of bubbles, lines, bars, filters, and scrubber bars, and expect readers to figure the story out by themselves, and draw conclusions from the data. That's not an approach to information graphics I like."*
>
> *— Jim*

Grimwade

The most fascinating thing about the rise of data visualization is exactly that anyone can explore all those large data sets without anyone telling us what the key insight is.

―

Moritz Stefaner

Fortunately, the compromise position can be found in the Jim Grimwade interview:

[The New York Times presents] complex sets of data, and they let you go really deep into the figures and their connections. But beforehand, they give you some context, some pointers as to what you can do with those data. If you don't do this… you will end up with a visualization that may look really beautiful and intricate, but that will leave readers wondering, What has this thing really told me? What is this useful for?

― Jim Grimwade

Although the case scenarios considered in the preceding quotes are likely quite different from the Tableau work you are involved in, the underlying principles remain the same. You can choose to tell a story or build a platform that allows the discovery of numerous stories. Your choice will differ depending on the given dataset and audience. If you choose to create a platform for story discovery, be sure to take the *New York Times* approach suggested by Grimwade. Provide hints, pointers, and good documentation to lead your end user to successfully interact with the story you wish to tell or successfully discover their own story.

Document, document, document! But don't use any space!

In the previous section we considered the suggestion *provide hints, pointers, and good documentation…* but there's an issue. These things take space. Dashboard space is precious. Often, Tableau authors are asked to squeeze more and more stuff on a dashboard and are hence looking for ways to conserve space. Here are some suggestions for maximizing documentation on a dashboard while minimally impacting screen real estate.

Craft titles for clear communication

Titles are expected. Not just a title for a dashboard and worksheets on the dashboard, but also titles for legends, filters, and other objects. These titles can be used for effective and efficient documentation. For instance, a filter should not just read *Market*. Instead, it should say something, like *Select a Market*. Notice the imperative statement. The user is being told to do something and this is a helpful hint. Adding a couple of words to a title will usually not impact dashboard space.

Use subtitles to relay instructions

A subtitle will take some extra space but it does not have to be much. A small, italicized font immediately underneath a title is an obvious place a user will look at for guidance. Consider an example: *Red represents loss*. This short sentence could be used as a subtitle that may eliminate the need for a legend and thus actually save space.

Use intuitive icons

Consider a use case of navigating from one dashboard to another. Of course, you could associate an action with some hyperlinked text stating **Click here to navigate to another dashboard**. But this seems quite unnecessary when an action can be associated with a small, innocuous arrow, such as is natively used in PowerPoint, to communicate the same thing.

Store more extensive documentation in a tooltip associated with a help icon.

A small question mark in the top-right corner of an application is common. Currently, I'm composing this chapter in Word 2013 which has such a question mark. This clearly communicates where to go if additional help is required. As shown in the following exercise, it's easy to create a similar feature on a Tableau dashboard.

Exercise – tooltips for extensive help

This exercise demonstrates how to associate a small help icon with underlying detailed text:

1. Open the workbook associated with this chapter and navigate to the worksheet entitled Help.
2. Hover over the question mark on the worksheet and note the text that appears. (Note that *Lorem ipsum...* is commonly used by web designers who borrowed it from typesetters who have been using this Latin text as a placeholder for centuries. Visit http://www.loremipsum.com/ to learn more.)
3. The text in this worksheet was deployed via **Worksheet | Tooltip**. This worksheet could be thoughtfully placed on a dashboard (for example, in the top-right corner) to give very detailed documentation while minimally impacting space.

Keeping visualizations simple versus exploring esoteric chart types

Some tire of seeing the same chart types over and over. This leads to requests such as: *can we spice up the dashboard a bit?* Normally, such sentiments should be resisted. As stated at the beginning of this chapter, introducing variety for its own sake is counterproductive. Nonetheless, there are times when a less common visualization type may be a better choice than a more popular type. When are those times?

Use less common chart types in the following cases:

- The chart is used to catch the end user's attention
- The chart type presents the data more effectively

Sometimes a less common chart type can be effectively used to catch the end user's attention for some particular goal such as humour, making a salient point, or making the visualization more memorable. One such example can be found on the Tableau 404 error page. Navigate to `http://www.tableau.com/asdf` and observe Sasquatch in a packed bubble chart (note that this page changes from time to time, so you may see Elvis or aliens or some other clever visualization).

An example of the second point in the preceding information box is using a treemap over a pie chart. Both are non-Cartesian chart types (that is, visualizations with no fields on the **Rows** or **Columns** shelves) used for showing parts of a whole. Pie charts are the more common of the two but treemaps usually present the data better. There are at least three reasons for this.

- A treemap can represent more data points
- The rectangular nature of a treemap fits monitor space more efficiently
- Pie slice sizes are more difficult to distinguish than sizes of treemap segments

Sometimes using a less common visualization type may elicit complaints. *I like pie charts. Give me a pie chart!* In such cases, a compromise may be possible. Later in this chapter we will consider sheet swapping. As you will learn, sheet swapping can allow the end user to determine which visualization type to view. In the end, if a compromise is not possible and the person responsible for your pay check desires a less-than-ideal chart type, I recommend a chipper yes ma'am/sir!

Dashboard design

Now that we have completed our discussion of visualization theory, let's turn our attention to dashboard design. We'll begin by asking the question: *What is a dashboard?* The question is rather difficult to answer; however, its usage in everyday conversation in many organizations would suggest that people have a definite idea of what a dashboard is. Furthermore, search engine results provide no shortage of definitions. But those definitions can differ significantly and even be contradictory.

Why is it so difficult to define a dashboard? In part, it is because data visualization as a whole and dashboarding specifically is an emerging field that combines many other disciplines. These disciplines include statistical analysis, graphic and web design, computer science, and even journalism. An emerging field with so many components is a moving target and as such is difficult to define.

For our purposes, we will begin with Stephen Few's definition as it first appeared in an issue of *Intelligent Enterprise* in 2004. Afterward, we'll extend and adapt that definition for Tableau dashboards.

> *"A dashboard is a visual display of the most important information needed to achieve one or more objectives, consolidated and arranged on a single screen so the information can be monitored at a glance."*
>
> *– Stephen Few in the March 2004 issue of Intelligent Enterprise.*

Although this definition is quite good, Tableau takes a broader approach. For instance, a Tableau dashboard may be contained on a single screen but can be designed (and quite effectively designed) to require scrolling. More importantly, Tableau dashboards are typically interactive, which opens a world of exploratory, analysis, and design options. Therefore, let's attempt a Tableau-centric dashboard definition:

 A Tableau dashboard is a display containing one or more data visualizations designed to enable a user to quickly view metrics. This display may provide interactive elements such as filtering, highlighting, and drill-down capabilities that enable further exploration and analysis.

With this definition in mind, let's consider how to design effective dashboard layouts.

Dashboard layout

The layout of a dashboard is important for the same reason that the layout of a magazine foldout or a web page is important. Placing the right information in the right place helps the viewer quickly and efficiently garner information and draw conclusions. In order to appreciate this fact, consider the last time you had to hunt through a poorly constructed web page to find important information. That time could have been better used to actually apply that important information!

Now, we'll consider three dashboard layouts: the Golden Rectangle, Quad, and Small Multiple.

Golden Rectangle layout

You have probably heard of the Fibonacci sequence, the Golden Rectangle, and the Golden Ratio. Nonetheless, given that it may have been a few years since you attended a math class, a brief reminder may prove helpful.

The Fibonacci sequence is a series of numbers where every number is the sum of the previous two numbers. For example, 1, 1, 2, 3, 5, 8, 13, 21.

A Golden Rectangle is achieved where the ratio of the longest side to the shortest side of a rectangle approximates 1.618. This ratio is known as the Golden Ratio. Mathematically, the Golden Ratio is represented as follows:

$$\varphi = \frac{1 + \sqrt{5}}{2} \approx 1.61803398874989$$

The Fibonacci Sequence and the Golden Ratio can be seen to be connected when dividing each number of the Fibonacci Sequence by the previous number. For example,

0, 1, 1, 2, 3, 5, 8, 13, 21, 34

Leads to:

1/1=1, 2/1=2, 3/2=1.5, 5/3=1.67, 8/5=1.6, 13/8=1.625, 21/13=1.615, 34/21=1.619

As can be observed, the further the sequence progresses, the more exactly the Golden Ratio is represented.

Now let's consider a dashboard layout using the Golden Rectangle. The layout shown below is constructed of rectangles so that each is 1.618 times longer or taller than the next. The spiral (known as the **Golden Spiral**) is displayed to demonstrate the order of the rectangles:

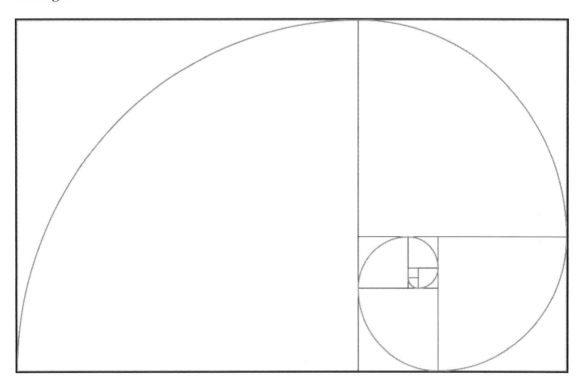

The Fibonacci Sequence/Golden Rectangle/Golden Ratio appears relentlessly in nature and throughout history. Many sea shells and flowers adhere to the Fibonacci sequence. The Great Pyramid of Giza appears to have been constructed with the Golden Ratio in mind. Phidias probably used the Golden Ratio to design his statues for the Athenian Partheon. Indeed the Partheon itself was designed with Golden Rectangle proportions.

So does the Golden Rectangle as pictured in the preceding image represent the ideal dashboard layout? Perhaps it's truer to say that this image represents one acceptable dashboard layout. The ideal is not so much found in the abstract as it's found in the application. Dashboard layouts may sometimes approximate the Golden Rectangle but, as will be considered later, other dashboard layouts may be superior for different scenarios.

The dashboard pictured here (which is also available in the Tableau workbook accompanying this chapter) utilizes the Golden Rectangle:

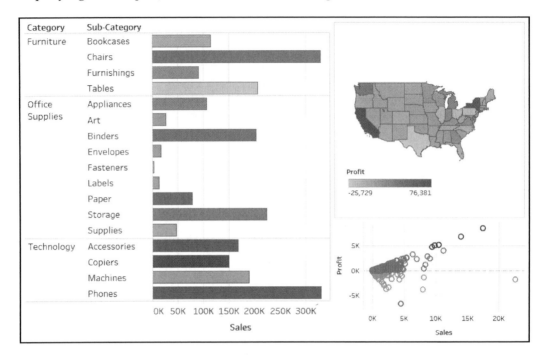

Notice that this example does not attempt to follow the Golden Spiral through to smaller and smaller rectangles. There are practical limits.

The Golden Rectangle layout is particularly good for guiding the viewer from courser to finer granularity. In the preceding example, the left-hand portion of the dashboard displays the coarsest granularity; 17 sub-categories. The map is next. Lastly, the scatterplot displays the finest granularity. Creating actions that follow this path would make a natural interaction for the end user. For example an end user might first click on Tables and next click on the state of Pennsylvania in order to observe outliers in the scatterplot.

Quad layout

The Quad layout divvies up a dashboard into four more or less equal quadrants. It's quite easy to implement. On a blank dashboard, simply double-click on four worksheets in the **Dashboard** pane. The result is a Quad layout though some small adjustments may need to be made to account for legends, filters and parameters. To observe a Quad layout, refer to the image located in the section titled *Rule – use pie charts sparingly*.

Small Multiple layout

A Small Multiple layout displays many views on a single dashboard. Like the Quad layout, a Small Multiple layout can be implemented simply by double-clicking on each desired worksheet in the **Dashboard** pane. Small Multiples are useful when viewing information that utilizes the same visualization type repeatedly. Also a consistent theme is helpful; for example, the following screenshot demonstrates a theme of profit performance per state in USA. Attempting to create a Small Multiple with multiple visualization types and multiple themes will probably be messy and difficult to interact with:

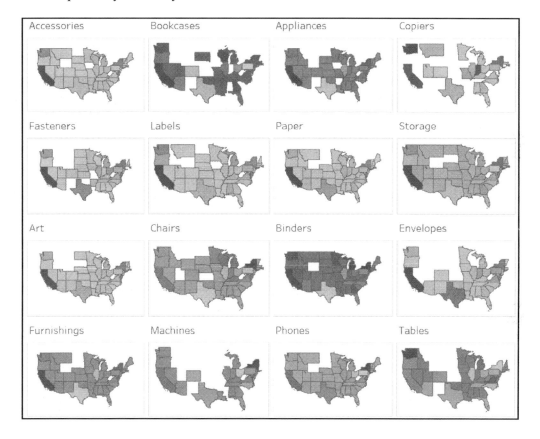

Some layouts are essentially variations on a theme. For instance, a layout displaying three views such that one view on the dashboard covers double the real estate of each of the other views is essentially a variation of the Quad layout. Other layouts defy easy categorization and are unique to a given dashboard. Regardless, the preceding points will hopefully provide food for thought as you design dashboards in future.

Sheet selection

Sheet selection, often referred to as *sheet swapping*, allows the Tableau author to hide and display visualizations as well as move worksheets on and off the dashboard. These techniques have been used in creative ways with some very impressive results. For example, Tableau Zen Master Joshua Milligan has built various games including Tic-Tak-Toe and Blackjack, using sheet selection. For our purposes, we will stick to using sheet selection to assist with creating dashboards that adhere to the design principles discussed previously.

Exercise – sheet swapping pie charts and treemaps

In the preceding discussion on pie charts and treemaps, we noted that a treemap is usually a better visualization but people are often more comfortable with pie charts. As a compromise, in this exercise we will review an example that allows the end user to choose whether to see a pie chart or a treemap:

1. Open the workbook associated with this chapter and navigate to the worksheet titled `Population Pie`.
2. Select the **World Indicators** data source and note the calculated field called **Blank**. The code is comprised of single quotes with a space in between.
3. Place **Blank** on the **Columns** shelf.
4. Non-Cartesian visualization types (that is, visualizations with no fields on the **Rows** or **Columns** shelves) require this step for sheet swapping to work. Otherwise, when placing the worksheet in a **Vertical** container on a dashboard, the worksheet will not properly stretch to fill the width of the container.
5. In the view, select all pie slices via *Ctrl + A* or by dragging a marquee around the entire pie.
6. Right-click on any pie slice and choose **Annotate** | **Mark**.

7. In the resulting dialog box, delete all text except `<Country>`.

8. Position and format the annotations as desired. Note that additional adjustments may be required once the pie chart is deployed on a dashboard.

9. Create a parameter named **Select Chart Type** with the following settings:
   - Data Type: String
   - Current Value: Pie Chart
   - Allowable values: List
   - Value and Display As:

Value	Display As
Pie Chart	Pie Chart
Treemap	Treemap

 Note that the preceding Current Value setting is important.

10. Create a calculated field called `Sheet Swap` with the code `[Select Chart Type]`; that is, the calculated field will simply reference the parameter.

11. Place `Sheet Swap` on the **Filters** shelf and select **Pie Chart** in the resulting dialog box.

12. Display the parameter by right-clicking on **Select Chart Type** and choosing **Show Parameter Control**.

13. In the displayed parameter, toggle back and forth between **Pie Chart** and **Treemap** and observe.

14. Navigate to the worksheet entitled **Population Tree**.

15. Place **Blank** on the **Columns** shelf.

16. Place `Sheet Swap` on the **Filters** shelf and select **Treemap** in the resulting dialog box.

17. If **Treemap** does not display as a choice, make sure that the **Select Chart Type** parameter is toggled to **Treemap**.

18. Create a new dashboard entitled `Latin American Population`.

19. In the **Dashboard** pane, double-click on **Vertical** to place a vertical container on the dashboard.

20. In the **Dashboard** pane, double-click on **Population Tree** and **Population Pie**.

21. Right-click on the titles **Population Tree** and **Population Pie** and select **Hide Title**.
22. Place **Population Map** and **Population Line** on the dashboard and position as desired.
23. Press Shift and drag the **Select Chart Type** parameter over the treemap in order to float the control and position as desired.
24. Delete all legends and quick filters.
25. Format, document, and position all dashboard elements as desired.
26. Now the end user can determine whether to view a treemap or a pie chart:

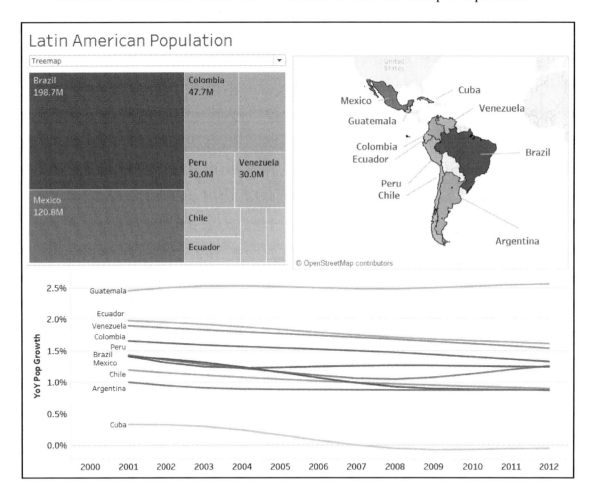

Exercise – collapsible menu

In the preceding section about documenting dashboards, the point was made that dashboard space is precious. In this exercise, we will review an example that will use sheet selection to allow the end user to show or hide filters and thus make more efficient use of screen real estate:

1. Duplicate the dashboard created in the previous exercise and name it Collapsible Menu. If you did not complete the preceding exercise, utilize the dashboard included with the Solution workbook provided with this chapter.

2. In the bottom portion of the **Dashboard** pane, select **Floating**.

3. Drag the **Menu** icon from the **Dashboard** pane onto the dashboard.

4. Right-click on the title and select **Hide Title**.

5. Set the fit of the **Menu** icon to **Entire View**.

6. Size and position the **Menu** icon so that it fits in the top-right corner of the dashboard. The following dimensions can be entered in the **Layout** pane:

Position		Size	
X	927	w	47
Y	4	h	23

7. In the bottom portion of the **Dashboard** pane, select **Tiled**.

8. Place the **Menu** worksheet anywhere on the dashboard. The filters for **Year** and **Country** should display on the right-hand side of the dashboard.

9. Navigate to the **Menu** worksheet and take a moment to explore the settings of each dimension on the **Filters** shelf. Particularly note that the **Latin America Countries** filter is set to **Context** and that **Country Copy** is displayed as a filter. Also note that the **Country Copy** quick filter is set to **Show All Values in Context**. It is necessary to display the **Country Copy** filter as opposed to the **Country** filter because **Country** displays the condition AVG([Population Total]) > 1000000.

10. Return to the **Collapsible Menu** dashboard.

11. Right-click on the **Menu** title and select **Hide Title**.

12. Make the Menu worksheet floating and then size and position with these dimensions:

Position		Size	
X	1	w	1
Y	1	h	1

 Note that the goal of this step is to make the Menu worksheet as small as possible. It is necessary for the Menu worksheet to remain on the dashboard so that the accompanying **Year** and **Country** filters can be used.

13. On the **Dashboard**pane, select **Floating** and drag a horizontal container on to the view in approximately the middle of the dashboard.
14. Within the **Layout** pane, set the width of the horizontal container to 400.
15. In the lower-right section of the dashboard, *right click on the* container that houses the **Country** and **Year** filters. In the resulting pop-up menu, choose **Edit Width** and set the value to 200.
16. Drag the container selected in the previous step and place it in the container that is floating in the centre of the dashboard.
17. From the **Dashboard** pane, press Shift, drag a vertical container, and place it inside the left-hand-side portion of the floating horizontal container.
18. Right-click on the newly created vertical container and select **Fixed Width**. The width of the vertical container should now be 200 pixels.
19. Place the worksheet titled **Expander** in the newly created vertical container. As in the preceding steps, be sure to press Shift and drag.
20. The **Expander** worksheet contains a small, transparent image that will be used to expand and collapse the menu we are creating. An image does not have to be used. For example, text could be used instead. However, since small, transparent images are sometimes used in web design to stretch tables, one is used here to assist readers with a web design background.
21. Set the fit for the **Expander** worksheet to **Entire View**.
22. Right-click on the **Expander** worksheet title and select **Hide Title**. The results should look similar to the following screenshot:

23. Within the **Layout** pane, select the horizontal container that contains the **Country** and **Years** filters and the **Expander** worksheet. Enter the following dimensions:

Position		Size	
X	800	w	400
Y	26	h	700

24. The results should look similar to the following screenshot:

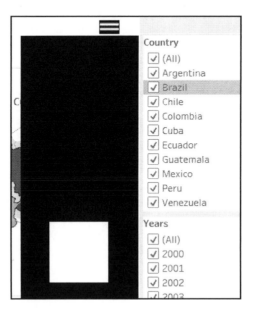

25. Select **Dashboard | Actions** and create the following filter action:

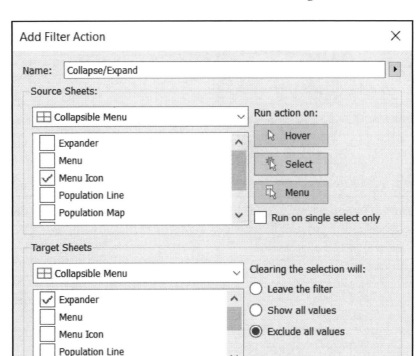

26. In the **Layout**pane, right-click on the vertical container that is housing the **Expander** worksheet and deselect **Fixed Width**.

27. This step is necessary so that the **Collapse/Expand** action will work properly. It was necessary to fix the container width previously so as to properly align the contents of the container.

28. On the dashboard, click on the **Menu Icon**. The **Expander** worksheet should appear and disappear, causing the filters to move on and off the dashboard. When you're finished with this step, make sure that the **Expander** worksheet is visible.

29. From the **Dashboard** pane, press Shift and drag two blank containers onto the dashboard. Position one directly above the **Expander** and one directly below. The results should look similar to the following screenshot:

30. Size the blank containers so that the black rectangle is as small as possible and is positioned so that it covers only a blank portion of the dashboard.

31. Be sure to continually test the **Menu** action as you adjust the size so as to not inadvertently break the collapsing functionality of the container.

32. Navigate to the **Expander** worksheet and select **Format | Shading**. Change the worksheet shading from black to none.

33. Navigate back to the **Collapsible Menu** dashboard. Click on the drop-down menus associated with both the **Country** and **Year** filter and choose **Apply to Worksheets | Selected Worksheets**.

34. In the resulting dialog boxes, choose **Population Line, Population Map, Population Pie**, and **Population Tree**.

35. Adjust formatting and positioning as desired.

After completing this exercise, you may think, *Okay, the filters do not technically display on the dashboard, but they are still visible to the side.* While this is true in Tableau Desktop, if you are able to upload the workbook to an instance of Tableau Server, you will note that when clicking on the menu icon, the filters appear and disappear and do not display to the side. Note, however, that the same is not true of Tableau Reader. As in Tableau Desktop, in Tableau Reader the end user will be able to see the filters to the side of the dashboard. Fortunately, this limitation is quite easy to overcome. In the solution workbook provided with this chapter, a worksheet entitled `Hider` has been floated off the right side of the dashboard to completely hide the filters from view. Review the `Hider` approach if your design needs require completely hiding material that is beyond the confines of the dashboard.

Summary

We began this chapter by considering theory on visualization design. We considered formatting rules, color rules, and rules about which visualization types to use and which to avoid. We also considered how to compromise when contradictory design goals are expressed by end users.

Next, we discussed dashboard design principles. We covered three popular layouts: Golden Rectangle, Quad, and Small Multiple.

Lastly, we considered how to use sheet selection techniques as an ally in good design. Specifically, we considered how to allow the end user to choose which visualization type to view and how to hide and display filters so as to make the best use of screen real estate.

In the next chapter, we will turn our attention to Tableau Server, where we learn how to build workbooks that perform well, have an efficient footprint, and are easy to maintain.

11
Improving Performance

Recently, while teaching a Tableau Desktop class, a gentleman approached me regarding a dashboard he had built that was performing inadequately. He stated that his dashboard probably flaunted several best practices for performance. Alas, he was correct! The dashboard had close to a dozen filters, most of which were set to show **Only relevant values**. Also, the dashboard was chock-full of worksheets, some of which included thousands of marks. Although we did not look at the underlying data sources, based on our conversation, some of those data sources probably included complex joins. I was amazed that the dashboard performed as well as it did! This underscores a truth that many Tableau authors have experienced: Tableau can perform abysmally if best practices are not followed.

This chapter will address various aspects of performance with the intent of empowering you with techniques for creating workbooks that load quickly and respond snappily to end user interaction. Specifically, the following will be discussed:

- Understanding the Performance Recording dashboard
- Hardware and on-the-fly techniques
- Single Data Source > Joining > Blending
- Efficiently working with data sources
- Intelligent extracts
- Using filters wisely
- Efficient calculations
- Additional performance considerations

Understand the Performance Recording dashboard

Previous to version 8.0, if a Tableau author desired to view queries and other performance-centric information generated by Tableau Desktop, deciphering raw log files was the only option. Another option was introduced in version 8.0; that is, the Performance Recording dashboard.

Exercise – exploring Performance Recording in Tableau Desktop

This exercise and the associated discussion points will survey various aspects of the Performance Recording dashboard, including how to generate it, how to use it to explore options for improving performance, and how it's constructed:

1. Navigate to `https://public.tableau.com/profile/david.baldwin#!/` to locate and download the workbook associated with this chapter.
2. Navigate to the worksheet titled `Types of Events`.
3. Go to **Help | Settings and Performance | Start Performance Recording**.
4. Press *F5* on Windows or *Command + R* on Mac to refresh the view.
5. Go to **Help | Settings and Performance | Stop Performance Recording**.
6. In the resulting `PerformanceRecording.twb` file that displays, drag the events timeline slider to the far left:

7. Note the **Timeline**. By referencing the **Events** legend, it can be easily understood, though the axis may be confusing. The axis in the following screenshot communicates that the recorded events took place in the 11653rd second; that is, the workbook had been open for over 3 hours when the recorded events took place:

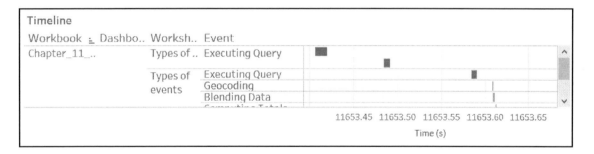

8. Within **Events Sorted by Time**, click on any green bar titled **Executing Query**. Note that the **Query** section now populates. The Query is in TQL since the `Types of Events` worksheet is pointing to an extract:

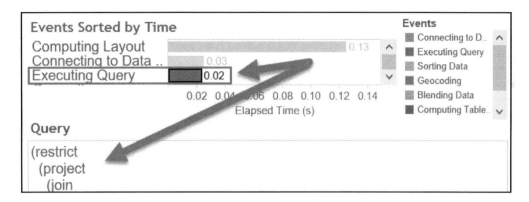

9. Navigate to the `Events` worksheet and right-click on the `Event` group located in the **Data** pane. Select **Edit Group**. Note the complete list of events that can be measured in Tableau. The most common events are listed and discussed later in this chapter.

10. To see the query in its entirety, navigate to the `Query` worksheet and set the fit to **Entire View**. Note that an especially long query may not be recorded in its entirety. In order to see every line of such a query, reference the log files located in `My Tableau Repository`.

Performance Recording dashboard events

In the first exercise of this chapter, the Events worksheet from the Performance Recording dashboard was accessed and the **Event** group was considered. The list of possible events is substantial. This section will not consider every event possibility but will instead focus on the most common events impacting performance and briefly consider how to address performance concerns:

Event type	Performance considerations
Connecting to Data Source	Poor performance when connecting to the data source could indicate network latency or database issues
Generating Extract	See the section titled Intelligent extracts for information regarding optimizing extract performance
Compile Query	Compile Query performance problems could indicate database issues
Executing Query	See the sections titled Using filters wisely and Efficient calculations for information regarding efficient queries
Sorting Data	Performance issues related to sorting issues may indicate too many marks in the view
Geocoding	Geocoding performance issues may indicate too many marks in the view or Internet latency issues
Blending Data	Blending data performance may be improved by reducing the amount of underlying data or by filtering
Computing Table Calculations	Since table calculations are typically performed locally, complex calculations may tax the end user's computer
Computing Totals	Computing totals' performance may be improved by reducing the amount of underlying data or by filtering
Computing Layout	Computing layout performance issues may be indicative of a dashboard with too many worksheets

Behind the scenes of the Performance Recording dashboard

This section explores what happens when performance recording is activated. Note that the following assumes you are working on Tableau Desktop not Tableau Server. As covered in the next chapter, the Performance Recording dashboard is also available on Tableau Server.

When recording performance, Tableau initially creates a file in `My Tableau Repository\Logs` named `performance.[timestamp].tab`. Upon completion of the recording, Tableau copies the resulting TAB file to the `TableauTemp` directory, for example, `C:\Users\DavidaBldwin\AppData\Local\Temp\TableauTemp\0nqsj2c0w2er7e194r x500aj9178`. The TAB file is renamed `perf_gantt.tab`. Additionally, there is a file named `PerformanceRecording_new.twb` located in the Tableau program directory, for example, `C:\Program Files\Tableau\Tableau 10.0\Performance`. That file is copied to the same temp directory where `perf_gantt.tab` is located and renamed `PerformanceRecording.twb`. That file is automatically opened once the recording stops, thus allowing the author to peruse the results.

Hardware and on-the-fly techniques

The number 1 performance inhibitor for Tableau Desktop that I have observed while training in many different organizations across the USA is underpowered machines. Developers almost invariably have excellent computers. Analysts and other business users, regrettably, often do not. In many cases, a few modest upgrades can make a significant improvement. Unfortunately, upgrading a computer may be impossible at many organizations due to a variety of factors, and procuring a new machine may also be quite difficult. Therefore, in this section, we will consider both optimal computer specifications and techniques for working with Tableau on underpowered machines.

Hardware considerations

The published minimum requirements for Tableau Desktop are as follows:

Windows	Mac
• Microsoft Windows 7 or newer (32-bit and 64-bit) • Microsoft Server 2008 R2 or newer (32-bit and 64-bit) • Intel Pentium 4 or AMD Opteron processor or newer (SSE2 or newer required) • 2 GB memory • 1.5 GB minimum free disk space	• iMac/MacBook computers, 2009 or newer • OS X 10.10 or newer

The specifications listed for Mac are adequate upon assuming sufficient RAM (a minimum of 8 GB). Those for Windows, however, are insufficient for many use case scenarios. Instead consider the following recommendations:

Recommended specifications for Windows computers	Notes
Microsoft Windows 7 or newer	Note that most Windows performance reviews will report, at best, modest gains when upgrading. Therefore, don't expect Tableau to run noticeably faster if upgrading beyond Windows 7. *Performance improvement expected by upgrading: Moderate*
64-bit OS	32-bit OS only supports up to 4 GB of memory. As noted later, 8 GB of memory or more is recommended. *Performance improvement expected by upgrading: High (provided the upgrade is accompanied by additional RAM)*
Intel i7 processor	The i5 processor works fine with Tableau but the larger cache and faster processing of the i7 processor enable better multitasking and improve performance overall. *Performance improvement expected by upgrading: Moderate*
8 GB memory or more	RAM is a major performance factor. In short, the more the better. 8 GB will suffice for most purposes but 4 GB is often unsatisfactory, especially if running multiple instances of Tableau. Note that a 64-bit version of Tableau is required to take advantage of RAM in excess of 4 GB. More RAM is particularly important when using a TDE file as a data source since a TDE file is typically loaded in RAM. *Performance improvement expected by upgrading: High*
SSD (solid-state drive)	An SSD outperforms an HDD by a wide margin. Part of the reason is simply better I/O (input/output) performance. Also, over time an HDD will fragment; that is, data is scattered throughout the drive and performance consequently suffers. Fragmentation is irrelevant for an SSD. *Performance improvement expected by upgrading: High*

NVIDIA graphics card	As of Tableau 8.0, rendering performance can be improved via OpenGL. OpenGL enables the Accelerated Graphics option within Tableau. This in turn allows Tableau to utilize a GPU (graphic processing unit) instead of a CPU (central processing unit) for some rendering operations. Accelerated Graphics requires a graphics card. NVIDIA is recommended here because, according to Dan Cory, a technical advisor to the Tableau Development leadership team, Tableau Software (the company) predominately uses NVIDIA graphics cards. Other graphics cards include ATI and Intel HD Graphics 2000, 4000, and 5000. Note that the Intel HD Graphics 4000 card requires updated video drivers for Tableau 9.0 and later. You can update video drivers via the device manager located in the Windows Control Panel. Accelerated Graphics is activated in Tableau by going to **Help | Settings and Performance | Enable Accelerated Graphics**. *Performance improvement expected by upgrading: Moderate*

You may have noticed that the preceding table mostly does not address specific brands. For instance, there is no mention of Dell or Lenovo or HP. Nor are there considerations of different brands of RAM or hard drives. Despite the proliferation of computer and component types (or perhaps as a result of this proliferation), computers and components have become commodities. In short, any name-brand should work fine. In fact off-brand equipment will often perform just as well although the relatively small price savings may not justify additional risks. A little research combined with common sense should lead to satisfactory results when considering which brand of computer or component to purchase.

On-the-fly techniques

Perhaps as a result of the preceding section you have ordered a new, optimal computer. Or, more likely, you may keep all of that in mind should you have the opportunity to obtain a new machine in the near future; but for now you have to make do with what you have. This section discusses tips that will help the Tableau author work more efficiently, irrespective of the equipment used.

Exercise – pause/resume auto updates

Auto updates can be accessed in any of these ways:

- Via the icon located on the toolbar
- By going to **Worksheet** | **Auto Updates**
- Using the shortcut key *F10* on Windows or *Option-Command-0* on Mac

Auto updates give the author the option of pausing/resuming auto updates for the worksheet and/or filters. The following exercise demonstrates how this works:

1. Open the workbook associated with this chapter and navigate to the worksheet titled `Auto Updates`.
2. In the **Data** pane, select the **Superstore** dataset.
3. Place **State** on the **Rows** shelf.
4. Deselect **Auto update** worksheet via the toolbar:

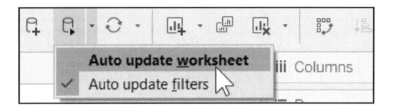

5. Place **City** on the **Rows** shelf to the right of **State**. Note that the view does not update.
6. Enable the `Auto Updates` worksheet via the toolbar. The view now updates.
7. Right-click on **State** on the **Rows** shelf and select **Show Filter**.
8. Now right-click on **City** on the **Rows** shelf and select **Show Filter**.
9. On the **City** quick filter, click on the drop-down menu and select **Multiple values (list)** and **Only relevant values**:

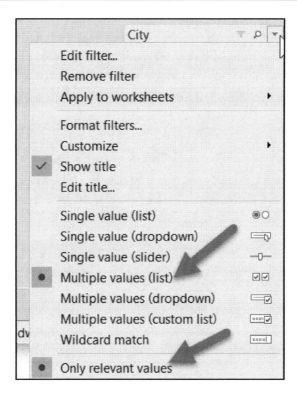

10. Deselect **Auto update filters** via the toolbar.
11. Within the **State** quick filter, select only Alabama. Note that the **City** quick filter does not update.
12. Enable **Auto update filters** via the toolbar. The **City** quick filter now updates.

In practice, **Auto updates worksheet** can be very helpful. The author may pause auto updates, make multiple changes, and then resume auto updates, thereby saving time.

In practice, **Auto update filters** are less useful. However, when using high-cardinality filters (that is, filters with many members), **Auto update filters** can be helpful.

Exercise – Run Update

The **Run Update** icon to the right of **Pause/Resume auto updates** can be confusing. The following brief example should help clarify this option:

1. Duplicate the previous worksheet, `Auto Updates`, and name the duplicate `Run Update`.
2. Pause all updates by clicking on the **Pause Auto Updates** icon.
3. Select several states at random in the **State** quick filter.
4. Click on the **Run Update** icon. As shown in the following screenshot, note that the shortcut key for **Run Update** is *F9* on Windows. The shortcut on Mac is *Shift + command + 0*:

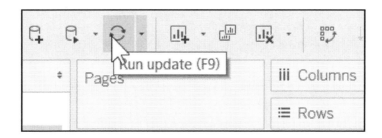

5. Select several more states at random in the **State** quick filter. Note that auto updating is still paused.

In short, **Run Update** allows the Tableau author to intermittently refresh the view while still keeping **Auto Updates** paused.

Exercise – small extracts

Although extracts will be discussed in more detail in the following section, it seems fitting to mention extracts in the context of performance considerations while authoring. Even under optimal conditions, working with large data sources can be slow. If constant access to the entire dataset while authoring is not necessary, consider creating a small, local extract. Author as much of the workbook as possible; and then, when all of the underlying data is truly needed, point to the original data source. The following is a brief example of this technique in action:

1. In the workbook associated with this chapter, navigate to the worksheet titled `Small Local Ext`.

2. Go to **Data** | **New Data Source** to choose a desired data source. This exercise assumes `Sample - Superstore.xls`, which installs with Tableau.

3. Drag **Number of Records** to the **Text** shelf. Note the resulting count.

4. Right-click on `Sample - Superstore.xls` and select **Extract Data**.

5. At the bottom of the **Extract Data** dialog box, select **Top** and choose **1000**:

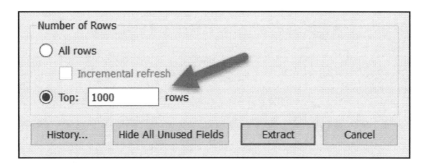

6. Click the **Extract** button and note that **Number of Records** now displays **1000** rows.

7. In the **Data** pane, right-click on **Superstore** and deselect **Use Extract**. Note that the **Number of Records** has reverted to the original value.

By creating a small, local extract, the Tableau author alleviates two performance inhibitors: network latency and dataset size.

Single Data Source > Joining > Blending

One of the beauties of Tableau is the ease with which you can connect to many different data sources in various ways. As mentioned earlier in this book, there are 50 connectors defined in Tableau 10 for interfacing with a variety of data sources. Furthermore, this flexibility extends beyond simply connecting to single tables or files. Previous versions of Tableau accommodated joining within data sources and data blending of disparate data sources. Tableau 10 can even accommodate cross-joining data sources.

Although Tableau makes it easy to connect to various data sources, it should be stressed that Tableau is not an **Extract, Transform, and Load** (ETL) tool. If complex joins and complex data blending are required to generate useful results, it may be advisable to perform ETL work outside of Tableau. Such ETL work will ideally lead to better data modeling and thus easier authoring and quicker performance in Tableau.

Three ways Tableau connects to data

Consider the following three ways Tableau connects to datasets. Tableau may connect to a single table. This is ideal as it allows the most functionality and easiest troubleshooting while enabling Tableau to send the simplest queries and thus perform optimally. However, it is not always possible to connect to a single table, and although ideal, it is not reasonable to have such a strict limitation. The relationship between data sources and reporting tools is constantly changing. A reporting tool that is inflexible in the way it can connect to data will likely not be successful no matter how elegant and beautiful the end results.

The second way Tableau may connect to data is via joining. One table may not supply all the necessary data but by joining two or more tables, all the needed data may be accessible. As joins become more and more complex, performance may be impacted and troubleshooting may become difficult. Fortunately, as we will explore in the following section, Tableau can assume referential integrity and thus work quite efficiently with even complex joins.

Lastly Tableau may utilize data blending.

 Data blending often performs admirably provided that not more than one of the blended data sources is large and dimensions that are used for blending have relatively few members.

When blending multiple, large data sources, performance can be seriously impacted. The problem is further compounded when blending on high-cardinality dimensions. Also, data blending limits some functionality such as the ability to use dimensions, row-level calculations, or LOD expressions from a secondary data source. For these reasons, consider this as a guideline that data blending should normally be avoided if a joining option exists.

Chapter 3, *All about Data – Joins, Blends, and Data Structures*, provides detailed information about joining and blending. For the purpose of this chapter, joining and blending discussions will be limited to performance considerations.

Referential integrity assumes that every key value in one table exists in a corresponding key in another table.

Using referential integrity when joining

Referential integrity is set via **Data | Assume Referential Integrity**. When selected, Tableau only includes a joined table if it is specifically referenced by fields in the view. As a result, queries to the data source are simplified and performance improves.

Ideally, referential integrity should be set at the database level as this will improve database performance as well as performance in Tableau. When referential integrity is set at the database level, Tableau will not include a reference to the joined table (unless that table is specifically referenced by fields in the view) even if **Data | Assume Referential Integrity** is not selected.

Exercise – referential integrity

This example explores how a query is altered when referential integrity is selected:

1. Consider the following two tables. Note that key C does not exist in the **Catalog** table. Also observe that the total sales amount in the **Music Sales** table is $19,500:

	Catalog		Music Sales	
Key	Instrument	Key	Sales	Date
A	Selmer trumpet	A	$3500	8/15/2016
B	Conn French horn	B	$4500	8/15/2016
D	Miraphone tuba	C	$2500	8/16/2016
		D	$9000	8/17/2016

2. In the workbook associated with this chapter, navigate to the worksheet titled `WO_Ref_Int`.
3. Download the spreadsheet titled `RefIntegrity.xlsx`, referenced in the caption of the worksheet.

4. Press *Ctrl + D* to connect to `RefIntegrity.xlsx` using the legacy connection option for Excel, as shown in the following screenshot. The legacy connection is necessary for Tableau to generate a SQL query when connecting to an Excel file:

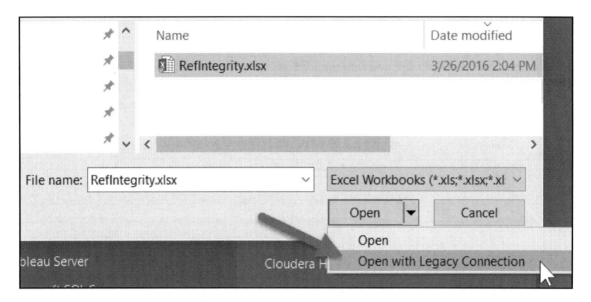

5. Create an inner join between **Music_Sales** and **Cat** using the **Key** field:

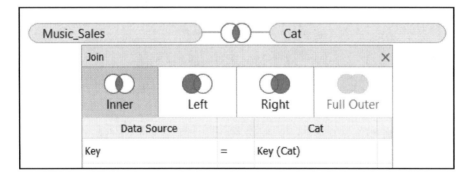

6. Rename the dataset `WO_Ref_Int`.
7. Within the worksheet titled `WO_Ref_Int`, right-click on the `WO_Ref_Int` dataset and ensure that **Assume Referential Integrity** is not selected.
8. Place **Sales** on the **Text** shelf and note the value $17,000.

9. Select **Help** | **Settings and performance** | **Start/Stop Performance Recording** to observe the following query Tableau sent to the underlying data source. Note the inner join:

```
SELECT SUM([Music_Sales$].[Sale Amount]) AS [sum:Sale Amount:ok]
FROM [Music_Sales$]
INNER JOIN [Cat$] ON [Music_Sales$].[Key] = [Cat$].[Key]
HAVING (COUNT(1) > 0)
```

10. The value of $17,000 reflects the inner join. Since the key *C* was not included in the **Catalog** table, the associated $2500 was not included in the total (Recall that the total sales amount in the **Music Sales** table is $19,500).
11. Navigate to the worksheet titled `W_Ref_Int`.
12. Right-click on the `WO_Ref_Int` data source to duplicate it.
13. Rename the duplicate data source `W_Ref_Int`.
14. Right-click on the `W_Ref_Int` dataset and ensure that **Assume Referential Integrity** is selected.
15. Place **Sales** on the **Text** shelf and note the value $19,500 (if the view does not display $19,500, refresh the view by pressing *F5* on Windows or Command + *R* on Mac).
16. Observe the query Tableau sent to the underlying data source. Note that an inner join is not included:

```
SELECT SUM([Music_Sales$].[Sale Amount]) AS [sum:Sale Amount:ok]
FROM [Music_Sales$]
HAVING (COUNT(1) > 0)
```

The value of $19,500 demonstrates that the **Catalog** table was not referenced. Tableau assumed referential integrity and simply reported **SUM(Sale Amount)** from the **Music_Sales** table.

When it's necessary or advantageous to blend

As mentioned previously, joining should be chosen instead of blending when possible. However, there are exceptions, two of which are discussed here. First, data blending is advantageous (and usually necessary) when there is no common key shared between two tables. Also, data blending may be necessary when it is easier to update a local spreadsheet than maintain an additional table in a database, although it is important to point out that this use of blending is somewhat deprecated with Tableau 10 since Tableau 10 can cross-join data sources. The following example, however, demonstrates an occasion when cross-joining will not work and a data blend is required.

Exercise – necessary blending

This example uses a small secondary dataset with quota information and no unique row-level keys. It illustrates a use case scenario in which it's easier to create and maintain a local spreadsheet rather than properly model the same information in a database:

1. In the workbook associated with this chapter, navigate to the worksheet titled Necessary Blending.
2. In the **Data** pane, select the **Superstore** dataset.
3. Place Region on the **Rows** shelf and Sales on the **Text** shelf.
4. In the **Data** pane, select the **Quota** dataset and make sure that **Region** has an orange chain icon next to it to ensure that **Region** is used as a linking field. Note that the **Quota** dataset contains no row-level keys and thus is not eligible for joining.
5. Double-click on the **Quota** measure to place it on the view.
6. At this point, the blend is working well. The correct numbers are displaying, the secondary dataset is quite small, and there is only one linking field.
7. In the **Data** pane, select the **Superstore** dataset.
8. Drag **Order Date** on the **Rows** shelf to the left of **Region**. Note that the correct numbers are not displaying for **Quota**.
9. In the **Data** pane, right-click on **Order Date** and select **Create | Custom Date**.
10. In the resulting dialog box, set **Name** to **Year** and **Detail** to **Years** and choose **Date Part**. Click on **OK**:

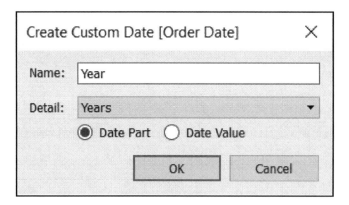

11. In the **Data** pane, select the **Quota** dataset.
12. Set **Year** as a linking field.

Quota now displays correctly. Note that both **Year** and **Region** are used as linking fields. Though necessary for the second half of the preceding exercise, linking on both fields is not ideal for performance because it requires Tableau to generate two additional queries. Follow the steps discussed previously to turn on performance recording in order to review the queries Tableau generates.

In the preceding exercise, is it possible to cross-join the **Superstore** and **Quota** data sources by joining on both the **Region** and the **Year** fields? No. The Year field is a calculated field and it is not possible to join on calculated fields in Tableau 10.

Working efficiently with data sources

This section will cover some basics of database tuning and ways to work efficiently with large data sources. Since the topic is more focused on data sources than on Tableau, no exercises are included.

Tuning data sources

If you are connecting to large data sources and are experiencing performance problems, a conversation with a **Database Administrator** (**DBA**) may be beneficial. Clear communication coupled with a small amount of database work could dramatically improve performance. The conversation should include database tuning points such as explicitly defining primary and foreign keys, defining columns as *NOT NULL*, and indexing. Each point will be discussed here.

Primary and foreign keys

Primary and foreign keys are essential for joining tables. A primary key comprises one or more columns in a table. The primary key should be unique for every row. Joining on a non-unique, row-level key may lead to erroneous results as explored in the exercise titled *A data blend versus a left join* in `Chapter 3`, *All about Data – Joins, Blends, and Data Structures*. Explicitly defining primary keys in the database helps ensure that each key value is unique:

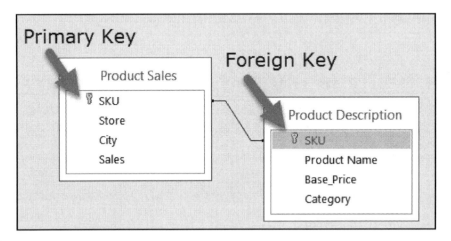

A foreign key is comprised of one or more columns in a table that uniquely identify rows in another table. This unique identification occurs as a result of the foreign key in one table referencing the primary key in another table. Explicitly defining foreign keys in the database enables Tableau to bypass many integrity checks thus improving performance.

NOT NULL

Tableau has published a PDF titled `Basic Performance Tips` which states: "*Programmers and Tableau Desktop do not like NULL data. Define each column in your tables with an explicit NOT NULL if possible.*" In practice, DBAs debate when it is and when it is not appropriate to define columns as NOT NULL; however, two things are clear. A primary or foreign key should be defined as NOT NULL. This is self-evident since primary and foreign keys must be unique by definition. Also, any column that is to be indexed should be defined as NOT NULL, since otherwise an index may be unusable. Indexing is discussed more fully in the next section.

What is an index?

Let's consider the following two questions regarding indexing:

- What is an index?
- What should be indexed?

The first of our two questions may be easily answered by a DBA, but is probably uncharted waters for the Tableau author.

 An index is a copy of selected columns in a database table that have been optimized for efficient searching.

Since these copied columns include pointers to the original columns, they can be accessed to quickly find given rows and return the required data. A small example may prove helpful.

According to the Boeing Company, the 787 Dreamliner has about 2.3 million parts. Imagine a table listing all of these parts in the Part_Name column. Your task is to search this column for every part starting with the string *fuse*. On a non-indexed column this would require the examination of every row of data in the database. Such a search could be quite slow. Fortunately, indexes can be used to reduce the number of rows searched, thus making the process much faster. One type of data structured used for indexing is B-tree. A B-tree data structure is sorted. Thus when accessing an index using a B-tree data structure to search for all parts starting with *fuse*, not every row has to be considered. Instead the database can skip straight to those products that start with the letter f and quickly return the desired rows.

What should be indexed?

Now let's move on to the second question about indexing. What should be indexed? As shown in the following information box, the question of what can be indexed can be answered fairly succinctly.

 Ideally, all columns used for joining or filtering should be indexed in the data source.

Later in this chapter, methods for efficiently using filters in Tableau regardless of indexing will be discussed. Although there are some basic performance considerations for creating more efficient joins in Tableau (for example, avoid an outer join when a left join will suffice), join performance is largely determined outside of Tableau. Therefore, it is typically more important to index columns used in joins than those used for filtering.

Working efficiently with large data sources

A colleague of mine recently consulted with a relatively small mobile phone service provider. Even though the company was small, the volume could be in excess of 1,000,000 calls per day. The management at the company insisted on the ability to interface with detailed visualizations of individual calls in Tableau workbooks. The performance of the workbooks was, understandably, a problem. Was such a low-level detail necessary? Might less detail and snappier workbooks have led to better business decisions?

In order to balance business needs with practical performance requirements, businesses often need to ascertain what level of detail is genuinely helpful for reporting. Often detailed granularity is not necessary. When such is the case, a summary table may provide sufficient business insight while enabling quick performance. In the case of the mobile phone service provider mentioned previously, a daily snapshot of call volume may have sufficed. Even an hourly snapshot would have greatly reduced the table size and improved Tableau performance. As will be discussed in the next section, Tableau can be used to create summarized datasets via extracting.

Intelligent extracts

This section will discuss what a **Tableau Data Extract** (TDE) is as well as how to efficiently construct an extract.

Understanding the Tableau Data Extract

A **Tableau Data Extract** (TDE) is a proprietary compressed data source created by Tableau Desktop. A TDE can be stored locally and accessed by Tableau to render visualizations. Consider the following points; they make a .tde file an excellent choice for improved performance:

- A TDE can be quickly generated at an aggregate level:
  - See the walkthrough of the **Extract Data** dialog box.

- A TDE is a columnar store:
  - Relational databases typically store data using a Row store methodology. A columnar store records as sequences of columns.
  - In the following example, note that Row store is excellent for returning individual rows, whereas Column store is much better for returning aggregated data:

	Table		
	Instrument	Store	Price
Row 1	Selmer Trumpet	North	$3500
Row 2	Conn French Horn	East	$4500
Row 3	Getzen Trombone	South	$2500
Row 4	Miraphone Tuba	West	$9000

Row store		Column store	
Row 1	Selmer Trumpet	Instrument	Selmer Trumpet
	North		Conn French Horn
	$3,500		Getzen Trombone
Row 2	Conn French Horn		Miraphone Tuba
	East	Store	North
	$4,500		East
Row 3	Getzen Trombone		South
	South		West
	$2,500	Price	$3,500
Row 4	Miraphone Tuba		$4,500
	West		$2,500
	$9,000		$9,000

- A TDE uses compression techniques to reduce file size while maintaining performance
- A TDE is architect aware. This means that a TDE tries to utilize both RAM and hard drive space for optimal performance

Constructing a TDE for optimal performance

This section will discuss the TDE from a performance point of view. Other aspects of extracts such as scheduling and incremental refreshes will not be considered here.

A TDE is created via **Data** | **[Data Source]** | **Extract Data.** Note that the numbers contained in the following screenshot indicate areas that are discussed in the text following the screenshot:

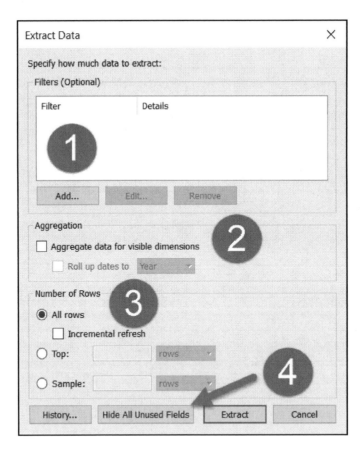

1. Filter the extract as needed:
    - Sometimes an extract that exactly reflects a data source is warranted, but often filtering various fields will still populate the extract with the required data while shrinking the size and improving performance. To add a filter simply click **Add...** to access a dialog box identical to the filter dialog box used within a worksheet.

2. Aggregate to the level of the granularity represented in the view:
    - Aggregation not only reduces the file size but can also be helpful from a security standpoint. Without aggregation, a TDE is constructed using row-level data. Therefore the Tableau author should note that if the extract is built without choosing to aggregate, any sensitive row-level data is accessible.

3. Reduce the number of rows:
    - As shown in the preceding section entitled *On the Fly techniques*, reducing the number of rows can allow the author to create a small, local extract for quick workbook building after which the original data source can be accessed for complete analysis.

4. Hide all unused fields:
    - This option excludes from the extract all columns that are not used in the workbook. This can significantly reduce the extract size and improve performance.

Exercise – summary aggregates for improved performance

The following exercise will use two aggregates from a single data source, one at the **State** level and the other at the **City** level. These aggregated data sources will be used to create two worksheets. Each of these worksheets will be placed on a dashboard along with a third worksheet with row level information. Finally, filter actions will be created to tie the three worksheets together. The purpose of the exercise is to demonstrate how small extracts might be used in conjunction with a larger dataset to create a more performant dashboard:

1. Open the workbook associated with this chapter and navigate to the worksheet titled State Agg.
2. In the **Data** pane, select the **SS – State Agg** data source.
3. Create a filled map using state by placing **State** on the **Detail** shelf and selecting **Filled Map** from the **Marks View** card.
4. Right-click on the **SS – State Agg** data source and select **Extract Data**.

5. Note that Tableau displays an error stating that it cannot find the referenced file. You can either point to the instance of **Sample – Superstore** that ships with Tableau, or use the instance provided via the link in the worksheet's caption.

6. After connecting to the data source, Tableau will display the **Extract Data** dialog box. Within the resulting dialog box, select **Aggregate** data for visible dimensions and **All Rows**.

7. Click on the **Hide All Unused Fields** button and then click on **Extract**. Note that the resulting extract only contains **State**. Also note that the data has been aggregated so that no underlying data is available:

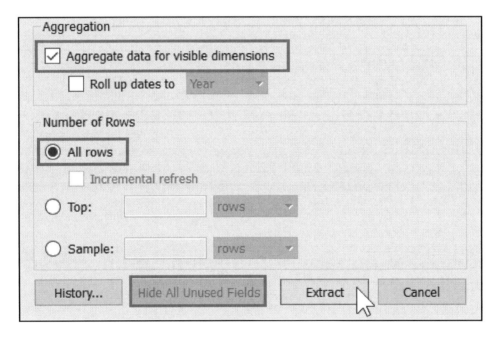

8. Navigate to the worksheet titled City Agg.

9. In the **Data** pane, select the **SS – City Agg** data source. Note that this data source has already been extracted and thus only contains **State**, **City**, and **Sales**. Also note that the data has been aggregated so that no underlying data is available.

10. Place **City** on the **Rows** shelf, **Sales** on the **Text** shelf, and **State** on the **Detail** shelf. Don't forget to include **State** even though it does not display on the view. It must be used so that the dashboard created at the end of the exercise works correctly.

11. Navigate to the **Row Detail** worksheet and select the **Superstore** dataset.

12. Create a crosstab view displaying **Customer Name**, **Order ID**, **Row ID**, **Profit**, and **Sales**.

> One quick way to create this view is to double-click, in order, on each field.

13. Navigate to the **Agg Dash** dashboard and place each of the three worksheets created previously on the dashboard.

14. Create the following actions via **Dashboard** | **Actions** | **Add Action** | **Filter**:

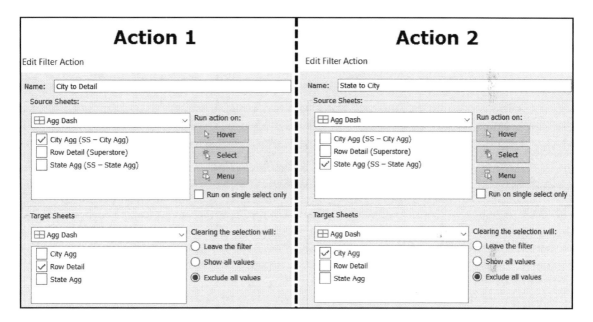

15. After creating the preceding two actions, in the dashboard, click on a state.

16. Next, click on a city.

17. Click in a blank portion of the `City Agg` worksheet to exclude all values on **Row Detail**.

18. Click on a blank portion of the `State Agg` worksheet to exclude all values on **City Agg**.

19. Format the dashboard as desired:

Having completed the exercise, note that the resulting dashboard is quite performant:

- When the user first opens the dashboard, only **State Agg** displays. This is performant for two reasons. First, displaying a single worksheet as opposed to every worksheet when opening the dashboard causes fewer initial queries and less rendering. Second, accessing a small extract is quicker than accessing a larger data source.
- Since the City Agg worksheet is also accessing a small extract, when the user clicks on a state, the City Agg worksheet will appear quickly.
- When the user clicks on a city, a call is made to the data source that only includes the information for that particular city. A relatively small amount of data is pulled and performance should be good for even larger datasets.

Another aspect of good performance practice, apart from using aggregate extracts, should be considered for the preceding exercise. The dashboard contains no quick filters. Often, using quick filters on a dashboard is unnecessary. If the worksheets on the dashboard can be used to filter, then those worksheets can essentially pull double duty. That is to say, worksheets can provide valuable analysis while simultaneously acting as filters for other worksheets on the dashboard. This represents a performance improvement over using quick filters since adding quick filters would cause additional queries to be sent to the underlying data source.

In the previous dashboard, each worksheet references a different data source. Therefore one might ask: *how are the action filters able to function across the different data sources?* The answer can be found in the **Filter Action** dialog box. As shown in the following screenshot, **All Fields** are considered **Target Fields**. Tableau simply matches any fields of the same name across each data source:

Optimizing extracts

Extracts can be optimized for even better performance results. To optimize an extract, simply right-click on a data source and select **Data** | **Extract** | **Optimize**. Optimization accelerates performance by materializing calculated fields when possible. This means that Tableau actually generates values for calculated fields in the extract so that those values can be looked up instead of calculated. Note that not all calculated fields are materialized. Fields that are not materialized include table calculations, changeable or unstable functions such as NOW() and TODAY(), and also calculated fields using parameters.

When an extract is first created, it is automatically optimized. In other words, calculated fields are automatically materialized when possible. However, over the course of time, calculated fields may be altered; that will cause the extract to drop materialized fields. At such times, **Extract** | **Optimize** must be selected in order to regenerate the materialized fields:

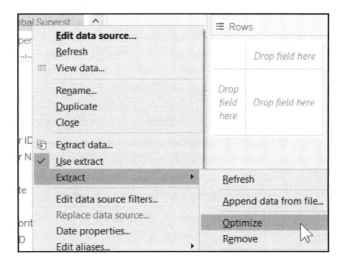

If an extract is set to refresh on Tableau Server, the extract is automatically optimized for each refresh. The following example demonstrates calculated fields that are materialized and those that are not.

Exercise - materialized calculations

This example demonstrates calculated fields that are materialized and those that are not:

1. In Tableau, select **File** | **New** to create a new workbook.
2. In the new workbook, select **Data** | **New Data Source** and connect to the **Sample Superstore** dataset located in My Tableau Repository/Datasources.
3. Connect to the Orders worksheet.
4. Create the following parameter:

Parameter	
Name	Select Sufficient Profit Ratio
Data Type	Float
Allowable Values	Range
Min/Max	0.25 – 0.5
Step Size	0.01

5. Create the following calculated fields:

Name	Calculation
Profit Ratio	SUM([Profit])/SUM([Sales])
This Year's Profit	IF [Profit Ratio] > [Select Sufficient Profit Ratio] THEN "Sufficient Profit" END
Window Sum	WINDOW_SUM(SUM([Sales]))
Profitable?	[Profit] > 0

6. Right-click on the data source and select **Extract data**.
7. Click the **Extract** button.
8. When prompted, save the resulting extract to a location of your choosing.
9. Open a new Tableau workbook and select **File** | **Open**; select the extract created in the preceding step.

10. Note the following in the data source:
    1. **Profit Ratio**, an aggregate calculation, was materialized.
    2. **This Year's Profit**, which references a parameter, has a value of null and was not materialized.
    3. **Window Sum**, a table calculation, has a value of undefined and was not materialized.
    4. **Profitable?**, a row-level calculation, was materialized.

Using filters wisely

Filters generally improve performance in Tableau. For example, when using a dimension filter to view only the West region, a query is passed to the underlying data source, resulting in returned information for only that region. By reducing the amount of data returned, performance improves. Basically, this is because less data means reduced network bandwidth load, reduced database processing requirements, and reduced processing requirements for the local computer.

Filters can also negatively impact Tableau's performance. For example, using *only relevant values* causes additional queries to be sent to the underlying data source, thus slowing the response time. Also, creating quick filters from high-cardinality dimensions can slow performance.

Navigating filter usage so as to maximize efficient usage and minimize inefficient usage will be the focus of this section.

Extract filter performance

Extract filters remove data from the extracted data source. Simply put, the data isn't there. Thus, performance is enhanced by reducing the overall amount of data. Performance may also be improved since extracted data uses Tableau's proprietary, columnar dataset. Furthermore, extracts are always flattened, which will have performance advantages over connecting to datasets using joins.

To create an extract filter, begin by selecting **Data** | **[Data Source]** | **Extract Data**. In the resulting dialog box, choose to add a filter.

Data source filter performance

Data source filters are applied throughout the workbook. For example, if you create a data source filter that removes all members of the **Country** dimension except USA, the **Country** dimension will only include USA for all worksheets in the workbook.

Data source filters improve performance in the same way as dimension and measure filters; that is, data source filters cause Tableau to generate a query to the underlying data source, which will limit the data that is returned. Less returned data generally results in quicker processing and rendering. A further advantage data source filters offer is ease of authoring. For example, if the Tableau author knows in advance that an entire workbook is going to be focused on the United States,, then creating a data source filter saves the trouble of applying a dimension filter to every worksheet in the workbook using that data source.

Also note that data source filters occur quite early in the process flow. All calculations (including calculations using Fixed LOD expressions, which are rendered before dimension and measure filters are triggered) respect data source filters.

To create a data source filter, click on the **Data Source** tab located in the bottom-left corner of Tableau. Next, click on the **Add...** link located in the top-right corner of the page:

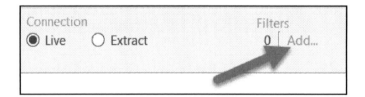

Context filters

A context filter is created simply by right-clicking on a field in the **Filter** shelf and selecting **Add to Context**.

Dimension and measure filters are independent. Each filter queries the data source independently and returns results. A context filter, on the other hand, will force dimension and measure filters to depend on it. This behavior can be helpful (and necessary) for getting the right answer in some circumstances. For instance, if a Tableau author accesses the **Superstore** dataset and uses a filter on **Product Names** to return the 10 top selling product names in a single **Category**, it will be necessary that **Category** be defined as a context filter. Otherwise, the **Product Names** filter will return the top 10 overall.

But will a context filter improve performance any more than a dimension or measure filter? The answer to that question changed with the release of Tableau 9.0. Consider the following SQL generated from Tableau 8.3 and 9.0. Note that in each case, the Superstore dataset is used; **Product Name** is constrained to the top 10 by **Sales** and **Category** is cast as a context filter, displaying only **Furniture**:

SQL generated by Tableau 8.3	SQL generated by Tableau 9.0
`SELECT [#Tableau_Context].[Product Name] AS [none:Product Name:nk] FROM [#Tableau_Context] INNER JOIN ( SELECT TOP 10 [#Tableau_Context].[Product Name] AS [none:Product Name:nk] ...`	`SELECT [Orders$].[Product Name] AS [Product Name] FROM [dbo].[Orders$] [Orders$] INNER JOIN ( SELECT TOP 10 [Orders$].[Product Name] AS [Product Name] ... WHERE ([Orders$].[Category] = 'Furniture')`

The 8.3 query references `[#Tableau_Context]` and does not reference `[Category]`. This is because `[#Tableau_Context]` is a temporary table that has been created in the data source (in this case, SQL Server). Since the temp table only contains data for **Furniture**, a WHERE clause is not needed.

The 9.0 query references `[Orders$]` and does contain a reference to **Category**. This is because `[Orders$]` is not a temp table, and therefore a WHERE clause is required to constrain the results.

This illustrates that when using Tableau 8.3 and previous, if a context filter can be used that will produce a significantly smaller table than exists in the source database, then performance might improve. However, since no temp table is created after 8.3, there may be no corresponding performance improvement in Tableau 9.0 or later, including Tableau 10.0.

At this point, a question may be raised: *are there still some scenarios for which a temp table may be created for a context filter?* The Tableau documentation states the following:

> As of Tableau 9.0, context filters no longer create temporary tables, except for generic ODBC data sources and customized data sources.

The end result is that context filters are still necessary for some visualizations to get the right answer, but performance enhancements beyond what is normally expected for dimension and measure filters may be unlikely. Of course, individual circumstances may differ and it's worth trying a context filter for performance improvement.

Another question may be raised at this point: *why did the Tableau development team change the way context filters are realized?* Consider these answers. First, in some environments, granting Tableau permission to create temp tables may require additional rights and thus make Tableau more difficult to deploy. Also, if a context filter creates a temp table that is not significantly smaller than the source table, performance may actually degrade.

Dimension and measure filters

Dimension and measure filters can improve performance. Since either a dimension filter or a measure filter will cause Tableau to generate a query to the underlying data source which will limit the data that is returned, performance is improved. Simply put, the smaller the returned dataset, the better the performance.

Dimension and measure filters can degrade performance. Since Tableau not only generates queries to the underlying data source in order to display visualizations but also generates queries to display filters, more displayed filters will slow performance. Furthermore, displayed filters on high-cardinality dimensions can inhibit performance (a dimension with many members is referred to as having high-cardinality). Consider the example of a filter that displays every customer in a dataset. Performance for such a filter might be slow because every customer in the underlying dataset must be located and returned and then Tableau has to render and display each of these customers in the filter.

When using two or more dimension or measure filters on a view, a relevant filter may be used to limit the choices that display. For example, if a view includes a filter for **City** and **Postal Code**, the later might be set to show **Only relevant values**. This is advantageous to the end user in that it adjusts the number of **Postal Codes** that are displayed to reflect only those pertinent to the cities selected in the first filter. However, using relative filters will cause additional queries to be sent to the data source and thus may degrade performance:

Table calculation filters

Using table calculations as filters do not have the same corresponding performance enhancements as dimension or measure filters. As discussed previously, dimension and measure filters reduce the returned dataset. Table calculation filters do not. In the Tableau process flow, table calculations are not rendered until after data is returned from the data source. This means that table calculations cannot be used to generate queries to limit returned data. Or, to put it another way, table calculation filters cause all data related to a given dimension or measure to be returned, after which Tableau executes the filter on the returned dataset.

Exercise – late filter

This exercise demonstrates how to create and use a table calculation filter:

1. Open the workbook associated with this chapter and navigate to the worksheet titled Late Filter.
2. In the **Data** pane, select the **Superstore** data source.
3. Create a calculated field named **Cust Name Tbl Calc** with the following code:

   ```
   LOOKUP( MAX( [Customer Name] ),0 )
   ```

4. Place **Customer Name** on the **Rows** shelf.
5. Place **Cust Name Tbl Calc** on the **Filters** shelf and constrain to show only **Aaron Bergman**:
6. Place **Sales** on the **Text** shelf.
7. Right-click on '**Sales**' and select **Quick table calculation** | **Rank**.

In the previous exercise, the entire list of customers is returned to Tableau, after which Tableau deploys the filter. Essentially, using **Cust Name Tbl Calc** as a filter merely hides the underlying data. This is useful because the rank returned for **Aaron Bergman** is correct. Merely filtering on **Customer Name** would return a rank of 1 for **Aaron Bergman**. Unfortunately, the correct results come with a performance hit. Running the performance recorder on the preceding exercise will show that the table calculation negatively impacts performance.

Fortunately with the advent of **level of detail** (**LOD**) calculations in Tableau 9.0, using table calculations as filters is often not necessary. See the exercise titled *Practical Fixed* in Chapter 6, *Level of Detail Calculations*, for more information.

Efficient calculations

Calculations may be constructed differently and yet accomplish the same thing, for instance:

Scenario I	Scenario II
• Create a calculated field with the following code: `IF SUM (Profit) > 0 THEN 'Profitable' ELSE 'Unprofitable' END` • Place the calculated field on the **Color** shelf.	• Create a calculated field with the following code: `SUM (Profit) > 0` • Place the calculated field on the **Color** shelf. • Right-click on **True** and **False** in the resulting legend and rename as **Profitable** and **Unprofitable**.

Since either of the preceding scenarios will return the desired results, which should be used? The deciding factor is performance. This section will explore what to do and what to avoid when creating calculated fields in order to maximize performance.

Boolean/Numbers > Date > String

As this header suggests, calculations that use Boolean values or numbers are more performant than those that use dates. Calculations that use dates, in turn, are more performant than those using strings. This is not only true of Tableau but also in computer science as a whole.

Based on this information, Scenario II listed in the preceding table is more performant than Scenario I. Scenario I causes Tableau to create a query that requires the data source engine to handle strings for reporting profitability, whereas Scenario II sends only 1s and 0s to determine profitability. The third step for Scenario II (that is, aliasing **True** and **False** to **Profitable** and **Unprofitable**) is merely a labeling change that happens after the aggregate dataset is returned from the data source. Labeling is quick and easy for Tableau.

Exercise – an efficient and an inefficient way to determine N figure salary

The following exercise uses two calculations to determine the number of integers in individual annual income. The first method, while perhaps using more easily readable code, uses the STR function and is thus slower. The second method avoids the STR function and is thus quicker:

1. Open the workbook associated with this chapter and navigate to the worksheet titled `Salary`.
2. In the **Data** pane, select the data source named `Salary`.
3. Place **Tax Payer** on the **Rows** shelf and **Salary** on the **Text** shelf.
4. Create the following calculated fields:

Name	Calculation
X Figure Salary 1	`LEN(STR([Salary]))`
X Figure Salary 2	`INT(LOG([Salary]) + 1)`

5. Complete the view with both newly created calculated fields:

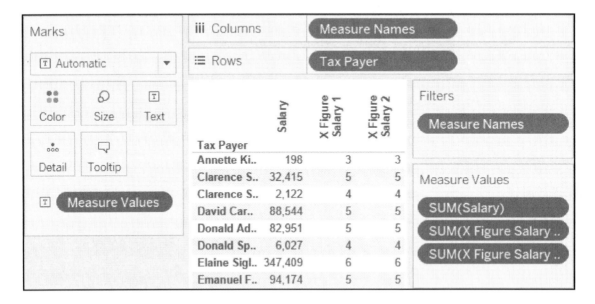

Exercise – date versus integer

The following exercise uses two calculations and two parameters to determine sales in the **Superstore** dataset. One parameter is set to **Date** and the other is set to **Integer**. The calculations associated with the parameters handle each data type accordingly. Even though the resulting query that is sent to the data source is much the same in each case, a potential performance boost is realized when Tableau uses integers as opposed to dates:

1. Open the workbook associated with this chapter and navigate to the worksheet titled `Chosen Year - Date`.
2. In the **Data** pane, select the **Superstore** data source.
3. Create the following parameters:

Parameter 1		Parameter 2	
Name	Select Year – Date	Name	Select Year – Int
Data Type	Date & Time	Data Type	Integer
Display Format	Select **Custom** and input yyyy	Display Format	Select **Custom** and input 0;-0
Allowable Values	Range	Allowable Values	List
Min/Max	Set from field **Order Date**	Value/Display As	2011 2012 2013 2014
Step Size	1 Year		

Note that the display format 0;-0 in **Select Year – Int** is needed so that a comma is not displayed, for example, 2,013.

4. Create the following calculated fields:

Name	Calculation
Chosen Year – Date	`IF YEAR([Order Date]) = YEAR(   [Select Year - Date] ) THEN [Sales] END`
Chosen Year – Int	`IF YEAR([Order Date]) = [Select   Year - Int] THEN [Sales] END`

5. Place **State** on the **Detail** shelf and **Chosen Year – Date** on both the **Color** shelf and the **Text/Label** shelf.

6. Right-click on the **Select Year – Date** parameter and choose to show the parameter control.
7. Set the parameter as desired.
8. Navigate to the worksheet titled **Chosen Year – Int**.
9. Place **State** on the **Detail** shelf and **Chosen Year – Int** on both the **Color** shelf and the **Text/Label** shelf.
10. Right-click on the **Select Year – Int** parameter and choose to show the parameter control.
11. Set the **Select Year – Int** parameter the same as the **Select Year – Date** parameter.

The displayed results of both the Chosen Year – Date and Chosen Year – Int worksheets are the same; however, Chosen Year – Int performs better.

Additional performance considerations

To conclude this chapter, let's consider a few other possibilities for improving performance.

Avoid overcrowding a dashboard

Often, end users want to see everything at once on a dashboard. Although this may be perceived as beneficial, it often is not. Consider the inclusion of a large crosstab on a dashboard. Does scrolling through pages of details add to the analytical value of the dashboard? Perhaps, the answer is no. Furthermore, an excess of information on a dashboard may obscure some important insight. Diplomatically arguing for leaner dashboards may lead to better decision making as well as better performance.

Fix dashboard sizing

Dashboards can be set to an exact size or to **Range** or **Automatic**. Exact size results in quicker performance because once Tableau Server has rendered a view for one end user, that render stays in cache and can be reused for the next end user who accesses that dashboard. **Automatic** and **Range**, on the other hand, cause Tableau Server to attempt to determine the resolution size used by each end user and render the dashboard accordingly. This means that Tableau Server does not use the instance of the dashboard stored in cache for the next end user, and this, in turn, impacts performance.

Set expectations

If an end user is expecting near-instantaneous performance, then, of course, anything less is disappointing. Explaining in advance that a complicated, detailed-oriented dashboard may not be performant can help in at least two ways. First, upon explaining the likely performance problems, a compromise may be reached that results in the creation of a less complicated dashboard that nonetheless delivers valuable information. Second, if it is absolutely necessary for the dashboard to be complicated and detailed-oriented, at least the end user has been warned that patience may be needed when interfacing with the dashboard.

Summary

We began this chapter with a discussion on the Performance Recording dashboard. This was important because many of the subsequent exercises utilized the Performance Recording dashboard to examine underlying queries. Next was a discussion on hardware and On-the-fly techniques where the intent was to communicate hardware considerations for good Tableau performance and, in the absence of optimal hardware, techniques for getting the best possible performance out of any computer.

Then we covered working with data sources, including a section titled Single Data Source > Joining > Blending and another titled `Efficiently working with Data Sources`. This was followed by a discussion on generating and using extracts as efficiently as possible. By focusing on data sources for these three sections, we learned best practices and what to avoid when working with either remote datasets or extracts.

The next sections, *Using filters wisely* and *Efficient calculations*, explored performance implications for various types of filters and calculations. Lastly, we covered *Additional performance considerations*, where we explored a few more thoughts about dashboard performance, as well as setting expectations.

In the next chapter, we will turn our attention to Tableau Server. Tableau Server is a dense topic, worthy of a book on its own. Thus, our exploration will be truncated to focus on Tableau Server from a desktop author's perspective.

12
Interacting with Tableau Server

Not too long ago I had a Tableau engagement in Houston, Texas with a relatively small company in the oil and gas industry. This company was not ready to purchase a copy of Tableau Server. I spent quite a bit of time considering how best to create and deploy a centralized repository to share packaged workbooks and data sources that could be easily shared among Tableau authors and also downloaded by end users for display on Tableau Reader. The security concerns, maintenance difficulties and functionality limitations caused me to really begin to appreciate Tableau Server. Although Tableau Server is not necessary for every environment in which Tableau Desktop is used, it is necessary for many environments, and even when not strictly required can be very helpful.

This chapter does not assume any knowledge of Tableau Server. Thus, when Tableau Server is the focus of a given section, basic information is provided. When Tableau Desktop is the focus, however, proficiency is assumed.

Given the preceding paragraph, let's begin with a brief explanation of what Tableau Server is. Let's paraphrase the help documentation:

Tableau Server is an online solution for sharing, distributing, and collaborating on content created in Tableau Desktop. Benefits include providing an environment where end users can securely view and explore data visualizations that are constantly updated from underlying data sources so that content is always fresh.

This chapter does assume access to Tableau Server with sufficient privileges for publishing data sources and editing in the web authoring environment. If you do not have access to Tableau Server but would like to work through the exercises in this chapter, consider downloading a trial version which, at the time of writing, is fully functional for two weeks. If you would like a longer trial, consider joining the Tableau Beta program at http://www.t ableau.com/getbeta, which will give you two weeks of access for each beta release in which you participate.

The scope of this chapter is limited to the Tableau Desktop author's interaction with Tableau Server. Topics such as installation and upgrades, authentication and access, security configuration, and command line utilities are not directly related to the Tableau Desktop author's interaction with Tableau Server and are thus are not included in this chapter. At the time writing I am unaware of any books focused exclusively on Tableau Server; however, the help documentation is quite good. If you have questions related to the topics listed or other Tableau Server centric topics, be sure to visit online help at `http://on linehelp.tableau.com/current/server/en-us/help.htm`.

This chapter will explore the following topics:

- Tableau file types
- Tableau Server architecture
- Tableau Server web authoring environment
- Tableau Server revision history
- User filters
- Accessing the Tableau Server Performance Recording dashboard

Tableau file types

We will begin our discussion of Tableau Server by considering the various Tableau file types. This may seem a surprising place to begin, but as you read you will discover that a clear understanding of file types provides the Tableau Desktop author with foundational knowledge for efficiently and effectively interacting with Tableau Server.

The file types discussed in the following section that are relevant for understanding how to interact with Tableau Server are considered in some depth. The file types that are not relevant for understanding Tableau Server are considered only briefly. Some file types (for example, those associated with license activation) are not considered.

Tableau Data Source (.tds)

- **File format type**: XML.
- **What it contains**: Metadata.

- **Why it is useful**: The .tds file is important because it allows the Tableau author to define default formatting and aggregation, calculated fields, data types, field types, and more. Furthermore, the .tds file can be published to Tableau Server and thus accessed by other authors in the environment. This effectively makes a .tds file a playbook ensuring consistency across the organization. This important feature will be explored more fully in the section on *Tableau Server architecture.*

- **How it's generated**: A .tds file can be generated by right-clicking on a data source in the **Data** pane and selecting **Add to Saved Data Sources...** followed by selecting **Tableau Data Source** in the resulting dialog box.
  A .tds file can also be generated when publishing to Tableau Server via **Server | Publish Data Source | [data source]**. Later in this chapter, an exercise is included that demonstrates how to publish a .tds file and also a .tdsx file.

- **How to access it**: The .tds file type is usually accessed in one of two places. First it can be stored in **My Tableau Repository | Datasources**. When stored in this directory, a .tds file will be displayed in the left-hand portion of the **Start Page** under the section entitled **Saved Data Sources**. The second place a .tds file is often stored is on Tableau Server. Selecting **Data | New Data Source** and choosing **Tableau Server** allows the Tableau author to point to the .tds and .tdsx files that have been published to Tableau Server.

Tableau Packaged Data Source (.tdsx)

- **File format type**: Compressed.
- **What it contains**: Metadata and a data extract.
- **Why it's useful**: The .tdsx file is useful because it can be accessed for both metadata and data. Tableau authors can access a .tdsx file located on Tableau Server as a data source thus eliminating the need for a workbook to connect directly to an external data source. A published .tdsx file can be placed on a schedule so that it is regularly updated from the underlying data source.
- **How it's generated**: A .tdsx file can be generated by right-clicking on a data source in the **Data** pane and selecting **Add to Saved Data Sources...** followed by selecting **Tableau Packaged Data Source** in the resulting dialog box.
  Like the .tds file, the .tdsx file can also be generated when publishing to Tableau server via **Server | Publish Data Source | [data source]**. See the following exercise for more details.

- **How to access it**: A .tdsx file is accessed in the same way a .tds file is. First, it can be stored in **My Tableau Repository | Datasources**. When stored in this directory a .tdsx file will display in the left-hand portion of the **Start Page** under the section entitled **Saved Data Sources**. The second place a .tdsx file is often stored is on Tableau Server. Selecting **Data | New Data Source** and choosing **Tableau Server** allows the Tableau author to point to the .tds and .tdsx files that have been published to a given instance of Tableau Server.

Exercise – publish a data source to Tableau Server

1. Navigate to `https://public.tableau.com/profile/david.baldwin#!/` to locate and download the workbook associated with this chapter.
2. Navigate to the worksheet entitled `Publish`.
3. Reference the **Caption** in the worksheet to download the content necessary to complete the exercise.
4. Select **Data | New Data Source** and connect to `My Superstore.xls`, which was downloaded in the previous step.
5. Connect to the **Orders** table.
6. Name the data source `My Superstore`.
7. Return to the `Publish` worksheet.
8. If you have not already done so, log in to an instance of Tableau Server.
9. In the **Data** pane, select the `My Superstore` data source.
10. Select **Server | Publish Data Source | My Superstore**.
11. In the resulting dialog box, choose your desired settings:

Note the bottom of the dialog box where you will see an option entitled **Include external files**. Selecting this box will cause Tableau to create and upload a package data source, that is, a .tdsx file. Deselecting this box will cause Tableau to generate and upload a .tds file. Of course, in this case, since the data source is an Excel file, deselecting **Include external files** would cause Tableau to create a data source that would only be accessible via your local machine.

Tableau Workbook (.twb)

- **File format type**: XML.
- **What it contains**: Metadata and schema. The schema defines the visualizations in the workbook. Note that schema, in this context, refers to the XML that defines the visual components of the workbook, including the visualizations displayed on worksheets as well as the layout of dashboards and stories.
- **Why it's useful**: The .twb file type is the file type most often used by the Tableau author. It is necessary for creating visualizations that point to a live dataset. Thus, real-time solutions will utilize this file type.
- **How it's generated**: A .twb file is created via **File | Save As** and selecting the .twb file type in the resulting dialog box.
- **How it's accessed**: A .twb file can be opened via Tableau Desktop or accessed via a browser pointing to an instance of Tableau Server. Since a .twb file is XML, it can be opened, viewed, and updated via a text editor.

Tableau Packaged Workbook (.twbx)

- **File format type**: Compressed.
- **What it contains**: Metadata, schema, and optionally, one or more data extracts.
- **Why it's useful**: The .twbx file type is required for use with Tableau Reader. It can also be effectively used with Tableau Server when accessing data sources to which Tableau Server does not directly connect such as flat files, Excel, and Access. Drawbacks to .twbx files will be discussed in the following section.
- **How it's generated**: A .twbx file is created via **File | Save As** and selecting the .twbx file type in the resulting dialog box.
- **How it's accessed**: A .twbx file can be opened via Tableau Desktop or accessed via a browser pointing to an instance of Tableau Server. Since a .twbx file is a compressed file it can also be unzipped via a compression utility such as WinZip or 7-Zip.

Other file types

The remaining file types the Tableau author should be familiar with are not particularly relevant for Tableau Server and will thus only be briefly discussed here:

- **Tableau Data Extract (.tde)**: The .tde file can be generated via the following: If a .twb file is opened in Tableau Desktop, a .tde file can be created by right-clicking on a data source in the **Data** pane and selecting **Extract Data**. After selecting the desired options, Tableau will provide a dialog box for the author to save the .tde file in a given location. The .tde file can be used to create a local snapshot of a data source for a quicker authoring experience. That same local snapshot is also portable and can thus be used offline. Often the data extracts compressed inside .twbx and .tdsx files are in the .tde format.

- An important clarification point should be made here. Often Tableau authors will refer to publishing an extract to Tableau Server. The extract that is published is not a .tde file. Rather, it is a .tdsx file. See Chapter 11, *Improving Performance* for additional information about the .tde file format.

- **Tableau Bookmark (**`.tbm`**)**: The `.tbm` file can be generated via **Window | Bookmark | Create Bookmark**. It can be useful for duplicating worksheets across multiple workbooks and also for sharing formatting across multiple workbooks.
- **Tableau Map Source (**`.tms`**)**: The `.tms` file is discussed in detail in `Chapter 8`, *Mapping*.

- **Tableau Preferences Source (**`.tps`**)**: The `.tps` file can be used to create custom color palettes. This can be helpful when an organization wishes to use its color scheme within Tableau workbooks. The `.tps` file that Tableau utilizes is called `Preferences.tps` and is located in the `My Tableau Repository`. Since it's in XML format, it can be altered via a text editor. Matt Francis has posted a helpful blog at `http://wannabeadatarockstar.blogspot.in/` that clearly communicates how to adjust this file. Also reference Tableau help.

Tableau Server architecture

Now that we have reviewed the various Tableau file types, we can use that information to understand various ways to architect a Tableau Server environment. Since this is not a book dedicated to Tableau Server, this architecture discussion is presented at a high level. The intent is to help the Tableau Desktop author understand how to interact with Tableau Server so that workbooks best serve the end user:

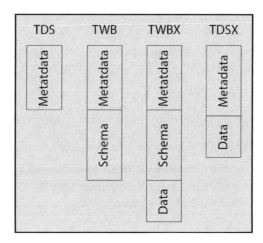

The preceding diagram visually represents the contents of the four file types that are most relevant when considering how the Tableau Desktop author should interface with Tableau Server. To be clear, the previous section of this chapter provided descriptions of the various file types. Each of these descriptions included the line **What it contains**. **What it contains** is visually represented in the preceding diagram.

Each of the four file types listed in the diagram includes metadata; two include data and two include schema.

Let's consider four approaches to Tableau Server architecture and how each presents advantages and disadvantages the Tableau Desktop author should be aware of. The first two approaches presented should generally be avoided. The second two approaches should generally be adopted. Of course, the four approaches listed do not encompass every possible approach. They do, however, provide a basic framework.

Tableau Server architecture approaches to avoid

If the following Tableau Server architecture approaches should be avoided, why mention them at all? Because they are often utilized! An administrator who hasn't had the opportunity to go to Tableau Server training, may default to these approaches and may even build out a large infrastructure before realizing that it's difficult to maintain and scale.

Tableau Server architecture – TWB Centric

The following diagram shows .twb files that have been published to Tableau Server. The diagram also communicates that, since the .twb files do not include any data, each workbook must access an external data source in order to display a visualization. Furthermore, this access will cause Tableau to return data in real time; that is, the latest data available in the external data source:

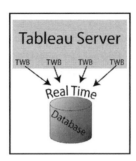

The TWB Centric approach to Tableau Server architecture results in various advantages and disadvantages:

- TWB Centric advantages:
    - Small footprint
    - Easy revision history
    - Real-time
- TWB Centric disadvantages:
    - Difficult maintenance
    - Potentially poor performance

The *Small footprint* advantage stems from small file size; .twb files are rarely larger than a few MB. Small file size leads to fewer issues for revision history. This is in contrast with .twbx files which can become quite large and thus unexpectedly overload a hard drive when storing many copies via revision history.

The Real-time advantage is as a result of a .twb file always pointing to an external data source. As the data source updates, the workbook that is based on a .twb file updates. Of course, Real-time in this case should not be mistaken with stock ticker; that is, updated results are not displayed in a worksheet unless the end user performs a manual refresh. (Note that even when manually refreshed, a worksheet may be regenerated from cache as opposed to making a call to the data source. This will depend on the settings in Tableau Server.)

Note the phrase *Difficult maintenance* in the preceding list. From one perspective, maintenance is fairly easy; that is, a .twb file can be quickly downloaded, edited, and then reupload. From another perspective, the TWB Centric approach can be quite a chore. Consider a change to a single foreign key in a data source that breaks every workbook in production. Editing dozens of workbooks (or more) to rectify the issue would not be trivial.

Another disadvantage of TWB Centric architecture is *Potentially poor performance*. This is because it requires .twb files to point to external data sources. Network latency and slow database servers will negatively impact workbook performance. It should be noted, however, that some data source engines (such as the **Massively Parallel Processing (MPP)** systems discussed in Chapter 4, *All about Data – Data Densification, Cubes, and Big Data*) can potentially outperform the architecture options discussed in the following section.

Verdict: Avoid TWB centric architecture. A TDS centric architecture maintains all the advantages of a TWB centric architecture and mitigates the maintenance difficulties discussed previously.

Tableau Server architecture – TWBX Centric

The following image shows .twbx files that have been published to Tableau Server. Assuming that the .twbx files contain extracts for each required data source, no call is necessary to external data to display a visualization:

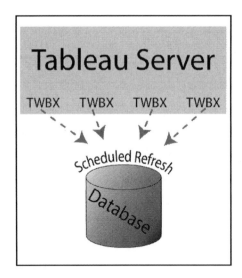

The TWBX Centric approach to Tableau Server architecture has a strong advantage and various disadvantages:

- TWBX Centric advantage:
    - Typically performant
- TWBX Centric disadvantages:
    - Large footprint
    - Very difficult maintenance
    - Potential problems with revision history
    - Not real-time

The TWBX Centric approach has at least one advantage: performance. Since a `.twbx` file can include data extracts, no calls to external data sources are required. This circumvents problems with network latency and slow database servers, thus enabling quick performance. Note that a `.twbx` file can be scheduled for refreshes, thus ensuring that the data is never stale.

Unfortunately, the TWBX Centric approach has major drawbacks. The *Large footprint* disadvantage listed previously can occur as a result of large `.twbx` files. These files can be as large as several GB. Such large files lead to *Very difficult maintenance* and can lead to *Potential problems with revision history*. Large `.twbx` files can be difficult and time consuming to download, update, and reupload. Also, as mentioned previously, revision history on large `.twbx` files may unexpectedly overload a hard drive. Furthermore, the TWBX Centric solution is *Not real-time*.

For most Tableau Server implementations, the TWBX Centric solution should be avoided. The Tableau Server administrator who observes a `.twbx` file in excess of 500 MB should probably contact the author who uploaded the file in order to seek a better solution. This is not to say that `.twbx` files should never be used on Tableau Server. If a Tableau author uses a local spreadsheet as a data source, then a `.twbx` file will almost certainly be used in order for the workbook to function on Tableau Server. However, this will typically not lead to large `.twbx` files. Thus the disadvantages listed previously would not apply.

Verdict: Avoid TWBX centric architecture. A TDSX centric architecture maintains all the advantages of a TWBX centric architecture and mitigates most of the difficulties discussed previously.

Tableau Server architecture approaches to adopt

In the previous sections, we considered two approaches to Tableau Server architecture to avoid. Now let's consider two approaches to adopt.

Tableau Server architecture – TDS Centric

The following image shows .twbx files that have been published to Tableau Server. Assuming that the `.twbx` files contain extracts for each required data source, no call is necessary to external data to display a visualization:

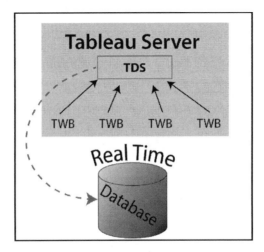

The TDS Centric approach to Tableau Server architecture results in various advantages and at least one disadvantage:

- TWB Centric advantages
  - Small footprint
  - Easy revision history
  - Easy maintenance
  - Real-time
- TWB Centric disadvantage
  - Potentially poor performance

Like the TWB Centric approach discussed previously, the TDS Centric approach has the advantage of a *Small footprint*, which stems from the small size of both .tds and .twb files. These small file sizes result in fewer issues for revision history.

By using .twb files with their corresponding small footprints, maintenance is relatively easy since .twb files can be quickly downloaded, updated and then reuploaded. Furthermore, pointing to a .tds file has an additional maintenance advantage. If changes are made to the metadata in the .tds file (for example, a calculated field is updated), those changes will trickle down to every .twb file that points to the .tds file thus allowing for an update in a single location to impact multiple workbooks. Previously, we considered a scenario in which a change to a single foreign key broke every workbook in production. By utilizing the TDS Centric approach, updating the metadata in a .tds file to account for the change to the foreign key could instantly fix the problem for every .twb file pointing to the .tds file.

As in the TWB Centric approach discussed earlier, the TDS Centric approach provides a *Real-time* advantage.

Lastly, the TDS Centric architecture has a disadvantage, that is, *Potentially poor performance*. This is because a .tds file must point to external data sources that could, in turn, introduce network latency and slow database engines that negatively impact workbook performance.

Verdict: Consider adopting the TDS Centric approach, especially when a real-time solution is required. The TDS centric architecture maintains all the advantages of a TWB centric architecture while providing easier maintenance.

Tableau Server architecture – TDSX Centric

The following image shows .twbx files that have been published to Tableau Server. Assuming that the .twbx files contain extracts for each required data source, no call is necessary to external data to display a visualization:

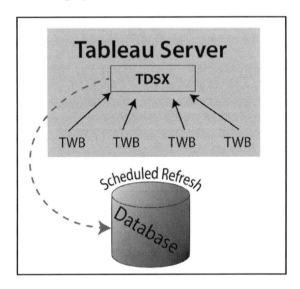

The TDSX Centric approach to Tableau Server architecture results in various advantages and at least one disadvantage:

- TDSX Centric advantages:
  - Typically quick performance
  - Smallish footprint
  - Easy maintenance
  - Revision history friendly
- TDSX Centric disadvantage:
  - Not real-time

The TDSX Centric approach allows for *Typically quick performance*. Since the .twb files point to a .tdsx file that resides on Tableau Server, problems with network latency and slow database servers are circumvented.

By using .twb files with their corresponding small footprints, maintenance is relatively easy since .twb files can be quickly downloaded, updated, and then reuploaded. Furthermore, pointing to a .tdsx file has an additional maintenance advantage. If changes are made to the metadata in the .tdsx file (for example, a calculated field is updated), those changes will trickle down to every .twb file that points to the .tdsx file, thus allowing an update in a single location to impact multiple workbooks. The term *Small footprint* is adopted in the list since .tdsx files can become quite large even though the .twb files remain small.

Verdict: In most environments a TDSX Centric architecture should be the approach most frequently used. Even the one disadvantage listed previously, *Not real-time*, can be mitigated via frequent updates. That said, a TDS Centric approach should be used when a real-time solution is required or when accessing a data source engine that outperforms Tableau extracts.

As previously stated, the preceding discussion of Tableau Server architecture is at a high level. Different environments require different approaches. Thus some combination of the previous two *to be adopted* approaches may often be appropriate. Also, there may be special cases that would utilize one of the *to be avoided* previous approaches. For example, it may be advantageous in some environments to programmatically generate a .twbx file for different end users thus allowing those end users to download .twbx files containing only their data.

Tableau Server revision history

In Tableau 9.3, revision history was introduced for workbooks, including .twb and .twbx files. In Tableau 10.0 revision history was extended to data sources, including .tds and .tdsx files. By default Tableau Server's revision history is set to 25. In other words, the past 25 versions of each workbook and data source are retrievable. Previous to Tableau 9.3, revision history was only available through third party tools such as InterWorks' Tableau Enterprise Deployment Tool.

In Tableau Desktop, if you attempt to upload a workbook or data source with the same name as a previously uploaded file, Tableau Desktop will display a warning such as *Data source is already in use*. Publishing will overwrite the existing data source. If you proceed with the upload, revision control will be activated and the previous version of the file will remain accessible as a revision.

To access revision history for individual workbooks and data sources in Tableau Server, simply select **Content | Data Sources** or **Content | Workbooks**, and click on the dropdown menu for the desired data source/workbook. In the drop-down menu, select **Revision History** to open a dialog box in order to choose which previous version to restore:

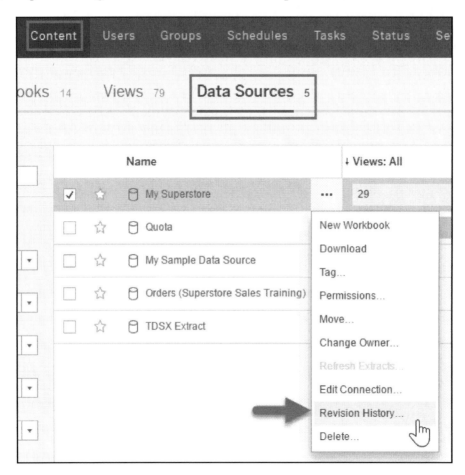

The Tableau Server browser interface provides easy access to adjust revision history settings and also access revisions of individual workbooks and data sources. To adjust revision history settings simply click on **Settings** and scroll to **Revision History**:

If you'd like to peek beneath the hood of Tableau Server to begin to understand how revision history works, do the following: on a computer with Tableau Server installed, go to the directory for revision history. By default, this is located at
`C:\ProgramData\Tableau\Tableau Server\data\tabsvc\dataengine\revision`. In the revision directory there are files with alphanumeric names. Simply rename one of those files with the appropriate extension (for example, `.twbx`) to open the file in Tableau Desktop.

Tableau Server web authoring environment

Web authoring is a Tableau Server feature introduced in 8.0 that provides an interface for authoring that is similar to Tableau Desktop. Originally, the web authoring interface was quite limited but more features are introduced with each version. Thus the capability gap between the Tableau Server web authoring environment and Tableau Desktop have shrunk. To mention a couple of examples of continuing improvements, in Tableau 10 the web authoring environment provides robust capabilities for creating and applying table calculations and also provides capabilities for creating dashboards, though the dashboard functionality is still fairly rudimentary. At the time of writing, some features are still missing altogether in the Tableau Server web authoring environment. For instance there is no interface for creating parameters or for connecting to data sources that have not already been published to Tableau Server. A fairly detailed comparison of the Tableau Desktop and web authoring environment capabilities is included later in this chapter.

The question of what one can and cannot do in the Tableau Server web authoring environment is quite important. After all, why pay for additional copies of Tableau Desktop when the web authoring environment will suffice? The following exercises provide an opportunity to explore some of the limitations and workarounds of the web authoring environment.

Basic web authoring instructions

The two very brief exercises demonstrate how to access the authoring environment within Tableau Server.

Exercise – edit an existing workbook on Tableau Server

1. Log in to an instance of Tableau Server.
2. Open an existing workbook within Tableau Server via **Content** | **Workbooks**.
3. Click on the **Edit** icon:

Exercise – create a new workbook on Tableau Server

1. Log in to an instance of Tableau Server.
2. Navigate to an existing data source via **Content | Data Sources**.
3. Click on the dropdown for the desired data source and choose to create a new workbook:

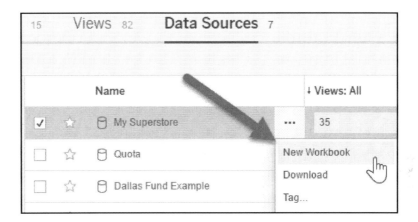

Exploring the capabilities and limitations of the Tableau Server web authoring environment

Although a comparison list is provided in the following section, a good understanding of the capabilities and limitations of the Tableau Server web authoring environment is most effectively explored by creating worksheets and dashboards in that environment. In that spirit, consider accessing the workbook associated with this chapter and referencing the worksheet entitled Sales & Quota in order to build out your own variation in Tableau Server. As you attempt to build the worksheet, you will discover the web authoring environment's exciting possibilities and sometimes frustrating limitations. Once you complete the build, compare your solution with the one included in the following section. This should help you understand which shortcomings can be overcome and which cannot.

Exercise – the Tableau Server web authoring environment

If you do not have access to the Tableau Server web authoring environment, the following step-by-step instructions and the subsequent commentary should be of help. Carefully reading through the exercise should allow you to begin to understand what can and cannot be accomplished in the web authoring environment:

1. Access the workbook associated with this chapter and note the worksheet entitled `Sales & Quota`:

Sales & Quota Desktop
Red represents a missed goal.

Region	Rank	State	
Central	1	Texas	106%
	2	Illinois	98%
	3	Michigan	100%
	4	Indiana	84%
	5	Wisconsin	100%
	6	Minnesota	96%
	7	Missouri	101%
	8	Oklahoma	86%
	9	Nebraska	93%
	10	Iowa	92%
	11	Kansas	97%
	12	South Dakota	132%
	13	North Dakota	92%
East	1	New York	100%
	2	Pennsylvania	92%
	3	Ohio	94%
	4	New Jersey	115%
	5	Massachusetts	106%

2. In the caption of the worksheet, you will note a Dropbox link with an Excel spreadsheet for **My Superstore** and **Quota**. Download and then publish both to an instance of Tableau Server. See the preceding, *Exercise – publish a data source to Tableau Server* for instructions.

3. Log in to Tableau Server and create a new workbook based on **My Superstore**. See the preceding, *Exercise – create a new workbook on Tableau Server* for instructions.

4. Click on the **Sheet 1** tab and rename the sheet `Sales & Quota`.

5. Add new data source via the **New Data Source** icon:

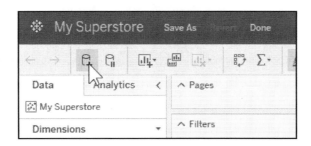

6. In the resulting window, choose the **Quota** data source.

7. Within the **My Superstore** dataset, create the following calculated fields. Calculated fields can be created in the web authoring interface by clicking on the dropdown next to the word **Dimensions** in the **Data** pane:

Quota	% Achieved	Quota Met?	Rank
SUM([Quota].[Quota])	STR(ROUND((SUM([Sales]) / [Quota]*100))) + '%'	IF SUM([Sales]) >= [Quota] THEN '✔' ELSE '✗' END	RANK(SUM(Sales))

8. From the **Data** pane:
    1. Place **Measure Values** on the **Columns** shelf.
    2. Place **Region** on the **Rows** shelf.
    3. Place **Rank** on the **Detail** shelf.
    4. Click on the drop-down menu on **Rank** and select **Discrete**.
    5. Move **Rank** from the **Detail** shelf to the **Rows** shelf after **Region**.
    6. Place **State** and **Quota Met** on the **Rows** shelf after **Rank**.
    7. Place **% Achieved** on the **Label** shelf.
    8. Place **Measure Names** as the last dimension on the **Rows** shelf and also on the **Color** shelf.

9. On the **Filters** shelf, click the drop-down menu associated with **Measure Names** and select **Show Filter**:

10. In the **Measure Names** filter, check only **Quota** and **Sales**.
11. Click on the drop-down menu for **Rank** on the **Rows** shelf and select **Edit Table Calculation**.
12. In the resulting dialog box select **Specific Dimensions** and check only **State**.
13. Click on the **Color** shelf to adjust colors as desired:

Sales & Quota

Region	Rank	State	Quota Met?		
Central	1	Texas	✓	Quota	106%
				Sales	106%
	2	Illinois	✗	Quota	98%
				Sales	98%
	3	Michigan	✓	Quota	100%
				Sales	100%
	4	Indiana	✗	Quota	84%
				Sales	84%
	5	Wisconsin	✓	Quota	100%
				Sales	100%
	6	Minnesota	✗	Quota	96%
				Sales	96%
	7	Missouri	✓	Quota	101%
				Sales	101%
	8	Oklahoma	✗	Quota	86%
				Sales	86%
	9	Nebraska	✗	Quota	93%
				Sales	93%
	10	Iowa	✗	Quota	93%

This worksheet looks rather different from the Tableau Desktop version. Let's consider some of the differences and similarities between the two environments that we discovered as a result of working through the exercise:

- Whereas Tableau Desktop provides connectivity to many data sources, the web authoring environment only provides access to data sources that have already been published to Tableau Server.
- The web authoring environment provides very limited formatting capabilities:
    - Consider the **% Achieved** calculated field. The STR function was included because the interface does not allow the number format to be changed.
    - Also note that label formatting is limited to show/hide.
- The table calculation functionality in the web authoring environment is quite robust.
- Data blending is functional.
- The shortcut for deploying **Measure Names** and **Measure Values** on a view utilizing an axis is not available:
    - To clarify, the Tableau Desktop shortcut referenced previously is as follows: an author can place a measure on the **Columns** or **Rows** shelf and then place a second measure on the resulting axis in the view to deploy **Measure Names** and **Measure Values** and thus view multiple measures on the same view type.
    - Note that in a new worksheet in the web authoring environment, placing a measure on the **Text** shelf and then double-clicking on a second measure will deploy **Measure Names** and **Measure Values**.
- Building a dual axis chart is not possible:
    - In the Tableau Desktop instance of the `Sales & Quota` worksheet, a dual axis is utilized.

- Reference lines are very limited:
    - Reference lines in Tableau Desktop are very flexible. Reference lines in the web authoring environment do not allow the modified bullet chart that was built in the Tableau Desktop worksheet example. Thus the previous exercise took a compromise approach.

- **Color** shelf functionality is different and more limited:
    - As you completed the last step in part II of the exercise, you probably noticed that the **Edit Color** dialog box is very different and somewhat more limited than in Tableau Desktop. There is no functionality for choosing specific colors for each dimension member, adding borders and halos, or defining individual RGB colors:

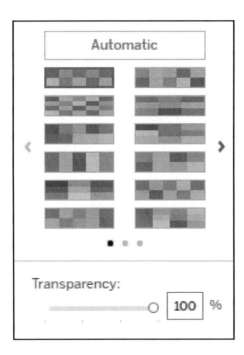

- Titles and captions can be hidden or displayed but not edited:
  - In Tableau Desktop, the title has been edited to display **Red represents a missed goal**. Also, the caption displays a dropbox link. This is not possible in the web authoring environment.

Comparing and contrasting Tableau Desktop with the Tableau Server web authoring environment

Sometimes it's unclear which individuals in an organization require a Tableau Desktop license and which only need a Tableau Server user license. For example, a technically-oriented executive with limited time to learn new software could go either way. On the one hand, she may want to delve into the details of the data but, on the other hand, she may not be able to invest the time necessary to learn enough about Tableau Desktop to warrant the price of an additional license. When the web authoring environment was released in Tableau Server 8.0, the features were fairly rudimentary. The busy executive may have been best served with a Tableau Desktop license. Since that time more and more capabilities have been introduced. Today, that same executive may be reasonably content with using the web authoring environment.

The following comparison and contrast list should help provide a quick way to decide who should receive which license type. Note that the list is primarily intended to communicate the major capabilities and limitations of Tableau Server's web authoring environment when compared to Tableau Desktop. Basic functionality capabilities such as the ability to place a field on a shelf are assumed and thus are not included:

Tableau Desktop feature	Available in Tableau Server web authoring environment?
Analytics Pane • Constant line • Average line • Median with quartiles • Box plot • Totals • Average/median with 95% CL • Trend line	✔ With limited or no customizability

• Forecast • Cluster • Custom Reference Line, Reference Band, Distribution Band, Box Plot	✗
Data Pane • Create extract • Replace Data Source • Connect/configure data sources outside of Tableau Server	✗
• Create folders • Edit Aliases • Find a Field • See Field Description	✗
• Duplicate, Show/Hide, Rename Fields • Convert to Measure/Dimension • Convert to Continuous/Discrete • Change Data Type • Change Geographic Role	✓
• Create Group • Create Set	✓ Groups and sets cannot be created via the Data Pane but can be created by selecting various marks on the view and interfacing with the tooltip command buttons.
• Create Bin	✓ Only by creating a histogram via 'Show Me'
• Create Hierarchy	✗
• Change default properties such as Comment, Color, Shape, Sort, Aggregation and Number format.	✗
• Create calculated fields including table calculations and LOD calculations	✓ With robust functionality
• Create Parameter	✗
• Group by Folder/Data Source Table	✓

View • Adjust Measure Aggregation • Create Basic Visualization Types such as Bar, Line, Area, Crosstab, Map, Treemap, Pie. • Create New Worksheet • Enable/Disable Sheet and Dashboard Highlighting • Fit Options (Standard, Fit Width, Fit Height, Entire View) • Show Mark Labels • Show/Hide Caption/Title • Utilize Measure Names/Measure Values	✔
• Create Intermediate to Advanced Chart Types such as Dual Axis, Bullet, Bar-In-Bar, Sankey, Control. • Edit Axis • Hide Legends • Map Layers and Format Windows • Map Options • Turn on/off Stack Marks	✘
• Adjust Color, Shape, and Size via Marks View Card • Sorting	✔ With Limited Functionality
• Formatting	✘ With Very Limited Functionality
Filters • Deploy Measure and Dimension Filters • Range – **At least** and **At most** • Only Relevant Values • All Values in Database • Display/Hide Filter • Include/Exclude • Choose filter type (Single Value, Multiple Values, List, Dropdown, Slider, and so on) • Search a filter for specific values • Apply to **All Using Related Data Sources** • Apply to **All Using This Data Source** • **Apply to Only This Worksheet**	✔

• Extract filter • Context filter • Special (Null, non-null values) • Row level filter • Data source filter • Wildcard filter • Conditional filter • Top/Bottom filter • Customize (Show **All** Value, Show Search Button, Show Apply Button, and so on.)	✗
Dashboard • Create New Dashboard • Add Horizontal, Vertical and Blank Objects • Add Objects as Tiled or Floating • Adjust Position of Floating Objects • Adjust Dashboard Size • Use a Worksheet as a Filter • Deploy Highlighters • Hide/Show Legend • Hide/Show Filter • Download crosstab, data, image, pdf, workbook • Save/Save As… • Fit Options (Standard, Fit Width, Fit Height, Entire View)	✓
• Add Image, Web Page and Text Objects • Create Custom Actions • Device Preview • Adjust Size of Floating Objects	✗
Story	✗ No creation or editing capabilities

User filters

Students often ask me questions such as the following:

> *"I have sales managers over various territories. It's important that the sales managers see only their metrics, that is, not the metrics of the other sales managers. In order to accomplish this, do I have to create separate workbooks for each sales manager?"*

Fortunately, the answer is no. Tableau provides user filters which allow the Tableau author to make sure that each of those sales managers sees only the information for which they have clearance.

Exercise – deploying a view level user filter

This exercise assumes a new, default install of Tableau Server. By default Tableau installs with a JaneDoe and a JohnSmith user. Both are used in this exercise:

1. Access the workbook associated with this chapter and navigate to the worksheet entitled `View Level User Filter`.
2. Note that the view is a field map of the USA with **State** on the **Detail** shelf, **Region** on the **Color** shelf, and **Sales** on the **Label** shelf.
3. Log in to an instance of Tableau Server via **Server** | **Sign In**.
4. Select **Server** | **Create User Filter** | **Region**.
5. Within the resulting **User Filter** dialog box, select **JaneDoe** and check the **Central** region. Also select **JohnSmith** and check the **East** region.
6. Name the user filter `Sales Manager` and click OK.

Note that **Sales Manager** is actually added to the **Sets** portion of the **Data** pane.

7. Click on the **Data Source** tab to access the **Data Source** page:

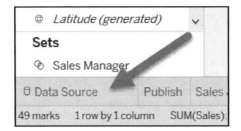

8. In the upper right-hand corner of the **Data Source** page, click **Add** to add a data source filter.

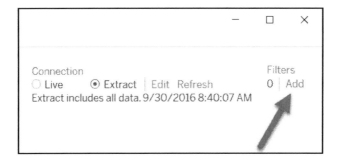

9. In the resulting dialog box, click the **Add** button to add a filter on **Sales Manager**.
10. After completing the data source filter, return to the worksheet and in the right-hand portion of the status bar click on the dropdown to access **Filter as User**:

11. Choose **JohnSmith** and note that the results display only the **East** region:

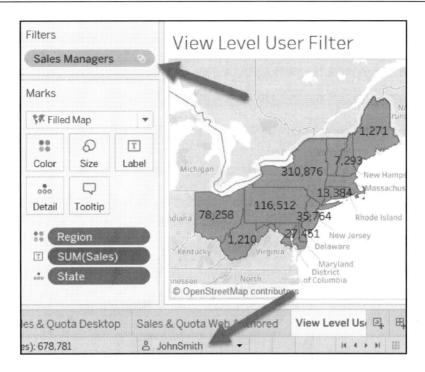

Once the workbook is published to Tableau Server, users who access the workbook will only see the information the filter allows.

You may have noticed in the preceding exercise that a data source filter was added as opposed to simply adding a dimension filter to the **Filters** shelf. This is important because any user with web authoring permission can simply remove a filter from the **Filters** shelf. In the case of this exercise, the user would then be able to see metrics for every **Region**. Data source filters, however, cannot be removed via the web authoring environment and are thus more secure. Furthermore, a data source filter is workbook wide which further secures the data.

Also note that user and group filters can be published as part of the data source. In other words, the .tdsx and .tds files discussed previously can include data source filters based on users and groups. This allows for centrally maintained security that is transparent even to those users with editing privileges.

Accessing the Tableau Server Performance Recording dashboard

In Chapter 11, *Improving Performance*, the Performance Recording dashboard was discussed in detail. Sometimes a workbook may perform satisfactorily on Tableau Desktop but, mysteriously, may perform poorly when published to Tableau Server. In such cases accessing the Performance Recording dashboard on Tableau Server can be very helpful. The following exercise provides step-by-step instructions for doing so.

Exercise – exploring performance recording on Tableau Server

1. Navigate to an instance of Tableau Server.
2. On the toolbar, click on **Settings**:

3. On the resulting page, locate the section entitled Workbook Performance Metrics and select **Record workbook performance metrics**.
4. Click **Save**.
5. Navigate to a workbook of your choosing and open a view. Note that the ending portion of the URL is :iid=<n>.
6. Type :record_performance=yes& immediately before :iid=<n>, for example, http://localhost:8000/#/views/Finance/Taleof100Start-ups?:record_performance=yes&:iid=5. Note that the toolbar now includes a **Performance** link:

7. Click the **Refresh** icon on the toolbar. It is located to the left of **Pause**. Click on the **Performance** link and observe the resulting Performance Recording dashboard that is displayed.

Summary

We began this chapter by considering the various Tableau file types; in particular, the `.tds`, `.tdsx`, `.twb`, and `.twbx` file types. This provided a foundation for understanding different ways to architect a Tableau Server deployment. We considered four basic architecture scenarios and the advantages and disadvantages of each.

Next, we considered Tableau Server revision history, where we learned that version control features beginning in Tableau 9.3 can provide a safety net against inadvertently overwriting files. This was followed by a section on the Tableau Server web authoring environment that compared and contrasted that environment with Tableau Desktop. The primary purpose of this section was to establish a knowledge base for determining which personnel should have Tableau Desktop licenses and those for whom the web authoring capabilities of Tableau Server should suffice.

Lastly, we considered user filters and the Performance Recording dashboard. User filters enable the Tableau author to ensure that users are only able to access data for which they have clearance. Although the Performance Recording dashboard was covered in the previous chapter, in this chapter we learned how to access it via Tableau Server.

In the next and final chapter, we will branch outside of the Tableau world and consider how to integrate with R. Knowledge of R integration will help the Tableau author accomplish analytic tasks beyond the capabilities of Tableau while still using Tableau to visualize the results.

13
R Integration

In February 2015, a student of mine came into class and said, *"Tableau stock took quite a jump this morning! What happened?"* I soon found out. Gartner had just released their report for *Business Intelligence and Analytics Platforms*. As you can see in this image, Tableau was clearly marked as the leader:

Although Gartner clearly ranked Tableau far in front for Ability to Execute, note that at least five platforms scored better for *Completeness of Vision*. Why? One major reason can be found in the text of the report where Gartner states, *"other vendors, such as SAS, SAP, and Tibco, have more advanced native [analytic] capabilities."*

Tableau is by no means ignorant of this criticism and has answered in two ways, firstly by releasing increasingly sophisticated native analytic capabilities, and secondly by providing R Integration. Recent examples of native advanced analytics include clustering (10.0) and the correlation function (10.1, which, at the time of writing, is in beta). R integration has actually been around for a while now since it was released in Tableau 8.1.

So how does R integration empower Tableau? Via calculated fields, Tableau dynamically interfaces with **Rserve** to pass values and receive results. As `http://www.tableau.com/` states, combining R with Tableau gives you the ability to bring deep statistical analysis into a drag-and-drop visual analytics environment.

We'll take a look at the following R techniques in this chapter:

- Architecture, installation, and integration
- Using R functions
- Troubleshooting

For the content of this chapter I'm particularly indebted to my colleague at Teknion, Matthew Agee. Matthew has formidable R and Tableau skills and was very willing to lend a helping hand.

Architecture, installation, and integration

In order to adequately understand how Tableau and R work together, it's important to grasp the big picture. To facilitate that understanding, we'll cover high-level concepts and information in this section before delving into calculated fields and R scripting details.

Architecture

The basic Tableau-to-R architecture is quite simple. Tableau pushes data to Rserve and then retrieves the results. Naturally, whether you are viewing a workbook on Tableau Desktop or via Tableau Server, if you wish to run R calculations, then Rserve must be accessible:

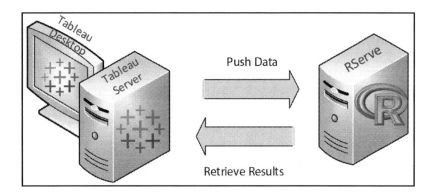

For a proper understanding of the R architecture, let's also look at the Tableau/R workflow. Terms used in the following diagram with which you may be unfamiliar will be discussed in this chapter:

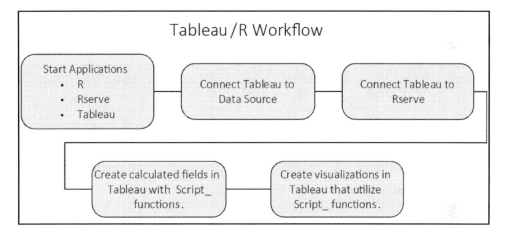

Installation

Installing R is typically not difficult, but it does involve more than simply double-clicking on an executable. In order to successfully connect Tableau with R, you will need to make sure that permissions are correctly set and that various components some required and some just nice to have are correctly implemented. We will cover the basics, review a couple of typical challenges faced during installation, and provide troubleshooting guidance.

Installing R

1. These steps provide the basics for downloading and installing R
2. Download R by visiting `https://www.r-project.org/` and choosing a CRAN mirror.
3. Note that R works best in a Linux or UNIX environment; however, in order to learn R and to begin working with Tableau/R functionality and complete the exercises in this chapter installing the Windows version is adequate.
4. Install R by double-clicking on the download executable.
5. Open R.

Various issues may arise while installing R. For example, you may experience problems due to insufficient permissions for the R working directory. This issue may first become evident when attempting to install R packages. To rectify the problem, first determine the working directory in R with the `getwd()` function. Next, either change the working directory via `setwd()` or, at the operating system level, set the appropriate read and execute permissions for the working directory.

Issues can also arise due to firewall and port configuration problems. By default, Tableau will connect to Rserve via port 6311, so make sure that that port is open and available. Alternatively, within Tableau, you can specify a different port when connecting to R.

> The documentation at `http://www.r-project.org/` provides detailed information regarding overcoming a variety of installation challenges.

Integration – starting Rserve, connecting with Tableau, and installing RStudio Desktop

To start R within a Windows environment, navigate to **Start** | **Programs** | **R x64 3.2.0** (of course, your version of R may differ from mine). This will open RGui, which can be seen in the following screenshot:

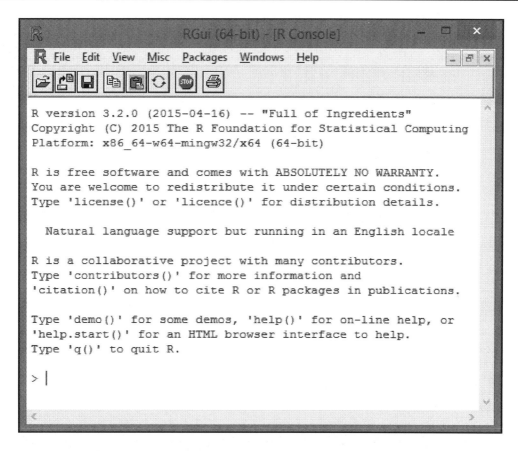

In order to establish a connection with Tableau, you will need to start Rserve. Technically, Rserve is a separate package; however, by default it is installed with R:

1. In order to make sure that the Rserve package is installed, within R, enter `rownames(installed.packages())`.
2. Several packages should be listed, including RServe.
3. If, for some reason, the Rserve package did not install with your instance of R, you can do so via `install.packages("Rserve")`.
4. To start Rserve, enter `library(Rserve); Rserve()`.

The semicolon (;) represents a new line of code in R.

Now that you have successfully installed R and started Rserve, you are ready to connect Tableau to R. Within Tableau, select **Help | Settings and Performance | Manage External Service Connection**. The default settings shown in the following screenshot will work for most local installations:

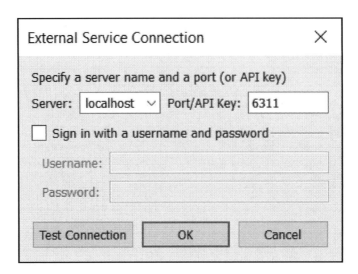

Although not required, RStudio Desktop provides a better user interface than the default RGui that installs with R. RStudio includes a console that features **Intelligent Code Completion** (that is, **IntelliSense**); a workspace browser that provides easy access to files, packages, and help; a data viewer; and much more. It's all within a single, unified environment. The open source edition of RStudio is sufficient for many uses. You can download the application via `https://www.rstudio.com/`:

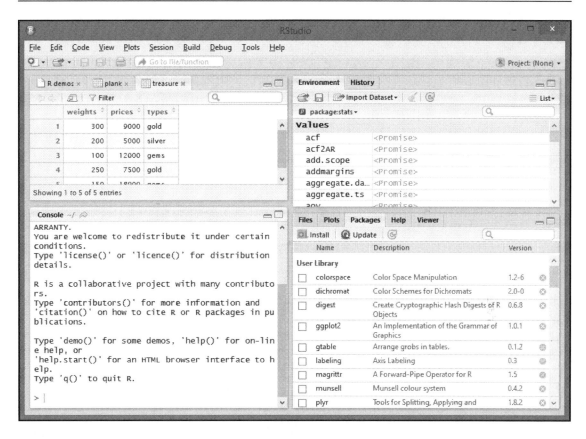

While integrating Tableau with R doesn't require any interaction with an R interface, you will probably often want to try out your R code in a GUI such as RGui or RStudio before embedding the code in Tableau. This will allow you to take advantage of useful accompanying features relevant to the R language, for example, help, examples, and sample datasets tailored to R. Note that the Calculated Field Editor in Tableau simply acts as a pass-through for R code and does not provide any support.

Using R functions

Now that we have successfully connected Tableau with R, let's write some code in Tableau to invoke R. Within Tableau, open the Calculated Field Editor. Notice within the functions panel those entries beginning with SCRIPT_, as shown in the following image:

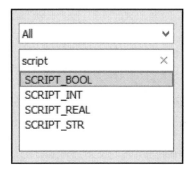

The SCRIPT functions are used by Tableau to invoke R. The function names communicate the data type of the returned results: SCRIPT_REAL returns float values, SCRIPT_BOOL returns T|F values, and so on.

The syntax of a SCRIPT function is represented in the following diagram:

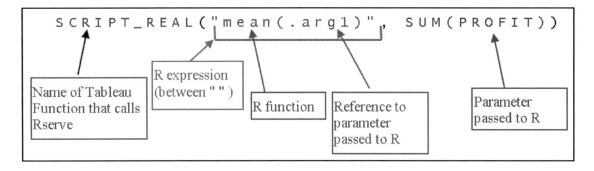

Exercise – reproducing native Tableau functionality in R

For our first example, we will use the AVG, MEDIAN, and STDEV functions in Tableau and compare the results with the mean, median, and sd R functions. This will allow you to practice the SCRIPT functions, begin to understand R syntax, and compare results generated by Tableau with those generated by R:

1. Navigate to `https://public.tableau.com/profile/david.baldwin#!/` to locate and download the workbook associated with this chapter.
2. Navigate to the worksheet titled `median/mean/sd`.
3. Select the **Superstore** data source.
4. Create the following Tableau-centric calculations:
    1. `Tab Avg`: WINDOW_AVG(SUM(Sales))
    2. `Tab Median`: WINDOW_MEDIAN(SUM(Sales))
    3. `Tab Stdev`: WINDOW_STDEV(SUM(Sales))
5. Place the **Region** dimension on the **Rows** shelf and the **Sales** measure on the **Text** shelf.
6. Place each resulting calculated field onto the view. Be sure that **Compute Using** is set to **Table (down)**:

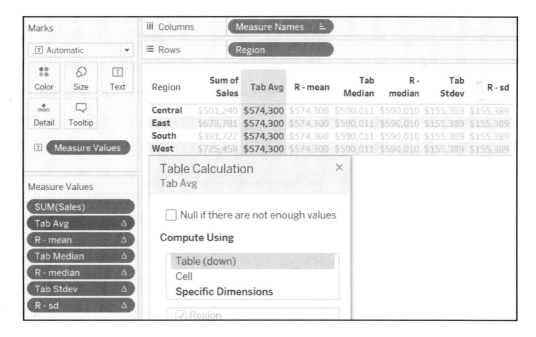

7. Create the following R-centric calculations. Note that R functions (for example, mean) are case sensitive:

   - R mean: SCRIPT_INT("mean(.arg1)", SUM(Sales))
   - R median: SCRIPT_INT("median(.arg1)", SUM(Sales))
   - R sd: SCRIPT_INT("sd(.arg1)", SUM(Sales))

8. Place each of the R calculated fields onto the view. Since SCRIPT functions are categorized as table calculations (more on that later), be sure that each instance of the R calculated fields has **Compute Using** set to **Table (down)**.

9. Observe that other than a slight rounding difference between Tab Median and R median, the results of the Tableau and R functions are identical.

10. To address the rounding difference, adjust the code for R median as follows:

```
SCRIPT_REAL("median(.arg1)", SUM( [Sales] ))
```

Note that INT has now been replaced with REAL thus demonstrating that, as the names suggest, SCRIPT_REAL works with float values and SCRIPT_INT works with integers.

Correlation

The preceding exercise was designed to get you started using R in Tableau. But of course there's no reason in a real world scenario to access the R engine to reproduce functionality that is native to Tableau. As shown in the architecture image represented earlier in this chapter, calling the R engine adds an extra process that could potentially slow performance.

The next exercise demonstrates correlation functionality that is not natively available in Tableau. At the time of writing, correlation is currently available in the 10.1 beta but this does not necessarily mean that the official 10.1 release will include such functionality.

A correlation is a number representing the degree of relationship between two variables. There are many approaches used to determine the degree of correlation but the most common is the **Pearson correlation coefficient** (**PCC**), which considers only the linear relationship between two variables. PCC is measured from -1 to +1, where -1 is complete negative correlation, 0 is no correlation, and 1 is complete positive correlation. In R, the cor function defaults to PCC and is what we will use in the following exercise.

Exercise – correlation

Our goal in this exercise is to determine the correlation between **SUM(Profit)** and **SUM(Sales)**:

1. Navigate to the worksheet titled `Correlation`.
2. Select the **Superstore** data source.
3. Build the initial view by placing **Category** and **Sales** on the **Columns** shelf and **State** and **Profit** on the **Rows** shelf, and filtering to **Top 5** by **Sum of Sales** on **State**.
4. Drag **Customer Name** to the **Detail** shelf:

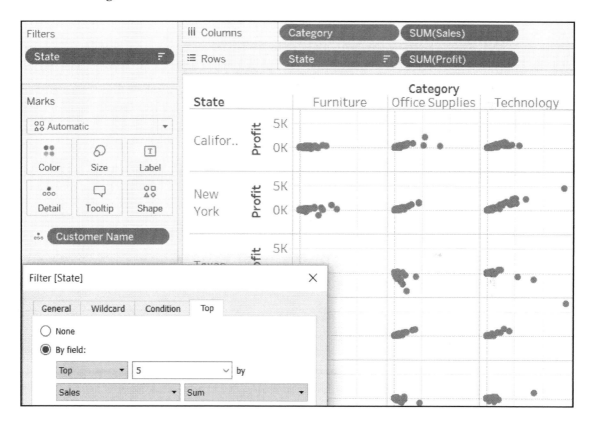

5. Create a calculated field named `P_S_Correlation` with the following code:

```
SCRIPT_REAL("cor(.arg1, .arg2)", SUM(Sales), SUM(Profit))
```

6. Create a calculated field named Negative P_S_Correlation with the following code:

```
WINDOW_MAX( [P_S_Correlation] ) < 0
```

7. Place P_S_Correlation on the **Label** shelf.
8. Place Negative P_S_Correlation on the **Shape** shelf.
9. After adjusting the worksheet for visual appeal, your results should look similar to the following screenshot. The take away, as a fictional **Superstore** business analyst, is that you've identified that by customer, some departments in some states actually have a negative Sales-to-Profit ratio. In other words, the more a customer buys, the lower the profit:

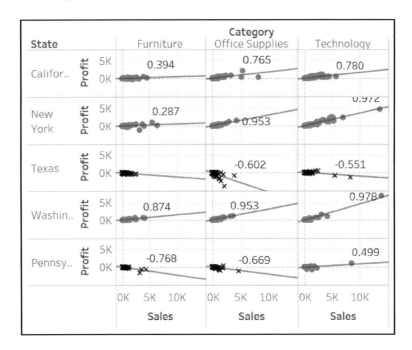

Regression analysis

Succinctly stated, regression analysis is a technique for estimating variable relationships. There are various types of regression analysis, the most popular of which is linear regression. As demonstrated in the following screenshot, linear regression estimates a line that best fits the data:

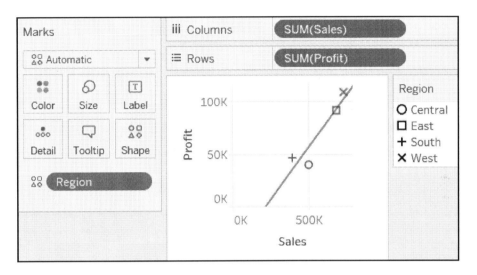

Notice that the preceding image is from Tableau and does not utilize R. It's a simple scatter plot with trend lines turned on. Trend lines, in Tableau, default to linear but also include logarithmic, exponential, and polynomial, which are all examples of regression analysis. By accessing **Worksheet** | **Export** | **Data** on a visualization utilizing a trend line, you can generate an Access database with predictions and residuals for marks on the view. But this is a tedious process and does not give a robust, dynamic solution for implementing more vigorous uses of linear regression. Using R provides much more flexibility.

Linear regression may use single or multiple variables. Single variable equations are great for learning, but multiple variable equations are typically necessary for real-world application. The following exercise includes multiple variable equations.

Exercise – regression analysis

Our goal for this exercise is to determine how closely a linear regression model of **Profit** fits **COUNT(Quantity)**, **SUM(Sales)**, and **AVG(Discount)**:

1. Navigate to the worksheet titled `Regression`.
2. Select the **Superstore** data source.
3. Build the basic layout by placing **Profit** on the **Columns** shelf, **State** on the **Rows** shelf, and filtering to **Top 10** by **Sum of Profit** on **State**.
4. Create a calculated field titled **Profit_Expected** utilizing the following code:

```
SCRIPT_REAL("
x <- lm(.arg1 ~ .arg2 + .arg3 + .arg4)
x$fitted",
SUM(Profit), COUNT(Quantity), SUM(Sales) , AVG(Discount)
)
```

5. Create a calculated field titled **% Diff** that calculates the percent difference between **Sum(Profit)** and **Profit_Expected**:

```
SUM(Profit)/Profit_Expected - 1
```

6. Create a calculated field titled **Profit_Expected (residuals)** to return the difference between **Sum(Profit)** and **Profit_Expected** in terms of dollars:

```
SCRIPT_REAL("
x <- lm(.arg1 ~ .arg2 + .arg3 + .arg4)
x$residuals",
SUM(Profit),COUNT(Quantity), SUM(Sales), AVG(Discount))
```

7. Place **Profit_Expected** on the **Profit** axis.
8. Move the instance of **Measure Names** from the **Rows** shelf and place it on the **Color** shelf. Also take an instance of **Measure Names** from the **Data** pane and place it on the **Size** shelf.
9. From the menu, navigate to **Analysis | Stack Marks | Off**.
10. Drag the calculated fields **% Diff** and **Profit_Expected** to the **Label** shelf:

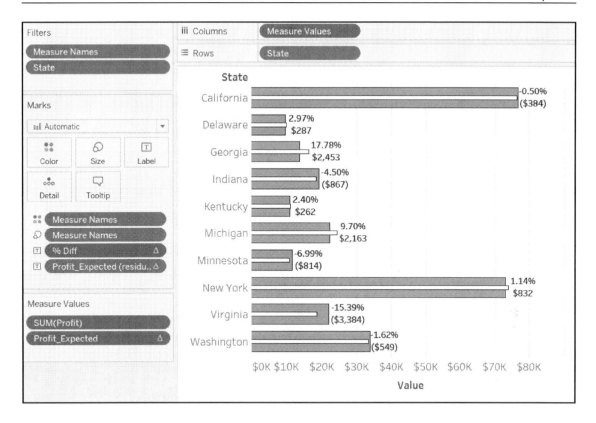

Now that we've completed the exercise, let's take a moment to consider the code. We'll focus on the code in step 3 since that will provide the necessary insight to understand the code represented in the other steps:

Code	Commentry
`SCRIPT_REAL`	This Tableau function calls the R engine and returns a float value.
`"x <- lm(.arg1 ~ .arg2 + .arg3 + .arg4);x$residuals"`	This is the R expression that houses a variable, a function, and an argument and returns predicted values.
`x <-`	This is the variable to be populated by the subsequent R function.

`lm`
`(.arg1 ~ .arg2 + .arg3`
`+ .arg4)`
	This R function is used to fit linear models. It can be used to return regression based on variables provided by the argument.
	
	The information within the parentheses is referred to as an 'argument' and is used to fit the model. Specifically, the response is to the left of the tilde (~), and the model is to the right. Thus, this is a multi-variable linear regression where `.arg1 = SUM(Profit)`, `.arg2 = COUNT(Quantity)`, `.arg3 = SUM(Sales)`, and `.arg4 = AVG(Discount)`. In English the argument could be read as "`SUM(Profit)` is modeled as the combined terms `COUNT(Quantity)`, `SUM(Sales)`, and `AVG(Discount)`."

`x$fitted`	The `lm` function returns many values as part of its model object including coefficients, residuals, rank, and fitted values. `x$fitted` references the fitted values generated as a result of passing data to the model.

`", SUM(Profit),`
`COUNT(Quantity),`
`SUM(Sales) ,`
`AVG(Discount))`
	These are the parameters used to populate the `.arg#` variables.
	
	Note that the double quote (") designates the end of the code passed to R and the comma (,) designates the second half of the Tableau function; that is, the expression.

Clustering

Clustering is used to select smaller subsets of data with members sharing similar characteristics from a larger dataset. As an example consider a marketing scenario. You have a large customer base to which you plan to send advertising material; however, cost prohibits you from sending material to every customer. Performing clustering on the data set will return groupings of customers with similar characteristics. You can then survey the results and choose a target group.

Major methods of clustering include Hierarchical and K-means. Hierarchical clustering is more thorough and thus more time-consuming. It generates a series of models ranging from 1, which includes all data points, to *n*, where each data point is an individual model. K-means clustering is a quicker method in which the user or another function defines the number of clusters. For example, a user may choose to create four clusters from a dataset of a thousand members.

Clustering capabilities were included with Tableau 10. According to Bora Beran, the Tableau development team had a few non-negotiable goals for a clustering implementation in Tableau: Solid methodology, repeatable results, quick processing time and ease of use. By utilizing the Howard-Harris Method and the Calinski-Harabasz Index within a K-means framework, the team succeeded on all accounts. Be sure to read Bora Beran's blog to learn the details.

There are numerous ways the Tableau development team could have approached clustering. R, for instance, provides many different clustering packages utilizing different approaches. A Tableau author may have good reason to choose one of these different approaches. For example, clustering results are always identical when using the native Tableau clustering capabilities. But they do not have to be. By using R for clustering, the underlying data and the view may remain unchanged, yet clustering could differ with each refresh. This could be advantageous to the Tableau author looking for edge cases where marks may switch between clusters. The following example explores such a case.

Exercise – clustering

Our goal in this exercise is to create four clusters of the countries of the world based on birth rate and infant mortality rate:

1. Navigate to the worksheet titled `Cluster`.
2. Select the **World Indicators** data source.
3. Build the initial view by placing **Infant Mortality Rate** on the **Columns** shelf, **Birth Rate** on the **Rows** shelf, and **Country** on the **Details** shelf.
4. Right-click on each axis, select **Logarithmic**, and deselect **Include Zero**.
5. This will spread the data points more uniformly and will help make the visualization more aesthetically pleasing and easier to read.

6. Note the null indicator in the lower-right corner of the view:

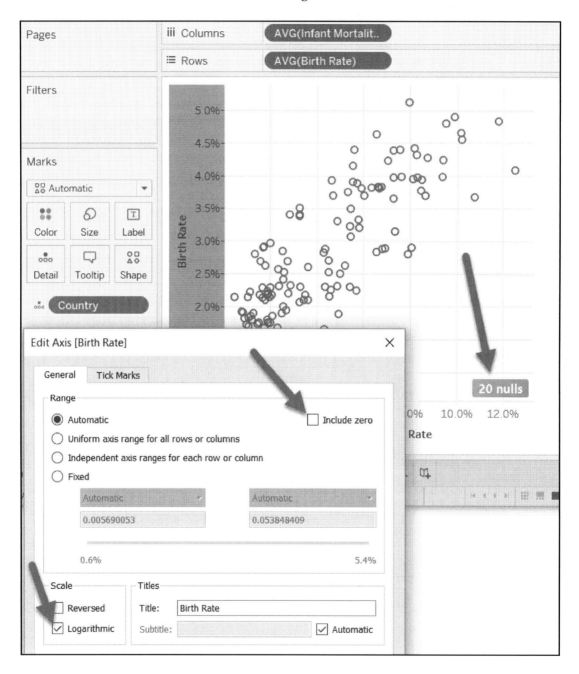

7. Create a calculated field named Cluster with the following code:

```
SCRIPT_INT("
m <- cbind(.arg1, .arg2);
kmeans(m,4,nstart=5)$cluster",
AVG( [Life Expectancy Female] ), AVG([Life Expectancy Male]))
```

8. Drag the **Cluster** calculated field you just created to the **Shape** and **Color** shelves. Note that the Rserve engine throws an error. This is because nulls exist in the underlying dataset. For example, the data does not include an Infant Mortality Rate for Puerto Rico.

If nulls exist in the dataset, Tableau displays a warning in the lower-right corner of the view. R, however, throws an error.

9. To rectify the error, drag instances of both the **Infant Mortality Rate** and the **Birth Rate** fields onto the **Filters** shelf. Within the **Filter** dialog box, select **Special | Non-null Values**.

10. Note that R still throws an error. The error states cannot take a sample larger than the population. R is expecting to cluster all countries, but the Cluster calculated field is set to **Compute Using | Table (across)**.

11. The error states, *"cannot take a sample larger than the population"*. R is expecting to cluster all countries, but the Cluster calculated field is set to **Compute Using | Table (across)**.

12. Set **Cluster** to **Compute Using | Country**.

13. The resulting view should look similar to the following screenshot:

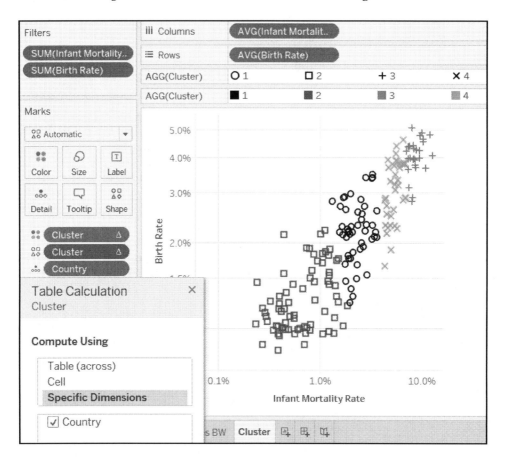

14. Press *F5* and observe that the clustering changes with each refresh.

Now that we've completed the exercise, let's take a moment to consider the code:

Code	Commentry
`SCRIPT_REAL`	This Tableau functions calls the R engine and returns a float value.
`"m <-    cbind(.arg1, .arg2);` `kmeans(m,4,nstart=1)$cluster"`	This is the R expression that houses a variable, a function, and an argument and returns clusters.
`m <-`	This is the variable to be populated by the subsequent R function.
`cbind`	This R function combines the following `.arg#` variables into columns.
`(.arg1, .arg2)`	The variables within the parentheses are referred to as an `argument`. Each variable contains vector information. Specifically, `.arg1 = AVG( [Infant Mortality Rate] )` and `.arg2 = AVG([Birth Rate])`.
`kmeans(m,4,nstart=1)$cluster"`	`kmeans` declares the method of clustering. `m` contains the vector created by the `cbind` argument discussed before. The integer 4 declares the number of clusters. `nstart` declares the number of random sets.
`", AVG(    [Infant Mortality Rate] ),` `AVG([Birth Rate]))`	These are the parameters used to populate the `.arg#` variables. Note that the double quote (") designates the end of the code passed to R and the comma (,) designates the second half of the Tableau function; that is, the expression.

Quantiles

Quantiles are often thought to be synonymous with quartiles. They are not. Quantiles are the sets that make up an evenly divided population of values. A quartile is a type of quantile, as is a quintile, a tercile, a decile, and so forth. To understand how quantiles evenly divide a population of values consider the following example from Tableau:

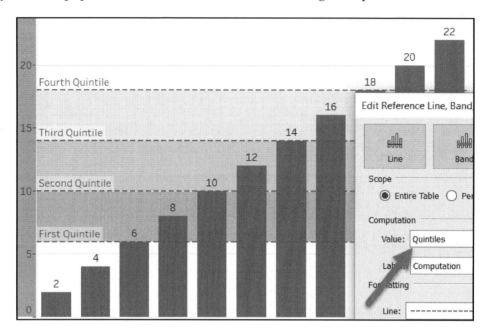

In this example our data points are 2 to 22 by even numbers. Quantiles are set to Quintiles. The **Fourth Quintile** is calculated thus: *22 * (4/5) = 17.6*. The closest value in the population when rounding up is 18. Therefore, 18 is set as the rank accounting for approximately four-fifths of the values of the total sorted population.

As evidenced in the preceding screenshot, Tableau allows you to view quantiles via right-clicking on an axis and choosing **Add Reference Line** | **Distribution** | **Computation** | **Quantiles**. The functionality of quantiles thus accessed, however, is quite limited. Primarily this is because reference lines do not generate measures that can be placed on shelves. This limits visualization options. Generating quantiles via R greatly expands those options.

Exercise – quantiles

Our goal for this exercise is to create n quantiles via R in order to view Customer distribution by sales. We will further expand the exercise by creating parameters that restrict the number of members in the total data set to a given percentile range. Lastly, we will fine tune the visualization by adding jittering:

1. Navigate to the worksheet titled `Quantiles`.
2. Select the **Superstore** data source.
3. Change the view type to **Shape** on the **Marks** view card.
4. Drag **Sales** to the **Rows** shelf, **Customer ID** to **Details** shelf, and copies of **Region** to the **Color** shelf and the **Shape** shelf:

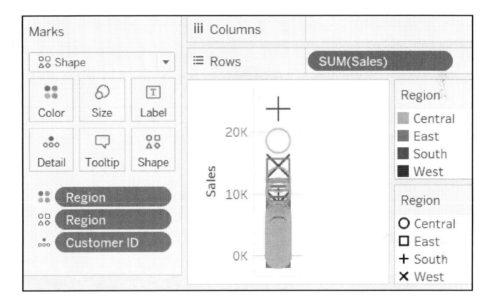

5. Create and display a parameter titled `Number of Quantiles` with the following settings:

Data Type: Integer	Allowable Values: All

6. Create a calculated field titled Quantiles with the following code:

```
SCRIPT_REAL("
x <- .arg1;
y <- .arg2[1];
m <- c(1:y)/y;
n <- length(x);
z <- c(1:n); for (i in c(1:n)) z[i] <- 0;
for (j in c(1:y))  for (i in c(1:n)) z[i] <- if (x[i] <=
quantile(x,m)[j] && z[i] == 0 )  j else z[i];
z;"
, SUM(Sales), [Number of Quantiles])
```

7. Right-click on the newly created calculated field `Quantiles` and select **Convert to Discrete**.

8. Create and display two parameters, **Select Percentile Bottom Range** and **Select Percentile Top Range**. Use the following settings:

Data Type: Float	Allowable Values: Range	Minimum: .01
Maximum: 1	Step size: 0.01	• Data Type: Float • Allowable Values: Range • Minimum: 0.01 • Maximum: 1 • Step size: 0.01

9. Create a calculated field titled **Percentile** with the following code:

```
RANK_PERCENTILE(SUM([Sales])) < [Select Percentile Top Range] AND
RANK_PERCENTILE(SUM([Sales])) > [Select Percentile Bottom Range]
```

10. Drag **Quantiles** to the **Columns** shelf and set **Compute Using** to **Customer ID**.

11. Drag **Percentile** to the **Filters** shelf and set **Compute Using** to **Customer ID**. For the filter value, select **True**.

12. Adjust size, color, and fit and also set the parameter values as desired.

13. You may wish to add these extra steps to further enhance the visualization:

14. To utilize jittering, create an **Index** calculated field via `Index()` and place that field on the **Columns** shelf. Set **Compute Using** to **Customer ID**. Be sure to deselect **Show Header** so that **Index** does not display in the view.

15. Right-click on each axis, select **Logarithmic**, and deselect **Include Zero**.

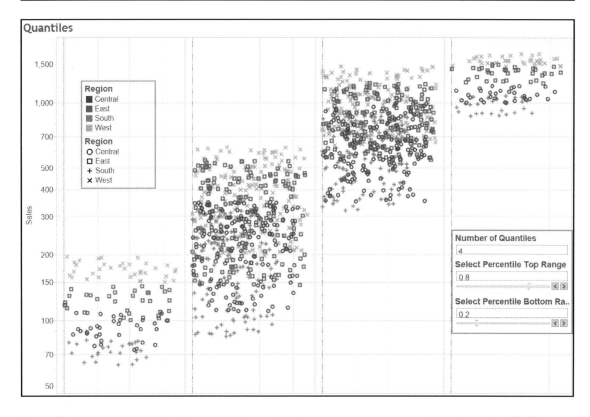

Now that we've completed the exercise, let's take a moment to consider the code. We'll focus on the code in step 5 since that will provide the necessary insight to understand the other steps:

Code	Commentry
`SCRIPT_REAL`	This Tableau function calls the R engine and returns a float value.
`x <- .arg1;`	x is the variable on which we'll create quantiles. The variable in this case is `[Sales]`.
`y <- .arg2[1];`	This variable sets the quantile count. The `[1]` forces a single number to be set and not a vector.
`m <- c(1:y)/y;`	m distributes probabilities evenly from 1:y.
`n <-length(x);`	This sets the size of the loops. The loops are discussed in the next section.

`z <- c(1:n);   for (i in c(1:n)) z[i] = 0;`	z sets the initial response vector by setting everything to 0.
`for (j in   c(1:y))  for (i in c(1:n)) z[i] = if (x[i] <= quantile(x,m)[j] &&   z[i] == 0 )  j else z[i];`	For each quantile, we go through the vector z, and for each entry, we test if the value of x is less than the upper limit of that quantile. If x has previously been set, we leave it. Otherwise, `z[i] = that quantile (j)`.

Troubleshooting

The interaction between Tableau and R can be challenging to negotiate. You may experience numerous problems that at first seem difficult to understand. These problems, however, usually stem from a few underlying causes. This section will address some of those underlying causes.

Give R what it expects

It's important to make sure that the variables you pass to an R argument line up with what R is expecting. Consider the following example based on code from *Exercise – correlation:*

`SCRIPT_REAL("cor(.arg1, .arg2)", SUM([Sales]), SUM([Profit]))`	**Initial code from Exercise 2**
`script_real("cor(.arg1)", SUM([Sales]), SUM([Profit]))`	Adjusted code from Exercise 2. Note that `cor` now only receives one variable.
`Error in cor(.arg1): supply both 'x' and 'y' or a matrix-like 'x'`	The adjusted code throws this error.

It's certainly no surprise that R would throw an error in this case. The `cor` function requires two variables, but the adjusted code provides only one. As stated in the returned error message, a second variable is required.

Be sure that the number of variables you pass to R matches the number of expected variables. Otherwise, you may receive an error or unexpected results.

R Scripts are table calculations

R Scripts are table calculations. Like all table calculations this means that you can only utilize fields that are on your view. Also, it's important that you set partitioning and addressing correctly, otherwise, you may receive unexpected results. Let's adjust the partitioning and addressing from the *Exercise – correlation* section and observe the results.

Note in this screenshot that **Compute Using** is set to **Customer ID**. This is necessary to correctly calculate the correlation between **Sales** and **Profit**:

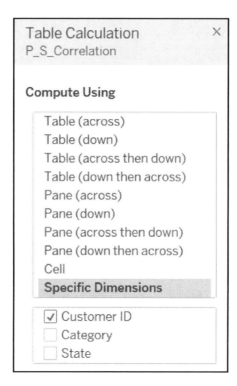

Adjusting **Compute** Using to State will result in very different and fairly meaningless results:

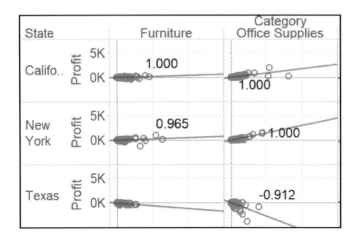

Performance challenges

In *Exercise – quantiles*, you may have noticed that the greater the number of quantiles set with the **Number of Quantiles** parameter, the longer it takes the results to be displayed. This is because R runs the loops in the Quantile calculated field one iteration for each quantile. For example, if the Number of Quantiles parameter is set to 1, the loop is instigated only once. If it is set to 2, it runs twice, and so on.

The rule of thumb is that R code is executed once for every partition. The more the partitions, the slower the performance. Therefore, when using R code, reduce the number of partitions whenever possible.

Summary

R is often cited as the most popular statistical package. Indeed, it's more than a package; it is a development platform dedicated to advanced statistical analysis. As mentioned at the beginning of this chapter, according to the 2015 Gartner Report for Analytics and Business Intelligence, Tableau is the leading software solution in its space. Thus, the integration of R with Tableau is arguably a union of best-breed tools.

This chapter just scratched the surface regarding the options of working with R. Although we've covered architecture, workflow, installation, as well as some of the more popular R functions such as `lm`, `cor`, `cluster`, and `quantile`, there is much more to explore. In fact, the possibilities of Tableau R integration remain largely uncharted territory in the BI community. The intrepid in data visualization are pushing the envelope, but there's much to be done. For those readers looking to enhance their career options, expertise in both packages could open vistas.

Index

Made in the USA
Lexington, KY
13 December 2019